# Tracks in the Snow

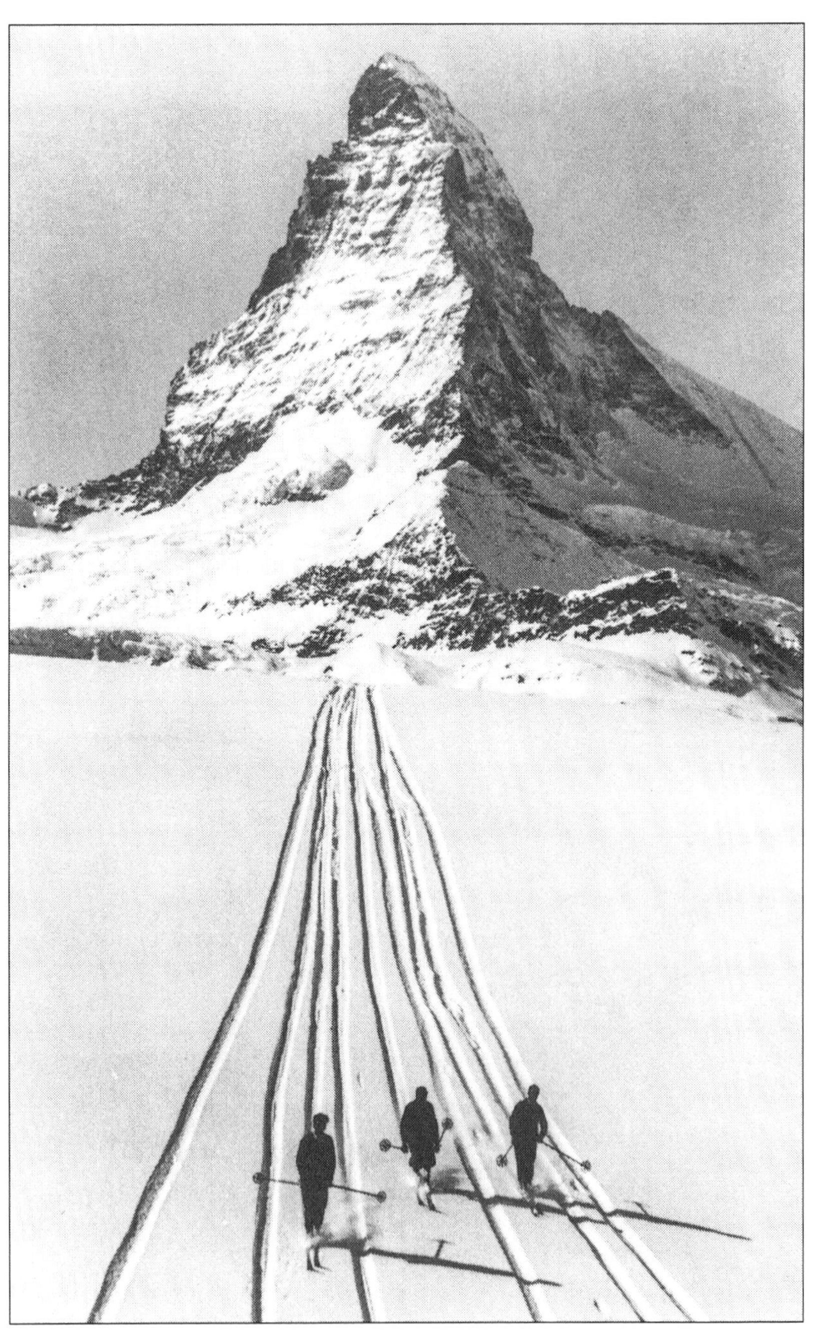

# Tracks in the Snow

*stories from a life on skis*

Peter Shelton

Western Eye Press

2017

*Tracks in the Snow*
*is published by*
*Western Eye Press,*
*a small independent publisher*
*(very small, and very independent) with*
*a home base in the Colorado*
*Rockies and an office in Sedona, Arizona.*
Tracks in the Snow *is also*
*available as an eBook*
*in various formats.*


*Western Eye Press*
*P O Box 1008*
*Sedona, Arizona 86339*
*1 800 333 5178*
*www.WesternEyePress.com*

*First edition, 2017*
*ISBN13 978-0-941283-47-2*

*Cover photo*
*Robert Chamberlain*

*remembering*

*Robert Hale Shelton*

*1923 – 2016*

# Contents

# Foreword

LET'S START with some philosophy.

Time + Space = Existence

Skiing = Time (as measured in gravitational fluctuation) + Space (in which space is a snowy inclination)

Skiing = Existential Experiences of Time & Space

Peter Shelton's writings are a crystallization of skiing as an experience of time and space.

Some of his writings are synchronic, some are diachronic, and some are both.

His synchronic recreations are deep remembrances of very particular times and very particular spaces, often in the company of highly, sometimes extremely particular people (see "On the Brink" or "Large Mouth Bass").

The diachronic dimension of Peter's work is a thread that ties together all these pieces, the thread being the underlying ski life that Peter has led and that gives foundation and context to all of his perceptions and his writings. Yielding a state of grace. See "Highlands," in which an experience of the present gives access to joys of the past.

Skiing is essentially evanescent, and if we ski soulfully, we experience skiing as the passing of time, each turn a moment that is gone the moment the turn is done. There's a certain underlying melancholy in that, but there's also consolation, because if you made the turn with full feeling, you made the most of that moment in time. You were fully alive for it. And one turn is, if you live and ski right, followed by another.

Peter Shelton has skied for these last 60 some years in order to be alive in time, and he has written about skiing for these last 40 years or so in order to recapture, preserve and plumb those times.

In "Code White," toward the end of this collection, he says about his beloved Volkl Code Speedwall S's, "Sometimes, riding them, I feel as if I've been given the code for bending space-time."

*Tracks in the Snow* captures a big arc of American ski history and ski journalism history.

When Peter made his first turns at Mammoth in 1956, at 7 years old, American skiing was about 25 years old, if we date the start of "modern" American downhill skiing to the arrival of the Arlberg Method in Franconia, New Hampshire, around 1930, where and when Sig Buchmayr and others started teaching Bostonians and New Yorkers to ski at Peckett's on Sugar Hill. When Peter skied at Mammoth in 1956, his new sport was only 22 years separated from America's first uphill conveyance, a rope tow, strung in 1934 in a Woodstock, Vermont pasture. Two years after that, in 1936, Averell Harriman, who learned to ski at Peckett's, would open Sun Valley.

In 1956, American skiing was still being founded (other than Aspen, most big Colorado ski areas didn't exist yet) and the founders of everything – ski mountain construction, ski operations, ski teaching, ski conviviality, etc – were setting the tone and creating the spirit of American ski culture.

Certain intrepid members of Peter's generation, generally War Babies or early Baby Boomers, moved to the mountains in the 1960s and 1970s as a variant of the "Back to the Land" movement. They were willing and able to pour cement, bang nails, teach skiing, throw avie bombs and otherwise make the livings they could in order to lead the lives they wanted. They experienced the mountains with others who devoted their lives to knowing the mountains as home ("Buddhist Road Patrol") and became deeply knowledgeable in their own right. Peter did all of the above.

Peter skied and worked with a lot of founders and mountain scholars, and when in the early 1980s he began writing about skiing, he wrote for established titles like *SKI* and newly-founded fresh expressions like *Powder*.

He also had the good fortune to begin writing for ski publications when the sport and business of American skiing were reaching their peak (which, in "real" or per capita terms, happened in 1986, just before Baby Boomers began wandering off to form families and careers).

Through the 1980s and into the very early 1990s, the American ski industry was flush, as captured so well in "Gear and Clothing in Las Vegas". Big ski equipment and ski clothing companies bought ad pages by the truckload, and the big "non-endemic" advertisers (car companies, liquor companies, cigarette companies, etc) still had flush advertising budgets, with very few media outlets to spend them in (cable TV still getting established, no internet yet). September gear issues could run to 300 pages.

Ski writers were given lots of space to fill, and the very best ski writers, like Peter, were able to publish frequently and fully enough to build genuine followings.

And then things began to change. Snowboarding arrived. Newsstands began withering. Younger people didn't pick up the magazine subscription habit, while new media proliferated and fragmented audiences.

But the essential experience of skiing – feeling the forces of nature, time and space on a snowy hill in winter – didn't change.

And Peter kept writing.

All of these pieces make me happy, but perhaps his latest pieces make me happiest, because he continues to learn to ski ("Code White") and he continues to explore past the boundaries ("Summit Day"), and this continuing learning and this continuing exploration continues to lead to great writing about ski time and ski space and how to experience them in a way that is life-changing.

Ed Pitoniak, former editor of *SKI* magazine
Exeter, Rhode Island
July 2017

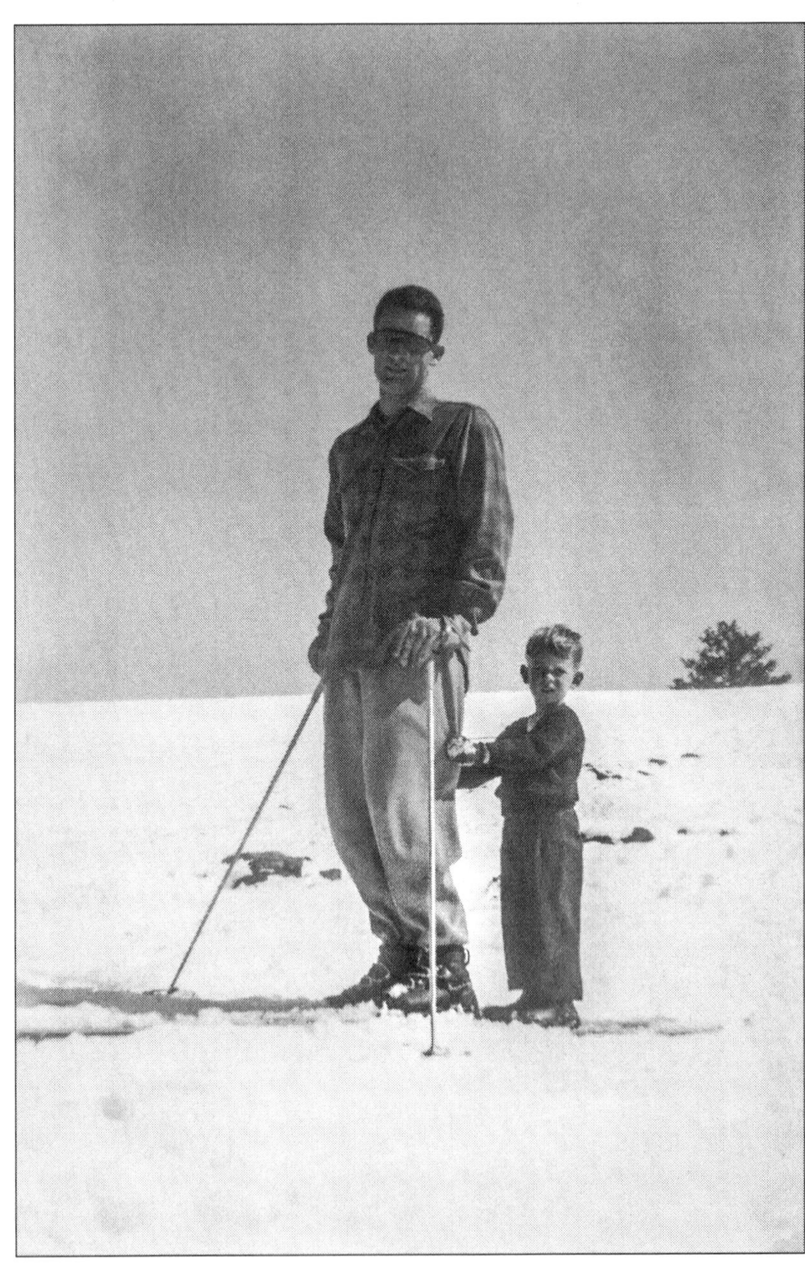

# PART I

# All Go Anywhere

# A Kind of Grace

The first place they tried to land our airliner was at LAX, the very same airport from which we'd taken off more than three hours earlier.

But L.A. was too windy to risk it, the captain told us, over the intercom. He checked with the nearby airports at Burbank and Ontario, but neither of them had the emergency equipment needed, he said. So, on we flew, across Southern California, eventually to the El Toro Marine Corps Air Station in Orange County, not far from the home where I'd dressed and packed my ski clothes and had my breakfast cereal that morning.

El Toro had the right stuff, apparently. And the wind wasn't bad. The captain's calm, Texas-inflected voice was by then a fixture in the cabin. We just needed to circle around now for a while, he said, to give ground crews time to lay spark-retardant foam on the runway. And to use up some of our remaining fuel.

It was the day after Christmas, 1966. I was 17, on my way to Salt Lake City to visit a new friend and to ski in the Wasatch for the first time. I wasn't a skilled skier, having grown up on the coast. Tony had come late to it, too, despite his address at the foot of the mountains. We were enthusiastic, though, and excited. And it was nice of his family to invite me to stay with them over the second week of school break.

Tony and I had met the summer before on board the SS Seven Seas, an aging, one-class passenger liner chartered by the American Field Service, and we'd hit it off right away. He had the bunk above mine. We were exchange students bound for three-month home stays in West Germany. As the ocean "veteran," I encouraged him to get out on deck where the fresh air helped his seasickness. Below decks, he taught me the guitar chords to "House of the Rising Sun."

The airplane flew in big, counterclockwise circles. Each circuit brought the Western Airlines turboprop over the Marine base, where from my left-side window seat I watched a thin white line, like a line of toothpaste squeezed out on the tarmac, growing a little longer with each pass. At the far end of the loop, we banked right over my house, on a bluff above the Corona del Mar State Beach. I could see the Monterrey pines in the front yard, the cedar-shake roof on which I flung my swim trunks to dry, the lines of surf breaking on the jetties.

I asked myself with a newfound self-consciousness if this weren't one of those times you hear about when a person's life flashes before his eyes. It had been a privileged life, a mostly charmed childhood – a childhood still. If our crash landing didn't work out as planned, shouldn't I be replaying cherished scenes in my head? Like, when I was seven, and the family had gone skiing for the first time at Mammoth Mountain. When, ambushed by the newness, I'd fallen in love with everything: the piney air, the roof-to-ground icicles, the mysteries of slippery gravity. I remembered the satisfaction I felt when I made it all the way to the top of the rope tow without falling off or slipping back. I remembered my mother on the lodge deck in the high-altitude sunlight applying Sea 'n' Ski to my cheeks and ears.

The plane completed another circle. In my short life there had been little need for reflection. Should I now be making some kind of peace? Saying thanks? Saying goodbye?

The young grandmother in the aisle seat had been crying for a while. Her three-year-old granddaughter slept between us, her head in Grandma's lap. She woke up now and began crying, too. "It took weeks to convince my daughter to let her go with me," the woman had told me earlier. "I so wanted to bring her to Salt Lake. And now..." Her tears drowned the rest.

Of course, none of us had anticipated this turn of events. Everything seemed perfectly normal as we approached our one scheduled stop on the way east and north to Utah. "Ladies and gentlemen," the stewardess crooned into her microphone, "we are beginning our gradual descent into Las Vegas. Please fasten your seatbelts and extinguish all cigarettes. We'll be on the ground shortly."

But then we weren't descending anymore, and the captain's voice came on the intercom. "Folks, we've got a little light up here on the dashboard that's telling us our landing gear isn't locked in the down position. So, we're going to drop down and buzz the tower, see if those boys can give us a visual on the nose gear. I'll get back to you when we know something more."

He didn't say anything more for what seemed like an eternity. After buzzing the airfield, we climbed back up to cruising altitude and headed west, back across the Mojave Desert from whence we'd come. Eventually he got on the horn again. "Well folks, the boys in the tower confirmed that the gear appeared to be down. But they couldn't be sure it locked, and we've still got this warning light. So we're heading back to L.A. where they're better prepared to handle an emergency landing. Meanwhile, please pay close attention to your cabin crew. They have some important instructions to impart. Thanks."

It took a second or two to sink in. But then the cabin erupted in a kind of low-level frenzy. I heard a couple of muffled shrieks, with the rumble of tense male voices underneath. The stewardesses came to the back of the plane, where I was seated, and asked the men there to please trade seats with women and children farther forward. Did that mean it was safer in the tail section? Pieces of conversation flew about like shards of glass: "Yeah, I read that somewhere about the tail." "Excuse me, sir. We're asking the gentlemen…" "This is my assigned seat! Why should I…?" "Sir, if you would just…"

The tension grew so thick it felt like a solid thing, like water or smoke. One guy wouldn't give up his seat. But then a couple of big, chivalrous fellows came back and stood above him, staring, until he finally got up and walked meekly forward.

My seat was quite close to the tail. But while all this was going on, one of the stewardesses leaned over and asked me to stay put. Asked if I'd be willing to hold the little girl in a special emergency-landing position since she was too small to do it herself. I said I would. The young grandmother fought her panic. She knew the child would take her cues from Grandma, and she knew she needed to stay calm, at least on the outside.

Things settled down then for an hour or so. There were quiet tears and a few audible prayers, but nothing angry. The stewardesses showed us the crash-landing position we were to assume: seat belt tight, head down on knees, arms wrapped around shins. I was to fold the little girl inside the comma of my body. We all had to practice and pass inspection. All but the little girl, who'd fallen asleep on Grandma's lap.

L.A. came into view and with it the bad news about the wind. Burbank. Ontario. The cabin crew remained professionally, even cheerfully, focused, like big sisters organizing an unusually important party. And the captain, with that preternatural Chuck Yeager calm, came through the speakers now and again to let us know what was going on – as if this sort of thing happened every other day. Without them, I think the collective fear would surely have cracked open before we reached the ground.

I still couldn't muster much in the way of a sense of doom. Maybe I was masking my fear. Or maybe it was just that I was so young and nothing potentially this bad had ever happened to me before. Bad luck was something that happened to other people. And the few instances that I could recall were not so bad, really. Like the time at Mammoth when Dad pointed out Linda Meyers, a pretty blond member of the U.S. Ski Team, who whipped by us on one ski, the other foot useless in a snow-white cast. She'd had the nasty luck to break a leg, but there she was skiing more beautifully, more effortlessly, than most of the two-legged humans on the hill.

Surely, this would all turn out fine.

The toothpaste strip of retardant grew until it stretched from one end of the runway to the other. I could see a collection of what looked like fire engines, and maybe an ambulance or two, gathered at the far end. The captain's voice said we were heading down now, that the cabin crew should take their seats, that we should all assume our positions. Whatever you do, he said, stay in your positions until the airplane has come to a complete stop. We'll have more instructions for you at that time.

Grandma cried quietly next to me. The little girl was crying, too, but not protesting. She seemed to settle into this stranger's embrace with a kind of instinctual understanding: even though Grandma was upset – maybe everyone was upset – this was not the time to resist.

Bent over, with the sweet smell of baby hair in my face, I waited a long time for the sound, or the feel, of the wheels touching down. I felt nothing.

Perhaps we were sliding on the foam the way a skimboard slides on the retreating foam of a wave? Maybe our captain was so good he'd put us down without the slightest tremor? Surely we were down by now. I waited some more but at last couldn't stand it any longer and lifted my head and peered out the porthole.

I expected to see the landscape whipping by right-to-left. Instead I saw the tarmac rushing straight at me as if my window were a front windshield. Somehow the airplane had turned sideways 90 degrees as it slid along on the foam.

And then it stopped. And everything was quiet until the flight attendants sprung into action, popping the emergency doors with their yellow rubber slides down to the ground. I carried the little girl with me, jumping out as they had instructed us to do – not stepping – jumping out and landing on my backside and skidding down, then walked away toward the television cameras and the crowd behind.

Inside the unadorned military terminal, lines formed to use the pay phones. The mood was more stunned than jubilant or outwardly thankful. Had the nose gear collapsed? Had the foam saved us from a fiery belly slide? Or had the gear in fact held up? I surely knew the answer then. Or maybe, in the tumult, I didn't. I can't remember now. The important thing was we were down safe. An airline representative said they were flying another plane out from LAX. We were welcome to hop back on when it got there and continue our trip to Salt Lake City. Or not, of course, if anyone was disinclined – they completely understood.

My parents, when I reached them, left the decision up to me, and I climbed back on board along with everyone else, except for one honeymooning couple. Even Grandma got back on with her tiny charge. And with an orange sun setting into the smog behind us, we lifted off for the second time.

There was free champagne. I had a glass. The stewardess winked at me. But the odd mood in the plane didn't break until we were almost to Las Vegas, again. The stewardess who had served me champagne took up the microphone and started into her spiel. Only this time she misspoke: "Ladies and gentlemen, we are beginning our gradual descent into Las Vegas. Please extinguish all seat belts and…" And the cabin erupted in laughter, the flight attendants too, everybody helpless, the bubble finally burst, the hours of tension at last lifted.

Tony came out to meet me at the airport in Salt Lake. It must have been 9 or 10 p.m. by then. His parents had gone to bed. He said the family had watched the drama of our "emergency landing" on the evening TV news.

Next morning early the two of us drove up Little Cottonwood Canyon to Alta. It had snowed a foot overnight, and it was still snowing. We bought half-day tickets, planning to come back to the car at noon to eat our peanut butter and banana sandwiches.

I had never skied powder before. Tony wasn't much more experienced. We struggled, unable to see changes in the terrain, unable to see our skis beneath the snow, unable for the most part to make our skis do the pivots and skids we depended on for control. Meanwhile, from the chairlift we watched other skiers, Alta regulars, slipping gracefully down the hill wrapped in a kind of gauzy slow-motion cloud. The snow flowing up their nylon jackets made a delicate hissing/whooshing sound, while the skiers themselves appeared to be doing nothing to make the turns happen. Their steering movements were a mystery too subtle for me to discern. Their paths seemed preordained, their soft, blue-shadow tracks collapsing in behind them.

Near noon we got off the Germania chair and noticed a ski patroller turning a sign above us on the saddle dividing Collins Basin, where we'd been skiing, from the Sugarloaf side. Now the sign said OPEN. Tony and I looked at each other, looked around. There was no one else there. Why not, we said, and sidestepped the 15 or 20 feet it took to gain the ridge.

Panting, we surveyed a panorama like nothing I had ever seen. Clouds snagged and tore apart on peaks to the east, opening diaphanous patches for the sun to work through. And that golden, filtered sunlight lit an untracked field of diamonds falling away at our feet. There was not a single mark on it.

I asked Tony, if we skied down here, could we get back? He thought so. He wasn't sure. It didn't matter, we were going.

I don't remember who went first or if we pushed off together. I am quite sure I butchered that crystalline plane with my clunky stem-christie turns. That didn't matter either. I had seen something new, something I wanted, a particular kind of grace. My old life seemed very far away. The diamonds rushed up at me. I was floating, flying without wings.

# ChapStick Kiss

When I was 24 and had been ski teaching for a year, my father sent me a book he'd rediscovered in his father's garage. It was a slim, large-format paperback from 1936, with a bluish tint to its dazzling black-and-white photographs. The cover showed a lone skier crouched in schuss position, the sun behind him, chasing his own shadow down a sparkling orb of snow.

*Ski Fever*, by Norman D. Vaughan. Open Road Publishing Company, Boston. Price 50 cents. Every picture, every caption, every paragraph was bursting with enthusiasm for "this new sport that is taking the country by storm!"

Dad's note, which he stapled to the title page, says: "Here's a relic I thought you'd enjoy. I remember that my buddy Eugene and I devoured the contents before our first big ski weekend at Big Bear, where reality submerged fantasy. We're praying for snow, Love, Dad."

I have since practically memorized the book. (Skis are "winged boards." The skier has "the world at his feet.") But I have trouble, still, picturing my father struggling, as he promises he did, that first time on skis. Though he never claimed anything but intermediate skiing skills, I can only recall a kind of patriarchal perfection.

Dad started me skiing at Mammoth Mountain in 1956, when I was seven, and what I remember is a tall, hatless elegance as he stem-christied down Broadway, his wool gabardine slacks fluttering smartly in the wind of his speed. He and my mom both seemed at the time like mythological figures skimming the cloud-white surface.

We lived at the beach then – they still do – but for one week each winter

Mammoth was the magical place. Before we left home, Dad and I would steel wool the rust from our skis' edges and paint the bases with green FaSki lacquer. We'd get the clothes box down and sort through reindeer sweaters, Dachstein mittens, and try on boots slick with sweet leather grease. Anticipation threatened to burst with that first whiff of cold air as the station wagon climbed out of the desert above Bishop and into the suddenly snowy Sierra. Mammoth was where the first epiphanies had hit: Grip the rope and hang on! Snow is *cold*, especially down your neck. Skis *want* to go downhill.

It all came back like a waxy ChapStick kiss last March when Dad and I got together for a return trip to Mammoth, after a 30-year hiatus. We talked about it through the early season, long distance, Colorado to Southern California. I sent Dad a pair of well-worn K2 TNC's that I had replaced with new ones. He'd never been on a pair of properly tuned, modern skis. The day approached, and we both had butterflies.

The ticket line downstairs in the main lodge sounded exactly as I remembered it as a kid: a low-ceiling lid on clattering skis and excited chatter. Dad rides the lifts for free now that he's over 65, and the pleasure of proving it to the girl in the booth tickled him. We walked out to the snow beside Chair 1, both of us swishing and creaking in our Gore-Tex jackets and plastic boots. On our first run down easy Stump Alley I was pleased to see that the skis suited him. He was slow waltzing, slicing neat arcs across the soft-packed snow.

"They already knew how to turn," he said, deflecting my compliment. "You've trained them."

Dad, in motion, looked much the same, but the mountain didn't. We skied places neither of us had ever been: over on the big westside rollers under Chairs 13 and 14; down the cliff-lined gully of Dry Creek; up on the naked, alpine ridge of Chair 5. Mammoth had grown, and Dad was skiing as well as ever, not aggressive or fast, but upright and stately. He had not given me a lot of instruction back when I was scrabbling on the rope tow, preferring, I suppose, to let me work things out for myself. Now he seemed hungry for tips from me. He was tasting new possibilities, sniffing a breakthrough at age 68.

By midafternoon, though, he was tired, leaning in on his turns, and occasionally sliding down on a hip and a hand. We worked our way back to the lodge where Dad insisted I take a run from the top, from the cornice, where he had never been. He would sit on the deck facing the slopes and watch.

Dad has had powder-skiing dreams since before *Ski Fever* and his early trips to Big Bear. Silken, floating, invincible dreams. He's mentioned them more than once, amazement overtaking his words. He never skied enough to make those dreams happen. Instead, he went to war and to work supporting a family of six, and I was the one who caught ski fever.

Many's the day I've thought of Dad while flying down some billowy pitch, deep, trampoline snow slowing my descent, riding the winged boards. I thank him silently, and I wish we could trade bodies for a minute.

We didn't talk much on the long walk back to the car, just clunked along, skis on shoulders, the day's warmth infusing our legs and arms with a loose-jointed satisfaction. Finally, on the road down to Mammoth Lakes, Dad reached over and patted me on the knee.

"Thanks," he said. "It was perfect."

# All Go Anywhere

It's scary to meet your heroes. Will they measure up? Will they look you in the eye? Will they be nice? Or might they have hardened under the pressure of being heroes?

Will they bear any resemblance to the idol you have created in your mind?

I was a little nervous last spring in Telluride when I had the chance to meet Norman Vaughan, a man who has been for many years top *kanone* in my skiing pantheon.

*Kanonen*, as Vaughan explains in his exquisitely slim book, *Ski Fever*, from 1936, are "top notch racers." The literal German means "cannon," which is appropriate, too. The big guns.

Vaughan was hoping, back in 1936, to encourage Americans of all stripes to take up skiing. "All go anywhere!" he wrote of the magic when skis met snow. I wasn't around in 1936 to heed the call. But my father was. (He was 13.) He devoured the contents of *Ski Fever*, then passed it on to me in 1973 when I was a rookie ski instructor. Vaughan wrote about a sport in its infancy, when skiers all belonged to the same fraternity and the simple act of sliding on snow seemed a miracle. He was open to astonishment and willing to wax poetic. One photo is captioned simply: "Have you ever had the thrill of breaking trail through fresh fallen snow?" In an instructional chapter, in the caption accompanying a photo of a skier demonstrating the Stem Christiana, he wrote, "This [turn] when smoothly executed gives you the sensation of a swooping bird."

Most wonderful of all for me as a fledgling technician were shots of Dick Durrance and Otto Lang and Robert Livermore, Jr. carving whose old wooden skis, bending them like bows while balanced – feet and knees and hips and eyes – in the most natural, relaxed stances. *Ski Fever* became my bulwark against the nonsense in modern ski school dogma, my dog-eared bible of skiing's timeless essence.

Telluride's Mountainfilm Festival 1995 welcomed the then 90-year-old Vaughan as an honored guest. (He died four days after his 100th birthday, at home in Alaska.) As his *résumé* was recited, I realized just how heroic, how adventurous, he actually was. He dropped out of Harvard in 1928 when he learned about Admiral Richard E. Byrd's planned expedition to Antarctica. He famously talked his way onto the expedition as a dog musher, even though he had never handled a dog team in his life. Byrd named a 10,000-foot peak in the Queen Maud Range for Vaughan, a peak Norman returned to climb, at age 89. He drove a dog team at the 1932 Winter Olympics. He rescued, by dog sled, 25 Allied fliers forced down on the Greenland ice cap in 1942 and then went back alone to retrieve a radar system considered World War II's biggest U.S. military secret after the Manhattan Project. Later in the war, he took 217 dogs and 17 drivers to the Battle of the Bulge to help evacuate wounded solders. In his seventies and eighties, he spent a dozen summers back in Greenland resurrecting, bolt-by-bolt, one of the crashed P-38 fighter planes from beneath 268 feet of ice. He was a fanatic, an explorer from an age when chunks of the planet remained unexplored. A lover of snow and ice. A bridge to a time that will soon disappear from living memory.

A film about the Mount Vaughan climb titled *The Height of Courage: The Norman Vaughan Story* screened at that Telluride festival. Afterward, Vaughan leaned against the stage, took the microphone, and brought the hero rhetoric down to earth. He told the audience of a lunatic trip he'd undertaken at age 68 when he "just got the idea" to ride a snowmobile from his home in Alaska to his boyhood home outside Boston. "I nevah thought I'd get that fah," he said with Yankee self-deprecation. It took him "fohty days and fohty nights," he said. "And I was arrested fohty times!"

He recounted the time he took Pope Paul VI for a dogsled ride. "I apologized to the pontiff; two of my dogs were named Devil and Satan, and I offered to take them off hahness. But the Pope said it was fine, as long as I kept 'em under control." Later, as the pope was leaving, he blessed everyone:

the handlers, the sleds, and the dogs. "He said, 'That may be the first time I have blessed the devil!'"

The stories rolled on.

When he had finished and the crowd began filing out of the theater, I sidled up with my copy of *Ski Fever*. I told him his book had provided crucial epiphanies. That good, basic ski technique transcends eras and national schools and equipment revolutions. That great skiing is fundamentally changeless. And, perhaps more to the point, that skiing's adherents, far from being lunatics, were actually tuned in to something transformative. He took the book in his hands and began calling for his wife.

"Caroline! Caroline! Come look at this! My wife doesn't believe I wrote this book. Caroline! How wonderful of you to bring it. How thoughtful. There aren't many of these around. In fact, this is only the second one I've seen in years. The other one I recall is in a ski museum, back East, I believe. Caroline! Look! This gentleman, Mr. Shelton, has brought a copy of my book. Remember, I told you about a ski book? I believe it was the first book of ski instruction to be published in America. And Mr. Shelton says that he actually used my book in his own teaching..."

The man was intemperate. But then his obsessions have evidently kept his body and his spirit fresh. He signed the book, twice, once inside the front cover and again on the title page. "Dream Big and Dare to Fail" and then "The only death you die is the death you die every day by not living."

He dragged me around for the rest of the afternoon introducing me to the crew who had made the Antarctica film, to friends and acquaintances. And always he presented me as "the wonderful man who preserved and thought to bring along this book." He turned it around. The hero endeavored to make me feel special.

# Sanctuary

I WAS ABOUT TO BE DRAFTED INTO THE ARMY. In the spring of 1970, Vietnam was still a human meat grinder. It was the end of student deferments, the beginning of the lottery system. I picked up *The Daily Californian* on my walk to campus the morning after the lottery draw (my roommates and I didn't have a television) to find I'd drawn number two.

Number two. Out of three hundred sixty-five. Before the semester was out (I was finishing my junior year) I would receive my "notice to appear," my "Greetings from the President of the United States..."

I was not dreaming. Though at times it felt that way. I didn't want to go; I was not ambivalent. I had a friend in high school who'd flown helicopters in 'Nam, and he came back embittered and addicted to heroin. I decided I was a pacifist. I *was* a pacifist, having been a runner and a skier – not a fighter – most of my life.

A law student at the free legal clinic in Berkeley encouraged me to file for conscientious objector status, while predicting that my application would be denied out of hand. The previous year, he told me, my home draft board in Southern California had awarded only three C.O.s out of hundreds of applicants, ten of whom were bona fide Quakers.

He was right; my C.O. was denied. The law student said I had three options remaining: go to Canada; refuse induction and face trial (the conscientious objector application might help my case in court); or, three, try to get out on a physical deferment. This last seemed ludicrous. Except for a mildly finicky back, I was in the bloom of health. I could drive through the night up to Lake Tahoe, ski all day, and drive home again for a two-hour round of roommate Frisbee. And besides, nobody was getting the coveted 4F physical deferment. California had become a war zone when it came to fulfilling its draft quota. Guys were pulling everything – from phony religious convictions to self-inflicted gunshot wounds to the "hung-down, brung-down, strung-out" dissipation of Arlo Guthrie's character in "Alice's Restaurant" – and *still* passing their physicals.

So, the law student said, "If I were you, I'd move to a state where the quota is met by volunteers. Young guys desperate to get off the farm. Then if you had some borderline physical problem – your back, or something else – they wouldn't absolutely have to take you. Know anybody in the Rock Mountain states?"

My mind leapt instantly to Sun Valley, Idaho, America's first destination ski resort, a place already carved into memory. It was the first place I'd skied outside California, the first trip I had ever taken without my parents. The idea had originated with friends who had acquiesced to send their 15-year-old son on a spring-break lark, but didn't quite trust him to go alone; they wanted a companion to go with him. Bless them, my parents said yes, and supplied the rented Head Masters, the Henke Speedfits, and the train ticket from Los Angeles. (Union Pacific owned the Sun Valley resort in those days.)

Ted and I were in over our heads on the overnight train. The girls in our car were all college age. They had big hair and pale glossed lips, dark eyeliner and extra long lashes. The Beatles had just appeared on Ed Sullivan. "I Want to Hold Your Hand" was number one in the land, and we had no clue how to respond to female attention. At least I didn't. I fell asleep to the clickity-clack in Nevada somewhere and woke up at dawn as Idaho potato fields rolled by, furrow and fence posts so bright with new snow they were hard to look at.

We stayed in the hotel Hemingway had lived in while he finished *For Whom the Bell Tolls*. We heard our first Austrian accents. Most Sun Valley ski instructors then were Austrians. Ours was named Leo, and he was the most beautiful skier I had ever seen. I suspected him of bedding several of the girls in our class. They, at any rate, made it abundantly clear they wanted him.

Leo led us down Dollar Mountain, and eventually Warm Springs trail on the big hill, Baldy. He taught by example: reverse-shoulder traverse, arms wide, one knee tucked in behind the other. “Check hup!” The sun blazed, and late in the week the sky opened up and snowed goose feathers. To this 15-year-old, the world of Sun Valley was all white and blue and perfect.

And that summer of the draft, six years later, in 1970, I did in fact know people who had left school to go live in Ketchum, at the base of the mountain.

So I set up residency in Idaho, with a P.O. box in nearby Hailey. Three months later, when my new “notice to appear” appeared (this time the induction center had a Boise address) I still hadn't found much in the way of life-saving medical evidence. The lower back thing probably wasn't going to work; X-rays showed nothing extraordinary. I had, however, turned up records of an incident eight years previous when a bee sting on the bottom of my (bare) foot resulted in secondary swelling on my face. An anaphylactic reaction. It was my only hope.

In the endless, winding underwear line of the daylong physical exam, in a sweltering downtown Boise gymnasium, I found myself sandwiched, as the law student had predicted, by eager, potato-white 18-year-olds. One of them implored the recording sergeant at every station (height, weight, eyes, ears, groin, urine, blood, etcetera), “When do we find out if we passed? When do we find out if we passed?” Most of them would pass and would eventually go to war. Did they believe in the rightness of it? Was that even part of their decision? Their faces showed only ardor and innocence.

The big shock came during the mental fitness test, where we scribbled in long rows in an airless classroom. (What was my goal here? To pass, as was my good-student wont, with flying colors?) I sensed before I saw the proctor/sergeant looming over my writing shoulder. He leaned down, buttons straining his starched khaki, and whispered, “You think we don't know what you're doin', but we do. We even have a name for you. We call you the California Roadrunners.” My heart raced. He straightened, hands clasped behind his back, and recommenced his watchful stroll. I was doomed.

The day's final station was a meeting with the medical captain in his book-lined office. The air there was even more stifling than in the gym. I sat on a straight-backed chair, sweat pouring in rivulets down my back. Behind his desk, the doctor shuffled papers and scowled. “I regret to inform you,” he began, and I felt myself slipping uncontrollably out of the worn, wooden seat, "that you will not be able to serve in the armed forces of the United States of America." The bee sting had done it. Along with the state of Idaho, then and forevermore a place of even greater magic.

I remained in a daze for the bus ride back to Sun Valley, across the Great Basin desert, through the moonscape of the Shoshone lava beds, along the Big Wood River and up into the Pioneer Range. The next day my friends took me fishing on Silver Creek, one of Papa Hemingway's favorites. The cottonwoods were turning yellow, the autumn grasses tall and brittle gold. The first snowstorm to stick in the high country hinted at the full white blanket to come. I stood chest deep in the slow-moving water and watched helplessly as huge rainbow trout, fat as torpedoes, swam over and held position in the eddy behind my waders. No fish were rising to my flies. I couldn't cast to the ones sculling at my calves. There was no way in the world to catch them.

They seemed to know this. And I couldn't have cared less. I thought about Hemingway, a World War I ambulance driver, and a skier. (I tried not to think about the day he shot himself in his Idaho cabin, a broken man at 61.) In "Cross Country Snow," his shell-shocked alter ego Nick Adams hops out of a funicular in Switzerland and skis the wild slope below. "The rush and the sudden swoop as he dropped down a steep undulation in the mountainside plucked Nick's mind out and left him only the wonderful flying, dropping sensation in his body."

# Private Lessons

She was the queen of the ski school – beautiful, regal, athletic, and above all, elegant. Elegant the way she came out to lineup in the morning, somehow reorganizing the stiff heel-to-toe motion of walking in ski boots and making it sexy. Elegant the way she stood and stretched and leaned on her poles. She was most elegant in motion. Where other skiers, even very good ones, projected their sense of effort and weight, of working the skis on the snow, she was weightless, floating; her path seemed preordained. She once told me she had gone whole seasons, 120 days on skis, without falling down. On a cold, quiet Keystone morning, midway through my first winter as an apprentice ski instructor, I followed her turn for turn, my track on top of hers, and the revelations changed my life.

Before that winter it had never occurred to me that I could be a ski instructor. I grew up in Southern California, and although we made a few family trips to Mammoth Mountain in the eastern Sierra, the high mountains, the reality of snow, remained exotic. Air like clear creek water, the squeak of snow underfoot, yodeling music piped through speakers at the day lodge – they were all runes of another world, one I could only hope to visit from time to time. I hardly noticed the ski instructors; they were simply small mysteries within the larger one.

Things remained that way through high school and college, while I continued to ski an average of about one week a year, never becoming very proficient. Until, passing through Colorado east to west in the late summer of 1972, I stopped for the night at Uncle Hal's.

At 23, I had no idea what to do next. I'd graduated from UC Berkeley with a major in (cue Garrison Keillor's nerdy character) English. After graduation I'd gone east to the Big Apple, where my sister lived and danced with the New York City Ballet. She had the best of all reasons to be there: Stravinsky, Balanchine, Jerome Robbins; it was the pinnacle of the dance world. I had no reason, other than chasing ballerinas and pretending – or wondering honestly whether – I might someday fit in with the beehive energy, the artistic drive, the high-speed claustrophobia of the place. I bussed tables for a while then landed a job in the stacks of the research library at Time-Life. I lasted nearly a year before the big western spaces called me back.

Golden, Colorado, was the perfect mid-continent stop-off, and Uncle Hal was the perfect host. A mapmaker and a painter, he'd built his own home on the side of Lookout Mountain and raised his sons to fish and ski and camp deep in the high country. There were horses and rattlesnakes out back and a baby grand piano in the living room. He was easy to talk to. In the morning after I'd slept, he cooked us pancakes on an electric griddle right there on the table. He asked me what I would do next. I said I didn't know. He said, "What do you love to do?"

This threw me. Nobody'd ever asked the question before in the context of a job. I must have hesitated. "I love to ski."

This was true but off the subject, I thought, of a serious discussion about the future. Skiing was a faraway world of dissociative sensations. Childhood wonder. The crazy acceleration that had nothing to do with you. The occasional, and seriously addictive, feeling of control.

Uncle Hal flipped a couple of pancakes. He said that his son Stony was currently teaching skiing part time up at Loveland Basin and that he had started out as an apprentice instructor.

Apprentice. The word sounded Dickensian. Apprentice cobbler. Apprentice bookkeeper. But the notion was also strangely attractive. You mean someone could be an apprentice ski instructor?

It turned out you could. When I got to home I wrote to several Colorado ski areas. Keystone's hiring clinic was the first on the calendar. October 28. It was a clear, cold, snowless morning. There wasn't a flake of white on the autumn-brown slopes. (This was before snowmaking.) I crawled out of my sleeping bag in the back of the VW and dressed in the only warm thing I had, a Navy-surplus wool pea coat.

As I climbed the stairs to the orientation meeting, a young woman swept down past me. She was slim and athletic with big eyes and long auburn hair. She was too beautiful to be available. Turned out she had been teaching there for a couple of years, married to one of the ski school supervisors. Our glances met very briefly.

# The Curtains of Time

My wife has breast cancer. Or rather, we are hoping, following treatment, we can say she had breast cancer. Time will tell.

She's doing well now, but we have endured a hellish few months. I bring this up because of the change Ellen's cancer wrought in so many of our long-held assumptions – assumptions about womanhood, work, grandkids and growing old together. When your body betrays you like that, you begin to mistrust even your memories. Had we not really led the kind of charmed life we always thought we had?

All of these things swirled through my head on a trip to Keystone, Colorado, in the early days of this winter. Editors and contributing editors were meeting to hash out assignments for *SKI* Magazine's next publishing year. Ellen and I had met and fallen in love at Keystone, in 1973. Back then I was an apprentice instructor with Max Dercum's ski school. Ellen had been there for two winters already. Now, 21 years, two kids, and several mountain homes later, I was eager to see what ghosts, if any, might materialize from our long-mythologized first winter together.

The shuttle bus deposited me at the base of what is now called the Energizer Bunny Hill. Back when Ellen and I marched beginners up that gentle grade it was called Checkerboard Flats. In those days, Keystone's parent company, Ralston Purina, was more interested in selling dog food than batteries. The slope looked much the same to me, but the ski school meeting place out front, where we lined up first thing in the morning, had disappeared under new buildings. Morning lineup was where I'd first seen

Ellen in stretch pants.

The day lodge was still there but somewhat rearranged. The ski school office and locker room where we had spent so much time were gone, moved to a different location. But upstairs the big stone fireplace still warmed the bar area, and the cafeteria still opened to tables faintly lit by the shadow-blue snow of the north hillside, skinny lodgepole pines framing the final diving curve of Last Hoot.

I sat and spooned a plastic, fruit-at-bottom yogurt recalling another noon – clatter of trays, dripping gloves and hats, an afternoon class in the offing – and another yogurt, when Ellen had laced hers with black currant syrup from berries she had picked that autumn up at Arapahoe Basin. She let me taste, and it tasted like a wild, earthy, perfect thing, like some kind of timberline secret that not many humans are allowed to know.

Now I spooned and stared at a table of young employees on break, babbling excitedly the way we must have done early in the season, the smell of snow on the ground and the promise of more. But, for the life of me, I couldn't get all the way back, couldn't really place myself back there at age 24. The walls weren't talking. It was as if time had dropped an invisible curtain, and despite the Proustian clues, I couldn't find a way through. Maybe up skiing, I thought, I'd get closer to the past.

Terrain was limited so early in the season, but Keystone had done a good job blowing machine-made crystals, and the skiing flowed seamlessly down Schoolmarm and Frenchman. Through the trees to the left of Frenchman, as I rode the summit chair, I caught glimpses of the snow on Flying Dutchman, which apparently still had too many rough edges to open.

Dutchman was the run where, on a bitter cold morning, Ellen had touched my cheek with her ungloved hand to warm a white spot of frostbite. Or had that been some other Good Samaritan on an early-morning clinic run? Ours was of necessity a discreet affair; Ellen might not have risked touching skin to skin. I couldn't recall for sure. It fit the narrative of our romance, but… there was that fog of time again.

I was certain that the biggest epiphany of my young skiing life had happened there on Dutchman when, following Ellen turn for turn, barely a ski length back, I realized that the point of the game was not the technical perfection of the turn.

I had been attending the apprentice clinics, but I still didn't get it. I didn't understand what Ellen was doing to make those roundy curves of hers, and I didn't get what Max's son Rolf Dercum was telling me about "independent leg action" and "carving" versus "windshield-wiper turns." I thought the idea was to lock your legs together, one knee tucked behind the other in a mono-legged channeling of Stein Eriksen – or more particular to my experience, Sun Valley Leo. Perfect the form and somehow the function would follow, that's what I thought.

That first time I tried following Ellen exactly, and couldn't do it. Our tracks were clearly visible in the inch of new snow. Hers were continuous, like ribbon on the ground, the end of one turn blending seamlessly into the start of the next, where mine were angular – a Calder mobile – triangle swishes connected by straight lines.

Then it dawned on me: As beautiful as her form was, the technique was in service to something else. With hips forward and head up, with eyes looking well down the hill, she was reading terrain, anticipating it, using the shapes underfoot to control her speed. Where I needed, or thought I needed, to throw my edges sideways to slow down (the "windshield wiper"), she drew a curving line back up the hill – managing momentum, acceleration and deceleration, divining rather than imposing. Using the mountain, complementing it. Ellen understood the relationship between technique and grace.

I'd be hard-pressed to imagine a better place to learn this lesson than Flying Dutchman, which in Keystone's formative years was a rollicking sea of terrain changes, never very steep, but blessed with swells and waves and cross currents enough for infinite line variety. Max Dercum, who cut the first trails by hand, relished that terrain. He cut the stumps right down to the ground, ski-packed every new storm himself, and bragged that no bulldozer would quash the God-given playfulness there.

I dropped in at the mountaintop patrol room on the chance I could talk somebody into letting me duck the rope on Dutchman. "Tell me again why it is you want to go down there," asked a polite if dubious young man. I explained about the epiphany and frostbite and falling in love, and he tilted his head like a dog listening, grabbed his jacket and led the way out the door.

Dutchman was not the same run I remembered. The dictates of

snowmaking and big-machine grooming had ironed most of the quirks out of the hill. Gone were the hollows and rolls that had inspired Ellen's sensuous line, and our reveries.

Nevertheless, I stopped part way down, let my guide ski out of sight below, and settled into the stillness. With eyes open, I had the same feeling I'd had in the lodge: that the trees, most of which were there to witness our rapturous descents, had nothing to say about the past. The pale sky and the view to the sunny evergreen patchwork across the Snake River Valley were indubitably familiar, but also reticent. They are savants, I reminded myself, of the present moment.

I thought I might conjure the spirits at the level of my ski edges, but there was no way I could replicate, in 1993, the turns Ellen had demonstrated so beautifully years before; the topography had been sheered off. The connection only came when I closed my eyes and let memory paint its own path.

At the end of the day, walking to the bus, I spied old Max, 81 winters old, unbowed, shuffling purposefully across the plaza in ski boots. He had loved every one of those terrain idiosyncrasies and led us neophytes around day after day to sample and love them too. He had watched, with some pain but also with remarkable acceptance, as the nature of his mountain succumbed to changing times. He didn't rail against fate; he moved on.

He didn't hear my first call hello, and I decided against a second. Max was obviously on a mission, out to generate new memories. Not to replace old ones but to add to them. I thought about the evenings spent with fellow instructors in the rathskeller at Max and Edna's Ski Tip Ranch, and how excited Max had been projecting jumpy 8mm films of Austrian maestro Dr. Stefan Kruckenhauser and his pivotal 1950s teaching methodology. We apprentices, in our callow wisdom, considered it barely relevant, ancient history. Max knew better. He wanted us to know the links to skiing's past.

The physical therapy is hard. It's important to get the full range of motion back as soon as possible, to prevent lymphopenia in the arms, to minimize scarring. Ellen says it feels as if piano wire has been stretched tight around her ribs.

As I work my fingertips in swirls across her chest, in order to break up adhesions caused by the surgery, her face twists in pain. There is the pain of loss, the pain of uncertainty, the pain of embarrassment and of worry. Each of which alone is probably equal to the pain I am inflicting in the name of love.

Ellen and I are committed to creating some new memories this winter. Perhaps on new trails, on mountains we've never skied before. Or maybe they'll come on the most familiar pistes, which are never, memory notwithstanding, the same twice.

# The Education of a Ski Instructor

HARD TO BELIEVE THESE DAYS – and maybe even harder to believe of the free-love years of the early 1970s – but our secret affair, mine and Ellen's at Keystone, remained platonic, right up until the day she drove east near the end of that winter.

We had kissed once, standing toe-to-toe in her apartment one early morning before ski school. Another day she told me she had dreamed of my weight pressing down on her in bed.

At the time, I was housesitting a place on Ptarmigan Hill, alone, with the absent owner's cat. The cat seemed to sense my happiness, my happily sublimated physical desire. She slept most nights curled up between my feet.

The plan had been for Ellen to leave at the end of the season, when the ski area shut down in April. But by mid-March her home life had become too uncomfortable, and she decided to go sooner. She had been sleeping on the living room couch. Her husband knew she was desperately unhappy in the marriage. But we didn't think he knew about us.

We promised to meet back East later that spring, in the parking lot of the Lord & Taylor's department store in Manhasset, Long Island, where Ellen grew up. On a bright, chilly day we drove in tandem over Loveland Pass and down to Denver, she in her VW bug "Puce" (French for flea), me in "Tortuga," my '69 microbus. On the way, we stopped in to see my Uncle Hal and Aunt Mary, in Golden, prelude to our one night together before saying goodbye. Then Ellen would head off across the plains toward Kansas, into a late-season blizzard that closed the freeway behind her.

I drove back up to Keystone and a final two weeks of preparation for my PSIA Stage 1 exam, which would be held over one long day at Copper Mountain. Our clinicians laid out what to expect, what would be expected of us. We'd be asked to define and describe the parts of various maneuvers. We would have to traverse quickly across big mogul fields, legs like shock absorbers. (Could we have done it – à la finishing school – with books balanced on our heads?) We would be made to free-ski the nastiest snow the examiners could find. They would pose hypothetical teaching problems, and challenge us to detect errors in their demonstrations. Then they would scrutinize our final forms. These were the meat of the exam. Each demonstration was to be performed at a precise speed and with exact turn radii. They were like school figures in ice-skating except that we had no marks on the snow to guide us.

No one pretended that these forms had much to do with teaching. They were too difficult to present to a class, and they were much too formal to become a natural component of our own free skiing. So why do them at all?

Gods, you see, can require voluntary service. The Professional Ski Instructors of America, the certified-pin club, is a tight fraternity. Its members don't rush anyone. The final forms were a test of our adaptability, discipline, and desire. It took me well over 60 hours of practice to get the forms right, or as right as I could make them. A part of me rebelled. Form follows function, right? Or it should. These final forms – these performances – seemed like a throwback to the way I used to ski, the way I'd followed Leo around Sun Valley, parroting his form with little to no appreciation of the underlying function. I wanted ski teaching to be about epiphanies: can my ski instructor set up revelations of function, like my awakening to Ellen's path down the mountain? This strict imitation, the breaking down of movement into its component parts – wasn't this somehow backward?

In self-defense, I tried to see the final forms as other rigid structures I had studied – sonnets, perhaps. The iambics, the rhyme schemes, were given. My job was to fill in the blanks with perfect sentiment. I didn't have nearly enough miles under my skis to be truly confident about the skiing, but I went into exam day buoyed by a floating feeling, a certainty I'd never know before. It had begun back in January when I tried to match Ellen's sinuous ski track, and was confirmed by our one night in a friend's basement double bed.

The gods had marvelous names. Scooter LaCouter came over to the exam from Aspen where he had been a Kennedy family instructor and PSIA demo team veteran. There was Frenchman Dadou Mayer, a stalwart of the school in Taos, and former French downhiller Serge Couttet, whose fractured English once resulted in the classic line: "You are very happy to meet me." He drove up to Copper from Loveland Basin where he was the ski school director. And there was Ellen's husband. He was one of the examiners, and I'd drawn his group..

I searched for signs that he knew about Ellen and me, that he might (understandably) wreak a kind of revenge with his grading. But I didn't see any. If he knew, he remained professional, gentlemanly.

He and Scooter LaCouter put our group – one at a time, as if auditioning – through the final forms: linked wedge turns (formerly snowplow turns), stem christies with abstem, parallel turns with down-unweighting, the mogul traverse, and the dreaded high-speed sideslip. This one was a potential fail maker. On a steep slope you had to ski straight down the fall line right at the examiners and pivot your skis into a 90-degree sideslip while keeping your upper body facing down the hill. Then you pivot back to tips-down straight running. Then whip the skis the other way beneath your (ideally) imperturbable center. All while maintaining a steady speed and never deviating from a straight fall-line path. If your weight shifted even slightly fore or aft during the sideslip, your skis would hook up and start to turn. This was a test of high-velocity not turning.

I survived that one, did better on some of the other demonstrations, and fared pretty well, I thought, in the hypothetical teaching situations. Ellen's husband scored me about the same as the other examiners, and I passed with something like an A-. I don't remember how the numerical scoring went.

I floated down to Tortuga, skis barely touching the snow, and began preparations for the drive east. We did indeed meet at Lord & Taylor's, where the kiss rivaled in purity the one at the end of *The Princess Bride*. We both got jobs teaching skiing at Bear Valley in California's central Sierra, and then a few years later at the (very new) Telluride ski school. We both aced our Stage 2 certifications. And we married a year after Ellen's divorce was final.

At stressful moments during the exam at Copper Mountain, I thought about our brief visit to Hal and Mary on Ellen's necessary escape out of the mountains. Hal, a wide-roaming landscape painter, had been the one to suggest I apprentice at a ski school, to abandon the conventional job search and go for what I loved. I wanted them both to see this fantastic good luck, how following that advice had turned out so beautifully.

When they answered the door, it was as if they knew already. Hal took one look and wrapped his big artist's arms around Ellen as if to say, welcome to the family.

# Gliders of the Storm

THE FOLKS WHO MARKET SKIING are into some serious ambivalence regarding storms. On the one hand, of course, they admit there wouldn't be much sliding without them. And, when pressed, they will agree that the occasional tempest, once it's moved through, gives good ambience – everything from frosting-laden evergreens to the classic, powder-baptism cover shot.

But the storms that make these images possible are never mentioned or pictured in the company literature. Instead, it's always "Come ski our fresh-powder, blue-sky bowls!" Or "165 days of winter sunshine!" You'd think the stuff grew in the night or was delivered in the fall by Scandinavian elves. Storms are still considered "bad" weather by every TV weatherman and, sadly, by most skiers. Storms are inconvenient, messy to drive and fly in, cold, wet, and sometimes dangerous.

Storm days are also, I'm here to say, the very best days to ski. Bar none.

Early this season I was in Breckenridge to ski with a friend from the Front Range. It was pre-Thanksgiving and not much of the mountain was yet open. Members of various national teams trained on the steepest run, closed to the rest of us, roaring around the gates, edges cleaving ice, padded sweaters smacking poles like abused saplings in the morning sunshine.

The skiing was good, no question. Firm. A little noisy underfoot but, hey. Perfect for finding your feet on the first day of the season.

Then it started to snow. Just spitting to begin with, the sun playing peekaboo, the clouds slowly lowering. After a while, spitting gave way to a steady sprinkling of needles and dendrites, extremely fine dustings gathering on sleeves and thighs during lift rides. Then the sky closed in completely. The air grew dark and still, and big stellar crystals poured down at a rate of several inches an hour.

The skiing became quiet. That's one of the wonderful things about storms: it only takes an inch of two to cushion a scratchy surface and render your skis silent, spoons scooping flour. We couldn't see very well, so we hugged the tree edges where there was more definition. Mostly we let go of the vision thing and placed our trust in the subtler, and ultimately more important, sense, the sense of feel. Proprioception engaged, I remembered to stand up taller, relaxed my feet in my boots, and stopped trying to carve turns so much as react to the shapes as they came.

For the final hour, we were practically alone on the hill. Lift operators trudged out of their warm shacks, nodded imperceptibly from beneath their hoods. The ticket-buying public had mostly given up. Those who remained slipped through a mountain world utterly different than the one we had skied that morning. The racers were gone, so we ghosted the pampered rolls and steeps of their domain. We rode the chair like tortoises, hunkered into our collars for protection from the swirling flakes. We went right from the top, or left – it didn't matter. Every run was better, softer, quieter than the one before. The mountain was renewing itself, and we were there, privy to secret, giddy, nearly illicit pleasure. Every turn felt like a gift.

Storm skiing returns you to the foundation of the sport, to a merging of skier and mountain. A lot of everyday baggage sloughs away. How do I look? How am I doing? Are my skis too old? My boots too soft?

Inside the snowy bubble of a storm day, the questions become more elemental. Where is the snow deepest? Which trees offer shelter from the wind? How well is my kit sealing out the weather?

If it is working well, if you are zipped to the chin and wrapped at the wrists and impenetrable around the midriff, it's like being in a soundproof booth. (Summit County friends call this "the inside inside, outside outside.") You may hear snowflakes plinking against your goggles, but you are also free to hear nothing, like the sound of your ski bending in the angel food cake beneath you. You are free to hum, free to go slowly, free to be invisible, free to find yourself.

If there is measurable snow on the ground, you will also be freed of the need for sharp edges. In new snow, edges don't scrape and brake. They disappear into the body of the ski, now a much sexier toy. In new snow, skis become hydrofoils. You are no longer sliding across a two-dimensional plane; you are diving in and out (the lovely cliché is *porpoising*) through a shallow, pure-white sea.

Some skiers think that if life is so good during a storm, it will be that much better after the sun comes out the next day, as clouds part to reveal a sky impossibly blue and a snow surface that sparkles like broken glass. That is the stuff of ski movies, and of dreams. And those moments do exist, but they are gone in a blink as hungry hordes scarf up every scrap of untouched. Competition and hurry rule the morning. You may claim a virgin run or two, then it's over. What's left is called crud, for good reason.

Storm skiing grants the gift of time. The fiercer the storm, the more time you have. Private time. Sacred time. Even backwards time. During a good dump crud becomes powder instead of the other way around. Old tracks fill in and disappear. Choice expands: the best lines are everywhere waiting to be picked. Everybody else is crammed into the steamy lodge, breathing wet socks.

That's why when my buddy and I are the last ones in on a stormy afternoon, and we stand shedding snow from the folds of our jackets, with snow-caked hats and boots and ice-encrusted neck gaiters, and people say, "Man, you're crazy!" we just smile. Some of them know. And those who don't, fine. Fine, too, if the folks who sell the lift tickets don't want to advertise these miserable, bothersome occurrences between their packed-powder, blue-sky days.

Crazy. But fine with me.

# On the Brink

Ellen and I were looking for the next mountain, the next ski school where we could ply our trade. A fellow instructor mentioned Bear Valley in California's central Sierra. A skier's mountain, he said, a mini Squaw Valley. Lots of snow. The ski school director was named Peter Brinkman.

We liked him the minute we met. He was tall and animated, with an uninhibited high giggle for a laugh. I wouldn't say he had classic, movie star good looks – he was too goofy for that. But he was magnetic, broad-shouldered (he played football at the University of Washington), and the Bear Valley web site is not wrong to have described him as "one of the country's hunkiest ski instructors." He had a Hollywood connection: his brother was married to the actress Jeanne Crain (*State Fair, Cheaper by the Dozen*). Clint Eastwood, Merv Griffin, and Lloyd Bridges all spent time on Bear's slopes. During our first winter with the ski school, Peter brought his girlfriend Ann Pennington, a *Playboy* Playmate, up to ski. She promptly broke her leg.

As our boss, Peter was both father and child. Like a father, or maybe more like a big brother, he cared about everyone in his charge. The responsible adult Peter assembled a staff of skiing stars: filmmaker, author and technical guru Lito Tejada-Flores; ex-U.S. Team member and speed skiing world record holder Dick Dorworth; fiery, long-legged ski-movie star Jon Reveal and his French wife, Marie-Chantal; Swiss pro Narcisse Emery; a pipe-smoking Kiwi, Maurice Flutey, who taught year round in Australia and Bear Valley; and a couple dozen other smart, strong-skiing characters.

Here's an example of the locker-room humor in the Brinkman era.

Racer Tim Kennedy was fed up with people dribbling hot wax on the vice affixed to the ski-tuning bench. So he wrote DON'T WAX ON VICE! on the chalkboard one evening. Next morning someone else had scribbled the logical rejoinder: DON'T WANE ON VIRTUE!

Little Bear Valley dominated the annual Far West Ski Instructor Association certification exams during those years, outscoring, and outclassing, the much bigger schools at Mammoth and Squaw Valley.

To keep this talented bunch busy, Peter single-handedly kept the venerable, all-inclusive ski week alive. Almost everywhere else in ski country in the 1970s the weeklong lodging/lifts/lessons package was going the way of the dodo. But Peter the charmer, Peter with his contagious enthusiasm, successfully sold packages to ski clubs and groups across the West. He worked his tail off all summer and fall so that we could have work six days a week (seven if we wanted it) and not just at Christmas and Easter.

I'm not sure we told him often or directly enough how much we appreciated this. We did, however, make up in loyalty and tolerance what we might have withheld in formal thanks. Peter required tolerance. His child was irrepressible.

He skied under ropes into closed areas, infuriating the Bear Valley ski patrol. I remember one incident after a major storm when Peter was caught in Grizzly Basin just as a huge, explosives-triggered avalanche was winding its way down Flying Serpent. The patrol was livid. The scandal rocked the whole ski-area family. And Peter was chastened, though not squashed, when he told us at the next Saturday meeting: Do as I say, not as I do.

We took to calling him The Brink. He drove a Porsche, drove it fast, sometimes with a bowl of breakfast cereal on his lap. He bought boots a size too small and skied without socks, barefoot to maximize snow-feel. He was a bit of a health nut; he refused to dilute his gastric juices with a drink of any kind at lunch, even on the warmest spring day. He had a peculiar sense of the possible versus the realistic. This was manifest most dramatically when he expanded his business to include the ski schools at Kirkwood and Telluride.

In those days, ski schools could be a separate business; they were not necessarily a spoke of the corporate umbrella. It's still that way in Europe, where a major ski area is likely to have two or three ski schools from which a visitor might choose.

Peter charmed Telluride's founding developer, Joe Zoline, into giving him the ski school there in 1976. That's how Ellen and I came back to Colorado, along with a handful of fellow instructors from Bear Valley.

In return for the franchise, Peter promised to do for Telluride's mid-week business what he'd done for Bear Valley's, by taking his show on the road and selling ski weeks. But Telluride was so remote then, so far off the average skier's radar. And The Brink was seriously over-extended. He never stopped believing he could do it – zip back and forth between the Sierras and the Rockies, run the three ski schools, and maintain a full schedule of sales meetings for all three mountains – but it wasn't humanly possible.

I remember an afternoon on Telluride's Main Street. Peter was leaning an arm out the door of a sporty, rented convertible, not wanting to say good-bye. He had an hour and 15 minutes to make a flight out of Grand Junction. He was already too late – part of him must have known that – but he kept insisting he could make it: he was a good driver; it's only about an hour to Junction, right? (It's two and a half hours. On dry roads.) And still he lingered. The familial affection. The unreal relationship to distance and time.

Eventually he lost all three ski schools, Kirkwood and Bear Valley, too. He spent the last quarter century as sports director for Caesar's Palace hotel/casino in South Lake Tahoe.

As for Miss Pennington, she and The Brink took a hiatus after her broken leg on the slopes. But they got back together and married in 1995, by all accounts completely devoted to one another until Peter's death at 74 in 2005. I didn't find out about his dying until years after the fact. The obits have been few and far between, which surprises me. He was a force in the ski world.

I have learned recently that it was pancreatic cancer killed him so young. Too young for a skiing Peter Pan.

# Bear Lessons

MOUNT REBA AT BEAR VALLEY was a real skier's mountain. Like an actor's play, it was a vehicle loaded with challenge and opportunity, much of which remained beyond the ken of an occasional skier or ski-school student.

Most of the terrain was wild, ungroomable, heart-in-throat steep, and aptly named: Balls, Free-Fall, Uptight, Yellow Submarine, Strawberry Fields Forever. (Bear's opening in the winter of 1967-68 jived nicely with late-period Beatles.)

Ellen and I got our first look at the mountain in the fall when the aspens were yellow against a threatening sky. With the ski school director, Peter Brinkman, we peered down into the granite maw of Mokelumne Canyon. It was almost all rock – great gray slabs and cliffs, waterfalls and scree fields – a stunning contrast to the grassy, manicured corridors we had known at Keystone. When the snow came at Bear, it came in droves directly off the Pacific, three and four feet at a time. Soon all those rocky gullies and scree fields, even the waterfalls, were covered, softened into a playground of voluminous shapes, a giant's version of what Max Dercum used to call a "terrain garden."

Ellen and I had to learn how to hold on again. We realized what a gentle, and limited, place Keystone had been, a place (in the words of one of our fellow instructors) where "you dazzled yourself with your own footwork." Bear's steeps were humbling. They demanded precision short-and- medium-radius turns. My newfound joy in carving had to be tempered, replaced largely, by a skiing style that included quick pivots and hard edge sets. When it was working I felt like a Slinky descending stairs – platform to platform to platform. It's called short swing, a more effective, more dynamic version of my old windshield wiper, and it was the only comfortable way to survive 40-degree pitches of frozen granular on an early morning run down Hari-kari.

Carving was still the goal, to ride the curved edge of the ski with so little skidding that one's track appeared engraved on the snow. But it was a necessarily compromised ideal. Wide-open spaces, gentler pitches, and softer snow invited carving. Steeper slopes, tighter spaces, and harder snow meant coiled body positions, more emphatic pole plants, more skidding added to the equation. Conditions determine the skier's response. A t-shirt of the time read, SKIING IS THE ULTIMATE DANCE… AND THE MOUNTAIN ALWAYS LEADS.

Eventually I came to see sideslipping as the skill at the other end of the spectrum from pure carving – and just as valuable. (Ski and skid do derive from the same root.) At my Stage I exam we did the high-speed sideslip, a demo that had many candidates in a panic. It seemed to have no relevance whatever to the modern technique we were teaching and being taught. But of course it did. What do downhill racers do when they cross the finish line at 60 miles per hour? They throw it into a big, snow-plume skid. It's the best way to slow down in a hurry. And unlike using the terrain to slow you down, which works if you have the room, skidding is functional in tight situations – like crowds, or on narrow cat-tracks, and in ten-foot-wide couloirs in the backcountry. Slipping worked wonderfully when I needed to interrupt an arc to drop below an icy patch or an ugly mogul. Starting downslope from a standing stop, I found I had but to relax my edge hold and slip into gravity's embrace. Slipping/skidding, I saw, was just as useful a tool for learning to "let go" as was carving.

To prove it, I followed Ellen once more. There it was: soft ankles, subtle skidding, a soft touch. She adjusted the radius of every turn by a subtle tuning of the carve/skid ratio. When the situation called for drift, her skis went flatter to the snow and she drifted sideways. When she needed to tighten up a curve, to hold a line and get around the corner without losing too much altitude, she dropped her hips to the inside, tilted her skis on edge, and encouraged the carving action.

Years later in Telluride, I spent whole days drifting on skis, floating like a butterfly, stinging like a bee. The sting would be the occasional edge set, used only when absolutely necessary to change direction. I would float wherever I could get away with it, skimming surfaces rather than trying to scribe arcs on them. The ski-school powers admitted that it looked like fun, but my experiments were not viewed as acceptable style by the PSIA. This was not surprising. Racing technique, which naturally focuses on carving, dominates the theoreticians' thinking, and the professional instructors' association and I had made our separate peace by then... But I'm getting ahead of myself.

Back in Bear Valley, all argument about carving and skidding was shelved when the snow started to fall in fat compound flakes. Deep powder changes things, and in the Sierra it seemed to snow every three or four days all winter long – sometimes light and dry, sometimes heavy and wet, lots of new snow that was in between. Ellen and I found ourselves in the company of powderhounds.

The ski-school room buzzed early on powder mornings. Uncle Milt would be there first, preparing skis in his long johns and cawing softly to himself. (The crow call was our way of signaling to one another from the lifts, a secret greeting and wordless commendation awarded a particularly fine run or turn sequence.) The smell of hot wax mingled with Maurice's pipe tobacco and the more acrid perfume of burning P-tex dripped into yesterday's base gouges. Marie-Chantal and Narcisse bantered away in French. Sharky did his imitation of a boorish customer: "Hey, mister! How much it cost to rent you for t-day?" Lito might be scribbling furiously on the chalkboard trying to work through some technical question regarding excess edge angle and "chatter" in a ski turn. Men and women dressed on the same cramped bench, lived out of tiny, stacked lockers. We were a true family, linked by circumstance, affection, and a shared fascination with the mountain in all its moods.

One by one, booted and waxed and goggled, we'd leave the room early, well before lineup, for the one thing that still makes my heart pound in anticipation: powder. I followed the masters. Once again, it is the best way to discover The Way. It took most of the three winters we spent in Bear Valley for me to get the hang of it. Through it all – the falling and the losing of skis, the fogging goggles, the aching legs, the frozen fingers and utter frustration – shone the memory of the occasional perfect turn, the floating through sparkling, hissing, moving snow.

I believe powder is so addictive because it slows everything down. Deep snow acts as a natural brake. Holding on becomes less important, and letting go becomes easier. The lazy, lilting look of a powder skier's descent is due to this freeing combination. Steep slopes don't seem so steep. Tree lines that are otherwise unthinkable are easily navigated in powder. Runners and tennis players talk of transcendent moments when time slows down. Powder can do it to a whole mountain.

I rarely had a ski-school class become comfortable in powder in a day or two. There are no secrets; basic technique still applies. The big hurdle is learning patience, to wait a little longer for your turn to unfold. It needs an alchemy of repetition, many days and many turns in the soft. And unfortunately, powder disappears in a hurry at most ski areas. What the machines don't flatten, the local hounds ski out in a matter of hours – all but the narrowest edges of the trails and a few out-of-the-way patches. So the would-be powder skier must become a sleuth, an explorer. There is no other way to get the experience. Here I recommend a tip from the great Jean-Claude Killy: "Ski ze sides of ze trails." And a couple of my own. First, ski on stormy days when trails are uncrowded and growing coats of ever-deepening white. Second, get out early on powder mornings, and ask the patrol which intermediate trails have been left unrolled. Third, try a pair of short, wide skis; they'll feel like dancing slippers after your full-length boards. And fourth, go to the movies. Lose yourself in the latest from Dick Barrymore and Warren Miller. Imagine yourself doing it. Dream it.

Finding powder was the adventure, the draw, but full certification was the professional goal. I remember Ellen's Stage II test down at Mammoth Mountain, my old schussing grounds as a kid. Ellen had psyched herself into a state of hyperawareness and was skiing like never before. She seemed ethereal, the very soul of grace. Most of the time it looked like she wasn't touching the snow at all. Confronted with mortal genius, the gods shuffled their feet and rustled their papers and gave her near-perfect marks. After the test, she collapsed for days.

My own Stage II also went well. I was lucky to be taking the exam in the Far West rather than in the Rockies. The FWSIA test was broader-based. The examiners wanted to see teaching and class-handling skills, an understanding of the biomechanics and kinesiology of skiing, and teaching psychology, as well as physical mastery on the mountain. In the Rocky Division the emphasis was – and may still be – on brilliant, demonstration-team-like skiing. As a relative neophyte to the wonders of advanced skiing, I prospered under the more balanced system.

Looking back, it seems that certification was just the beginning. After that was out of the way, we could become individual skiers and teachers, idiosyncratic, eccentric if we wanted to be. But the PSIA, to be sure, is not in the business of sanctioning eccentricity. The official dogma is still rooted in right and wrong technique, and most ski schools are still run with paramilitary attention to rank and conformity. Things like lyricism may be little appreciated. Certified instructors, those who have jumped through the hoops, are usually allowed the freedom to evolve a personal style, but the profession systematically discourages some fine teachers – instructors who are unwilling or unable to mold their own skiing in the image of the gods. Without this imitative ability there is no hope of passing the prerequisite exams.

There is more to the career saga. Ellen and I moved to Telluride, where I proved the theory that a good teacher does not necessarily a good administrator make. I fought more battles over carving versus skidding ("Are you skidding me?"), short skis versus long (This is largely a macho argument. The gods accept that "easier is better" for beginners, but short skis for instructors? Unthinkable!), and private lessons versus class lessons (Ski schools make more money off privates, but people actually seem to learn more in the company of their peers, and one hour – the length of most privates – is a pitiably short time to learn anything). These arguments are still going strong.

The best classes are still the ones with the happiest-looking people. The technique being taught has less to do with it than the care the instructor takes in designing challenges for each individual. The best teachers are inspirational guides. They help people see and then feel for themselves what this ecstatic curving through space is all about.

# Ski Bum Alum

Twenty years ago this fall I entered Pomona College, a small, proud, liberal arts college in Claremont, southern California. I didn't graduate. (I transferred to Berkeley.) But that doesn't stop them from sending, like clockwork, the quarterly alumni publication *Pomona Today*. They do it, I'm convinced, to make me feel bad.

Everyone else, it seems, in the Class of '71 writes in with news of mega-success in the wide world, thanks always in large part to the wonderful preparation Pomona endowed.

You know the letters: "Performed Dvorak's D Major Mass for choir and seven-handed organ just minutes before the birth of daughter number two, Jessica Ann. New York law practice continues to challenge. Currently chair of the Litigation Delegation to the American Bars Association, though there is still time (somehow!) for the Beyond Peace Movement and our (mine and husband John's) new non-profit organization for the re-settlement of Central American refugees and the re-animation of the culturally inane."

And another: "Recently left my post as dean of UCLA Medical School to assume the Vice Chancellery for Ethics and Justice at R.M. Nixon University. Kids were National Merit Scholars, again. Wife June (Class of '73) publishes the third in her series this spring, *Cityscrapes: An Artist's Guide to Playground Architecture as Motordrive Development and Spatial Management*. Loving L.A.! Any old friends welcome to drop by!"

Well, I decided to write, finally, and let them know about my life progress:

Dear Class,

Just returned from the ski swap up in Telluride where I scored winter clothes for the kids. Yay! And somebody in the neighboring town of Ouray (population 787) gave my wife Ellen (you don't know her; she went to another college, Class of '68), a used Patagonia pile sweater. Man, those things last forever! So, it looks like we'll be warm again this winter!

Also, I was able to swap some of the swag I got as a freelance ski writer for upgraded skis and boots for the kids. Can you believe it, they keep growing! And my past gig with Telluride's ski school is still paying benefits in the form of day passes for the family, if I ask nicely. Otherwise, can you imagine the retail cost of taking a family of four skiing?

We're loving it here in Ridgway, Colorado (population 279), where I recently won the local Cord Splitter's Award for "the most aesthetically pleasing woodpile of six cords or more unsupported by any wall or fence." The super-high alpine of Red Mountain Pass is just 45 minutes away. Also, I've been mentioned in the paper lately – sure, for being warned again by the marshal about having a dog at large – but also for speaking up at the town meeting against the annexation of that swamp property across the highway. Even if it would mean some help, eventually, with the town's sewer problem. At least nobody here is trying to get the streets paved.

Maybe a bit of catching up is in order. After leaving Pomona I went East for a time, then back West, then back to the mountainous middle, to Rocky Colorado, where teaching skiing would be a kind of hollyhock stalk on which the blooms of career options would open up, and, as it happened, the unemployment checks in summer (especially generous during the salad days of Nixon) were often nearly enough to keep us in yogurt, and gas for the bus.

Oh yes. The bus is still running. Tortuga. Two hundred sixty thousand miles now, though the transmission is finally going and the heater defrosts only about a dollar-sized spot on the windshield on cold days. We spray-painted it ourselves a couple of years ago. A nice mouse gray. Looks sharp.

Ellen and I have tried to pass along to the kids the cultural/intellectual heritage we bear in trust from our college days. Little Cloe likes garlic. And Cecily seems to have her mother's gypsy genius for fashion. Both girls have been known to layer tutus and jammy bottoms for school.

We do have a television now. My mother arrived from Southern California with it last winter saying she would not have her grandchildren raised by wolves. Which reminds me, the Broncos are playing the Bears in a little while and I've got to wrap this up.

I've been thinking a lot about my forthcoming book. Maybe it'll detail the existential conundrums of chimney cleaning. Or cleaning trout. Anyway, I won't be attending the reunion again this year. The high-velocity spatial interrelationships in the city don't settle well with the old bus. And besides, the skiing's too good in the spring.

Ciao for now,

Peter

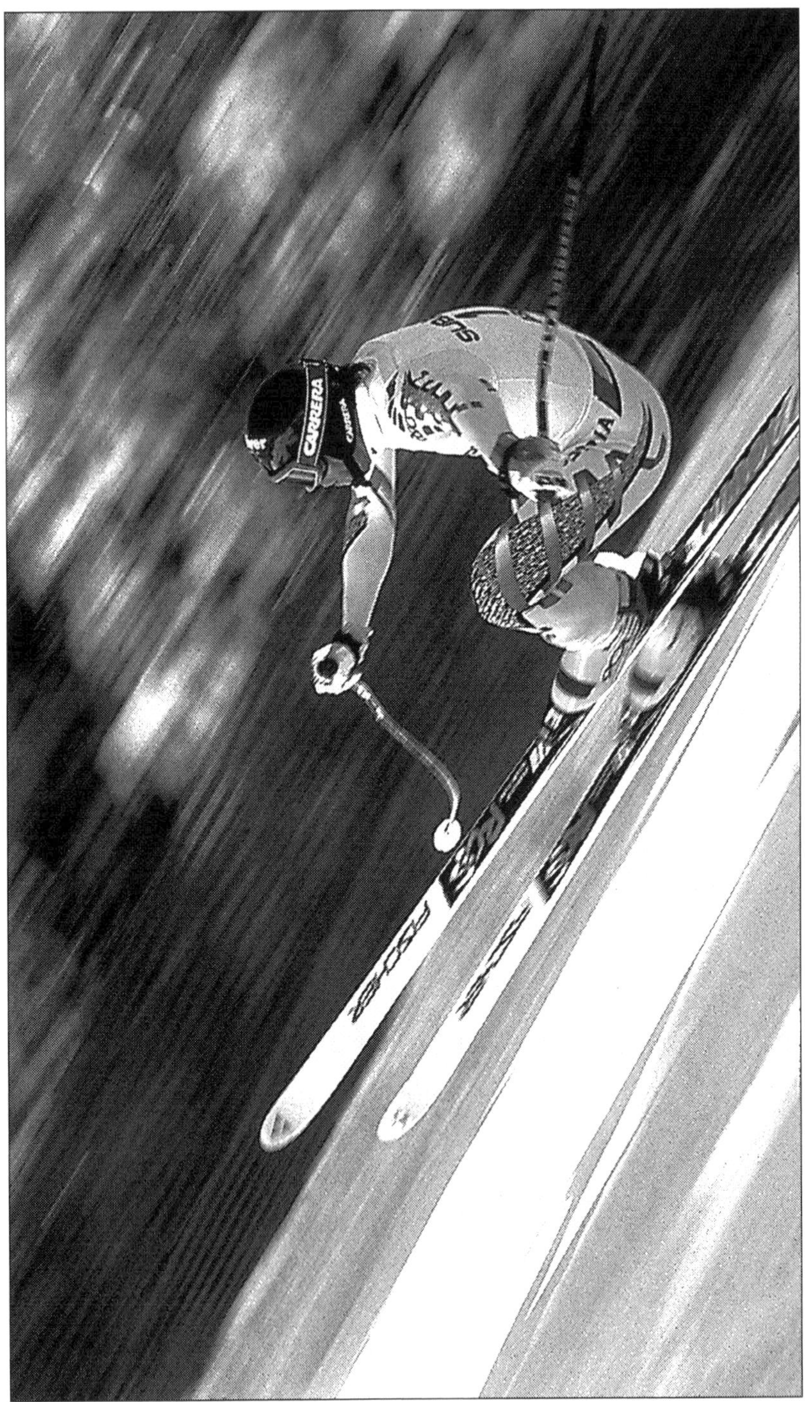
CARRERA

# PART II

# The Need for Speed

# Gear and Clothing in Las Vegas

*(with appologies to Hunter S. Thompson)*

Tooling along I-70 in the Gray Mouse just west of Green River, my attorney suddenly ripped off his pants.

"You crazy fool!" I screamed, remembering in my bones the sub-freezing dawn in which we'd left home.

"Hey," he said. "We're going to Vegas, man. Sun. Springtime. Tanness. As your attorney, I advise you to do the same." His snowy white gams stuck out of a pair of Patagonia stand-up shorts. Mine were still wrapped in Bean's woodsman's wool.

Las Vegas. Indeed.

Somehow for this week in March, the neon flower of the high desert would become the center of the ski world. The beating heart of the sport I love. Wayne "Fig" Newton. Slots. Girls. Free breakfast anytime. How was this possible? And what did it all mean? I didn't know. I only knew that, as a journalist, I had an obligation to cover the story.

"As your attorney, I advise you to drive faster." He was horribly twisted after fifteen hours at 55 miles per hour. I could see his point. But I was not about to push the Mouse. Loyalty like this should not be strained. Not after 15 years. The Mouse had been there when boots smelled of sweet leather grease, and skiers yodeled. No, it wasn't the Mouse – my faithful '69 bus – it was Las Vegas I was having my doubts about.

A rose-colored glow had been hovering on the desert horizon for the past few miles. At first I put it off to highway hallucinations. But it was getting brighter. Then, pulling over a final rise, the glare lashed through the windshield with the brilliance of a bomb blast. My attorney's eyes were slits in a glowing mask. "Ohmigod. They've dropped the Big One. Turn around! We'll all be killed!" He grabbed the wheel, but I beat him back.

"No, man." I said as soothingly as possible. "Vegas."

We pulled into a 76 station in North Las Vegas for gas and directions. It was 10 p.m. and as bright as midday. We told the man we were going to the Ski Show. He made a sweep with his arm across the blaze that was downtown and said, "I guarantee you'll see more there than you've seen in a long time."

We had both been to Vegas before, of course. But then it was just in passing. Late night coffee. A quick gas-up en route to Salt Lake City on the Wasatch powder pilgrimage. Always on the way to someplace else. Now we were really in it. Diving for the core.

In order to get acclimatized we cruised The Strip a few times. The Dunes. Caesar's Palace. The Flamingo. The Sands. The Grand Imperial. All battling to blot out the night. Light bulbs by the trillions. The very air hummed with electricity.

"Now we know why they put Hoover Dam where they did." My attorney was finally calming down.

Next morning we parked in the giant lot fronting the gold-domed Convention Center. My attorney insisted we carry our avalanche transceivers to locate the Mouse when we came out. It was no joke.

We got in line for credentials. There was a table about a mile long piled with programs and trade journals. A welcome letter featured a photo of the mayor, William "Bill" Briare, smiling awkwardly next to the President of the United States, Ronald Reagan. I began to read: "Welcome to Las Vegas and the 13th annual SIA (Ski Industries America) Trade Show and 3rd Annual Sports Exposition to be held here… [Last year] a total of 16,222 retailers, exhibitors, guests, and members of the press attended the SIA Ski Show… 9,316 buyers from 3,238 ski and sporting goods shops attended… to see and write orders for the 2,500 different product items and brands that were displayed in 335,000 net square feet of booth space."

I also learned that the 1984 SIA Official Trade Show sponsors were, among others: Adolph Coors Beer, "the official beer of the SIA Show," Maxwell

House Coffee, "the official coffee of the Show," and Velamints, "the official mint of the 1984 SIA Show." A wicked combination. I was going to have to keep a close watch on my attorney.

"Your affiliation?"

"Uh. I'm with *Powder* magazine."

"I don't find your name on my list under *Powder*."

"Well, I'm here to cover the story for them."

"That's okay. *Powder*'s an exhibitor; they have a booth. I can give you an exhibitor's tag. Just take this over to the typists…"

"Pssst! Ixnay, man." It was my attorney, resurfaced at my elbow. "You don't want the exhibitor badge. It's like leprosy. Exhibitors aren't supposed to go out of their booths. Might be out stealing trade secrets, dig? Get something else."

My attorney had me beat on experience. He'd once been to a mini show in Denver, so I had to go with his wisdom, such as it was.

"Uh, excuse me. I'm not really an exhibitor…"

"Are you a buyer?"

"Well, not exactly. How about press? Do you have something…?"

"You got a press card? Okay. Take this over to the typists, and put this sticker on your camera, and be sure to ask permission from the exhibitor first before you take any pictures. Some of them can be a little touchy."

"Better." My attorney appraised the red PRESS on my chest as we cruised by the guards and into the main hall. He had somehow got himself a blue BUYER tag. "But watch this!" he crowed. "They're all going to treat me like a king."

We got separated almost immediately. I stopped just long enough to work up sufficient embarrassment for a half-naked girl shilling for another ski magazine, and when I turned around, my attorney was gone. Thirty seconds later I got sucked into a crowd peeking through an opening in glossy white pre-fab walls that said Sport-Obermeyer on them. Fleetwood Mac was throbbing away inside, and every once in a while I could make out the models strutting it on the ramp – all hips and eyes and fingernails.

Then it was over and they hung out the sign: Next Show at 11:30. A show within the Show. Turned out there were hundreds of them. A different one starting every few minutes somewhere in the maze. Some were open to the passing world, like the Pacific Trail/Liberty Bell shows – just a stage with lights and sound and a bunch of kids break-dancing like crazy in nylon ski suits, spinning 'til they blurred on the slippery plastic floor. Others, like Obermeyer's, had walls or billowing tent sides with seating for buyers and just enough window space to attract peepers. Still others, like the Italian brand Fila, required reservations and made sure to protect next year's line from prying eyes.

I stumbled in on the tail end of the Gerry production billed "Raz Berry and G-TV," a takeoff on the kinky glitz of rock video. A pretty good Mick Jagger impersonator, shirtless and prancing, lip-synced "Beast of Burden" while wigged-out babes in ski togs flailed around him. Turned out I'd missed the Dolly Parton, Donna Summer and Boy George acts. I made a note of the next show time, then drifted away and promptly forgot it. I was already beginning to lose my mental muscle tone.

Models everywhere. Skinny. Punk hair and make-up. All exuding various combinations of the model's tools: sex, viciousness, boredom and playfulness. On their breaks, they'd zoom around in floppy-sweatshirt gangs, obviously thrilled to be out of their quilted, insulated tri-blend cocoons. Up and down the aisles they raced, past the conservatively dressed exhibitors, the company reps, all of whom looked like people I knew or should have known from somewhere – a chairlift shared perhaps? They, the reps, appeared semi-healthy, but a bit peaked, as if they hadn't skied enough this winter. There was a touch of resignation, too, around the corners of the eyes, as if to say: There was no other way to stay close to skiing and make a living, too.

Buyers covered the floor like worker ants building for the genetic future. That's exactly what they were doing, of course. Filling their big notebooks with orders for next year. Keeping the cycle rolling. I felt jealous. There they were picking out two dozen of these and four dozen of these and three gross of those. Like grown-up kids in Candyland. Every ski toy in existence under one roof. And not just one of each. The proper display effect was line upon line of identical items, like perfect teeth, like lines of time rippling out into space.

I felt myself swooning. Too much stimulation. I felt like I needed a whiff of my dad's old FaSki base varnish. That, or my mother applying a dose of Sea 'n' Ski to my nose. I wanted to be out there, doing it. Wind in the face. Where was the wind? Where was the movement? The skill? Where was the snow, for crissakes?!

I wandered about like a deranged bee, unable to stop but no longer able to distinguish one flower from another.

I became hopelessly lost. Was this North Hall, South Hall, or East Hall? Or the East Hall Exhibit Rooms, any one of which could be a hangar for a half dozen dirigibles. My feet were weary, and my mind ached. I was further away than ever, I thought, from understanding the story. In desperation, I had been popping official mints, but they seemed to have no helpful effect whatsoever. I sought solace in a familiar drug, the TV screen.

The Sarajevo Olympics were barely over, but here they were again, alive and repeating themselves all over the show. I plopped down in front of Dynastar's video monitor and zoned out on Debbie Armstrong's gold medal GS runs. Nobody seemed to mind. I watched them over and over and over and over. There was something soothing about her Day-Glo striped suit bopping left and right, up and down. All sense of time left me. Despite, or maybe because of, my weakened state, every gate on that course was permanently etched in my memory.

I have no idea how long I'd been slumped against that wall underneath that picture of downhill gold medalist Bill Johnson, staring at that row of Atomic skis – their perfect, even, matching, red sameness. Tip to tip and tail to tail, ad infinitum. They shone, as if buffed by an army of Austrian elves with Windex bottles. They glowed from within like the brand new Head Standards under my Christmas tree. Years ago. They had that same deep magic, the promise of graceful, slicing turns… I was sinking farther into irretrievable reverie when, suddenly…

"Pete! Hey, howya doin'? Say, I see you dressed for the Show." It was a fellow journalist, from Back East. He was looking natty in a blue blazer and tie. I glanced down at my faithful cords and best denim work shirt. "Pretty wild, eh? You ever been here before? Too much.

"Say, didja see those new stretch pants with the knee braces built right into them? They're promoting them for people who are too vain to wear braces on the outside and for bump skiers who are well on the way to ruining their knees anyway.

"Lotta boutique stuff this year. You know, the systems. Contact System. Variable Side-Cut System. Quatro. Thermo. Then there's the Nava knee-high binding so you don't ever have to get out of your after-ski boots.

"Say, are you going to the Mahres party? Everybody'll be there. Meeting Rooms Two and Three. Six oh five tonight. Yeah, come. The Mahres are going to talk about their future plans. They're going to be writing for *SKI* this year, you know. You can bet there's some money in that deal. Say, there goes Bill Johnson. He's a little shorter than I thought he'd be. Well, gotta go. See you tonight."

My attorney found me crawling in circles in the middle of the huge Salomon area – about a city block of blood-red carpet populated with thousands and thousands of matched boots and bindings. I was delirious, mumbling something about finding my lost ski. He'd been over in the Sports Expo wing, yet another 57,500 square feet of space for related businesses that don't belong to SIA.

"Yeah, it's business as usual over there." My attorney liked to hobnob with the dirtbag mountaineering types. "Some guy called me Pat, had a name tag that said Yule, and his name was really Dave. He said, 'I just borrowed this to get in. I need a job.' Business, man. I'd go up to some guy I used to climb with and say, 'How're your toes?' – frostbite – and he'd say, 'No problem. I've moved to Ventura.' I mean, all the hard guys have gone soft. Makin' money. Hey, wanna go back over to Gore-Tex with me and ask them what they thought about Chouinard's comments in *Outside*? You know, about there being no such thing as a waterproof *and* breathable fabric? Huh? Or we could go check out sailboards?"

"Sailboards?"

"Yeah. Contra-seasonal equipe. Keeps the retailers alive… Okay, how 'bout we go do a line."

"Whaaaa?"

"You know. Do a line. Go sit down and have the Helly-Hansen guy run through the line for us. I've got my buyer's tag, remember?"

"Uh, what time is it?"

"Six."

"Oh, wow. We've got to get over and meet the Mahres."

"Hey, amigo. Come on. Wake up." My attorney was slapping me on the cheeks and flicking flecks of the official beer of the Show on my neck. I struggled through the fog to come all the way back, but I kept slipping into this warm dark place where a voice I didn't recognize crooned softly: "Market share leaders Rossignol and Nordica... cost-effective Spanish and Italian factories... positioning your ski shop: high-volume, low-service discount shop or full-service, full-margin, specialty dealer... the threat of the gray markets, European retailers unloading excess inventory in the U.S., is greatly exaggerated... rear-entry versus overlap... *Hintereinstieg*... the question being the extent of its market penetration..."

"Wake up, man. We can't stay here." I recognized an urgency in my attorney's voice, but I still couldn't pull out of it. I drifted back to the Meet the Mahres reception. (We had made it after all.) There were these two magnificent athletes looking identically queasy in coats and ties as their manager/agent or whatever droned on about the new TWN line of skiwear – so new, it wasn't even at the Show. But it was available for viewing at a private room at the Frontier.

Then the Mahres themselves took the mic and spoke convincingly of their love for skiing and their hopes that their new television series and their new Ski-the-Mahre-Way Program and their new magazine columns would bring more families, like their own, to the sport. Man next to me: "It's too bad they didn't get life contracts with IBM or something instead of all this undignified scrambling." Retirement. Indeed. I felt a pain inside, somewhere between sadness and indigestion.

"Wake up. C'mon, man. We gotta get outta here."

The next scenes came as in a dream. They were fuzzy and unstuck in time. Maybe it was the Meet the Mahres reception champagne on top of the mints. Whatever. I remembered careening down long curving hallways with paisley carpets and chandeliers, hurrying to get somewhere – to a dinner engagement or some party or other – my attorney jerking my arm saying, "We gotta find Benihana Village." Right. The Benihana. Must pass through the casino first. Hum of coins and spinning machines. Oops! Watch out. Mirrors. Everywhere. Mirrors on the ceiling. Woman with cat eyes dealing cards. Fat man dripping sweat onto green crushed velvet table. Another man, his arm *becomes* the handle of the slot machine. Jerking down, then up. Again and again.

"Cigars. Cigarettes." A girl with too few clothes and earrings that blink red, on and off, like a beacon out at sea.

The Benihana chef suddenly very clear, knives dancing: "I Toyota. I check orders again, to be sure. Two shrimp, two chicken, two more shrimp, and two quarter pounders. Ha, ha! Where's the beef?!"

Rain falling from the ceiling into harmless pools, misting by the tables.

More curving halls. Trying to find *Powder*'s First Annual "Better Late Than Never St. Paddy's Day Party, Film and Slide Show." Hotel dick, grotesquely puffed up, cramming the doors shut against too many bodies. Saying to us, "No! Back off! Too many already!"

"But we have invita…" Slam.

Must be a way. Other doors. Empty ballrooms. Accordion walls. Squeeeezing through a crack into… BLINDING lights. Click and whirr of the projector. Damn. *Behind* the screen!

Press of warm bodies. Irish coffees. Cover-shot stars everywhere. Galen Rowell. Ned Gillette. Eric Sanford. Ron Dahlquist. Jan Reynolds. My god! I'm sitting on the floor next to Jan Reynolds!

Out into the bright sweet spring night air. Dragged through the streets to the Fly Away. The sign read: "MAN CAN FLY LIKE A BIRD. Now, In Las Vegas, The First Flying Chamber in the U.S.A., New Price $10.00 Per Person, 7 Days a Week, Spectators $2.00."

Totally wasted, I have no will, no sense. Somebody finds ten dollars in my pocket, and I am given a ticket, shoved down the stairs and dressed in a ridiculous parachute suit. Sincere young man is trying to tell me something about how to fly. Into the chamber. Terrific wind wails up through the screened floor.

"Jump! Jump!"

I hurl myself off the bench, arms out, body limp with acquiescence, mind blank with panic. But the air is a cushion, holding me up. I am soaring! Dipping. Swooping left and right. My mind clears to razor sharpness. I am at Alta for the first time. Storm breaking. Snow like diamonds. I am floating. Bouncing, left and right. Invincible, like Debbie Armstrong. I have happened upon gravity's secret, become one with it. I am free!

"C'mon, man. It's past midnight. They're trying to close up here. Let's go." My attorney sat me up. "Hey, you were great, man. They had to shut off the fan to get you down. Come on outside. The fresh air'll do you good."

On the sidewalk we had to go squinty again in the glare of artificial day. As my eyes got used to it, I spotted what appeared to be airborne lights. White pinpricks gyrating through the glow above the city. Then I realized that they were not electric at all but a flock of small birds pin-wheeling crazily and lit from below.

"Look," I pointed.

"Oh, wow."

Below the birds and a little off to one side was a well-lit billboard with letters ten feet tall spelling out: PHIL & STEVE FOR PRESIDENT.

Why not? I thought. Why not, indeed.

# The Need for Speed

Steve Fox, of ABC's *Good Morning America*, stood half way up the couloir, microphone in hand, balanced precariously on a shoveled-out snow ledge. Behind him sleek finned humans in rubberized suits and trout-face helmets bolted one by one down the Velocity Peak track, shrinking almost instantly to anonymous specks on the way to the basin floor.

"It is still hard for me to believe that these people literally dive straight down the mountain at speeds in excess of 100 miles per hour," Fox said, addressing the camera. "They are not good at describing why they do it. But for each of them, it is an awesome and compelling feeling."

Fox gingerly reaffirmed his footing, brushed back his hair, and said the words again. And again, at the behest of his director. With each repeat, his astonishment seemed to grow. It's hard not be awestruck by speed skiing.

Fox was wrong about the athletes being inarticulate on the question of why. But he was right to be astonished. Speed skiers go faster than a skydiver in free-fall. The sound of turbulence as they rip through the air has been likened to the roar of a jet engine. Or a forest fire. Last April 24 (1983), from a spot near the timing lights at this high-altitude track outside Silverton, Colorado, I thought it sounded like bacon frying, through stadium loudspeakers.

Fox and everyone else who had come to this remote basin for four days in spring was hoping for one thing: a new world record speed.

Speed skiing is by no means new. In 1860 a California miner named Tommy Todd was clocked at an average 88 mph (14 seconds from a standing start over a course of 1,804 feet) and achieved instant hero status in the

Sierra gold country. Competition among winter-idled miners often ran for days, with high-stakes gambling, secret wax concoctions applied by "dopemen," and a grand ball at the weekend. Speed records have been kept for the Kilometro Lanciato, the Flying Kilometer, on the Italian side of the Matterhorn, since 1931. World records have also been set in France and Chile. What is new is this thin-air Colorado venue that is almost certainly the best track of them all. And American fans are waking up to the spectacle.

Television is a part of it. Camel cigarettes and Coors beer have come on as sponsors. ABC's infatuation is understandable. There is the obvious danger, and the visuals are irresistible, the sweep of movement and color, the blurred flash of shiny speed-suit reds and whites and blacks against the snow and sky. Fully rigged, speed skiers look like something you'd find on the Bonneville Salt Flats. The fairings behind their calves are little stabilizer wings – to cut down on turbulence. Their swept-back helmets are cockpits. Their suits are so tight and slick they appear painted on. These are often plastered with sponsor logos, and the driver's name. The driver's name may be inscribed in florid script. The racers run on heavy, handmade, 240 cm skis. Their curved poles snuggle ergonomically around fiercely held tuck positions. Bulky ski gloves are out. Bare hands cleave the air in front of the racer's faces.

For seven of the last nine years the record holder has been Tahoe native Steve McKinney, a charismatic, enigmatic, bigger-than-life force. He's six-three and wiry, with blond hair flowing to his shoulders – a kind of rebel super athlete with Zen undertones.

McKinney was the first to break through the 200 kilometer-per-hour "barrier" – a mythical wall, like the sound barrier before Chuck Yeager – a speed beyond which the rules of nature were rumored to go haywire. His 200.222 kph (124.412 mph) run at Portillo in 1978 stood until a recent onslaught that has seen his seminal mark bettered 17 times. Most important perhaps in speed's current renaissance: In a world where everything is relative, or judged, speed skiing is absolute. The numbers may defy comprehension – try sticking your hand out the car window at 75 mph – but they preclude interpretation. And then there is this tantalizing notion from Canadian Terry Watts who owns the fourth fastest speed on record: "All the craziness of everyday life is worth it for the one pure moment when everything is perfect..."

Silverton represents a new chapter in the history of speed. For decades, the world's only track was the KL, on the Plateau Rosa glacier above Cervinia, with Monte Cervino (the Italian name for the Matterhorn) looming above. McKinney calls the KL a "classic" course out of deference to its long heritage and to the technical challenges of running there. He also calls it a "twilight zone," a "death zone," and a place where skiers are "launched into beautiful, weird flights down the mountain." Silverton's Chief of Race Dick Dorworth, a former record holder, watched a racer torn nearly in half at the KL by a cartwheeling, 100-mph fall, in 1964.

That course started out nearly flat at the top, crossed three wood-and-steel crevasse bridges, then plummeted over a 55-degree pitch before jackknifing to flat again at the bottom. Racers would lift off and fly as far as 300 yards over the steep drop (McKinney's "weird flight"), then get pummeled by triple G-forces in the transition, as they tried to stay on their feet through the finish. As speeds got higher, the track became more and more dangerous until it was ultimately closed.

Reno native Dorworth and Vermonter C.B. Vaughan, both former downhillers, spent weeks alone in the Chilean Andes, in 1963, preparing what they hoped would be a new record track at Portillo. They packed out the course themselves, sidestepping the entire slope, day after day. With the help of Chilean soldiers stationed nearby, they set up a 100-meter-long, electronic timing trap. And then, somewhat incredibly, on the last day before the snow deteriorated to mush, they clocked identical record runs of 106.520 mph.

Unlike the roller coaster KL, the Portillo course provided a continuous concave curve, smooth acceleration, and no killer transition at the bottom. It was also very high, 12,600 feet at the top, which, crucially, meant less air to press through. The Velocity Peak course is also high, about 12,500 feet depending on how far up the couloir the racers start. But it is not an easy track to get to, or to prepare. It's six miles up a dirt road from the depressed mining town of Silverton, population 600. Beyond the dirt, it's another two miles over the snow into Colorado Basin. Once there, the perfect teacup curve of the track comes into view. It starts high in a north-facing couloir and sweeps smoothly down, through the timing trap midway, then gradually moderates through the runout, past a milky turquoise lake melting out in the bottom of the basin. Early record attempts here were frustrated by weather (1980) and avalanches (1981), which tore the track down to the rocks. But April 1982 saw perfect conditions, and new records were set by Telluride ski instructor Marti Martin-Kuntz (111.114 mph) and Austrian tuckmeister Franz Weber, roaring like a bullet train to eclipse McKinney's record with a 126.238 mph.

This spring, with $270,000 from R.J. Reynolds Tobacco Co., Silverton's event managers brought in a snowcat to pack the bottom half of the course. That still meant the racers had to pack the top half themselves. Late afternoons, following training runs, a majority of them donned their short skis (the 223 cm downhill models), and sidestepped slowly up the mammoth curve – 1,200 vertical feet, over half a mile long. McKinney, one of the fraternity's hardest workers, was not in Silverton this time. He was busy climbing Mt. Everest. But he did send a postcard from the Potala Palace in Tibet, showing workers carrying huge loads up and down endless flights of stairs. The sidesteppers could relate.

Warm afternoons, and the time it takes to get back up the hill at Velocity Peak, kept practice runs to a minimum Thursday and Friday. Thursday's speeds were in the 80s and 90s. Friday, the best was 104 mph. B.C. native Watts was tops both days. The fastest woman was newcomer Melissa Dimino, from Squaw Valley. As the start moved higher and speeds began to increase, so too did the racers' spirits.

Saturday dawned clear and windless. The unspoken word was: record day. In years past, no one would dare predict a record – too many variables at the outer limits. But Velocity Peak, with its great, smooth shape and still-untapped potential, inspired confidence. Weber came back to top form and led the men through Saturday's first run at 116 mph. Dimino, still the fastest woman at 112 mph, said what many of the top guns were thinking, "I guess I just didn't think it would be that easy to go that fast."

The run was not without incident, however. Journeyman Charlie Row flipped before he reached the timing lights doing about 113 mph. He'd let a hand slip out from in front of his face and the force ripped him out of his tuck. Fortunately, his skis released and he spun safely to a stop 200 yards down the course. He even got a time: through the trap on his back at 89.585 mph. (At the 1982 event, I watched a racer go down and slide seemingly forever. In the finish area later he displayed the result: the black rubber of his suit welded grotesquely to his hip by the heat of the friction.)

Drag is the enemy. To reduce drag the racers roll their bodies into the tightest possible shape, the better to penetrate the stubborn air. The classic egg-shaped, downhill tuck is modified somewhat for speed skiing. The head is kept low to create a smooth line down the back. (Drop it too low and you can't see.) The chest is tight on the thighs, and the butt is held high to press the whole form forward into the wind. The position of the arms and hands in front of the face is especially important, for they part the air much as a diver's hands split the water. Some racers wear surgical rubber gloves. Others go barehanded, preferring to feel the wind on their skin. And, as McKinney says, "There are no seams in skin."

Anywhere there is a seam – wrists, ankles, boot buckles – is taped smooth with silver tape. Salt Lake City's Kirsten Culver forgot to have her wrists taped Saturday morning, and on her first run, the sleeves peeled off her forearms up to the elbows. The body suits themselves are so slick they would be illegal on the World Cup circuit. Getting suited up, booted up, taped up for a run will take half an hour, and requires assistance.

Piercing the wind. Anything that might help is worth a try. Fifty-four-year-old Kalevi Hakkinen, the grand old man of the sport, veteran of some 500 speed runs, stuffs bubble wrap inside his suit. "Golf ball effect," he winks. Hakki trains by bolting himself to the roof of a Saab and cruising the Finnish autobahns at 100 mph.

Everyone agrees that more important even than good equipment and a good tuck is a piercing mental attitude. Canadian gentle giant Kent Wills, second to Weber after the penultimate run on Saturday, said to Martin-Kuntz shortly before their third and final attempts, "At these speeds, you have to push. You're not just out for the ride, you have to *press* yourself down the hill." Or, as Dorworth, who has written eloquently about his own speed skiing, says, "You become an instrument of your will."

Somewhere in these two statements is at least the seed of an answer to *Good Morning America's* question: Why do they do it? It is beyond logic, of course. The answer is more elemental, more primitive, than that. Basically, it's the challenge: to forge your strengths, and overcome your weaknesses, to hold a precise and difficult position, on skis, in a battle with the air rushing up at you. And where the consequences of a mistake are unthinkable.

I'm convinced these people don't have a death wish. Like a lot of risk takers, they test for unusually low anxiety levels and high degrees of emotional control. And they can be morbidly funny. One t-shirt I saw read, on the front, "Speed Their Only God!" And on the back, "Too Stupid To Live." No, to survive and be good at this, you have to have a better than average grasp of reality, a strong ego, and a sense of calm in the face of tremendous forces. A run at speed is a transcendent event. Dorworth remembers it as "freedom in a perfect run for speed." McKinney has called it a search for "the center of light."

Following the second run on Saturday, warming temperatures caused several small avalanches to pour off the cliffs onto the top part of the track. A cameraman upended by a rolling snowball slid on his bottom a good eighth of a mile before he could dig in his heels and stop. Racers spent an hour ski-packing the slide debris. When it was finally smooth again, the women were well up the couloir beyond the world-record start from last year. It is so steep there (51 degrees plus) that in the lineup to start one girl's head was about level with the boot tops of the girl above her.

ISS rules permitted the record holder, Martin-Kuntz, and the fastest racer from the previous run, Dimino, to pick their start order. Dimino and Martin-Kuntz chose to go last. That meant their chief rival Kirsten Culver had to go first. She didn't care. More than most she seemed to relish each chance to go fast. She exhaled, jumped her skis into the fall line, and dove into her tuck. Her line was unwavering, her position low and tight, solid through the trap then up, arms first, before standing gradually, as if in a hurricane, braking, sweeping across the flats to the little tent city that is the helicopter base, waxing zone, computer center and scoreboard. Up on the screen: 120.785 mph, a new record. No one would catch her, though Martin-Kuntz came close with a 120.590 mph.

The women had made it look easy. The only exception had been the young Frenchwoman Veronique Nemitz, who fell on the outrun, while slowing to about 60 or 70 mph. Tossed about like a rag doll, she was knocked temporarily unconscious.

The men, as a group, had a harder time of it at their outer limits. At less severe speeds, near perfect tucks had been the norm. From this start, though, near the top of the chute, the most miniscule mistakes were exposed as disastrous. The bear-like Watts, trying hard to unseat Weber as champion, had an arm ripped back behind him as he entered the timing trap. He pulled it up. It was ripped back again. Spectators groaned in fear. Only Watts' great strength kept him from falling, but the bobble cost him. He ended up ninth with a speed of 123.656 mph.

So great are the forces at 120 mph that a ski delaminated tip to tail under Ty Fields, an unsponsored newcomer from Alaska. He stood up and rode his good ski for 300 feet before blowing up in a spectacular end-over-end crash. Miraculously, he escaped injury.

One by one the men roared down: buffeted, bounced, obviously struggling to maintain position. Big Sean Cridland from Aspen ran 124.412 – the best of his life. Kent Wills streaked to 126.096, just short of Weber's year-old record. Then Paul Buschmann – carpenter, father, seven-year speed veteran and Squaw Valley soul brother to McKinney – unleashed a 126.810, a new standard. Weber was next.

Franz had done some thinking up there at the start. The snow in the couloir proper, shaded by the rock walls, was cold, still wintry. While out in the sun below the rocks the snow was wetter, cornier – there would be more suction, especially in the glazed tracks of the previous racers. So Weber did an amazing thing. Streaking out of the couloir at 90 mph, he stepped to his left onto a clear line where the ribbed surface left by sidesteppers went "tickatickaticka" (as he later described it) under his skis. Then he held his tuck, generally conceded to be the tightest on the tour, through the lights at a resounding 129.303 mph.

"To be honest, I was nervous this morning," Weber, who speaks five languages, confided to Steve Fox, who remained gobsmacked. "This is the first time I have gone really fast since my fall [at Les Arcs last year]. But no, I was not afraid during the run. There is no fear, only concentration."

International Speed Skiing rules allow for one more run following a record, but the race jury decided to end the competition right there. They'd been lucky so far: new records, no one seriously hurt. Watts, and others who had hoped for another chance were disappointed, but conditions were changing fast in the basin, and the move seemed prescient when wet slides buried the access road the next day.

# E. T. and the mind of Expectation

EVA TWARDOKENS GRUNTS and throws her skis sideways coming through the delay gate. Edges chattering on the rock-hard snow, she muscles back on line, late for the next turn.

The steepest part of the racecourse, the place where her technical superiority usually tells, slips rapidly by, and Eva is not in sync. She grunts again, arms flailing. She's struggling, fighting every corner on the Copper Mountain course. It is not pretty. And it is not particularly fast. She stands eleventh after this, the first run of the 1987 National Championships giant slalom, a full second and a half behind the leader, Debbie Armstrong.

At the finish corral, Twardokens snaps off her skis and stomps quickly away, anger in her dark eyes. She has reason to be upset. At 21, she is, along with Armstrong and Tamara McKinney, one of the mainstays of the U.S. Ski Team. She is fresh from a solid, if not inspired, eighth place finish in the World Championships Combined at Crans Montana, Switzerland, against the world's best. And there is the memory, still vivid, of a GS bronze medal at the 1985 World Championships in Bormio, Italy, when she was just 19. To sit eleventh here behind American B- and C-teamers, behind 16 and 17-year-old comers, is more than Eva can bear.

What went wrong? The day before in practice, Twardokens had skied out of her mind. She had slashed down courses with abandon, nearly flying, not thinking at all – just the way coach Connie Reuprecter (known affectionately as Conan) wanted to see her – "a bit on the edge."

This morning she followed the same monastic routine she always follows: up at 6:00, stretch and warm up, dress, on the hill at 7:00 for an hour of free skiing before course inspection at 8:00. She had felt loose and ready, knowing inside that, "All I have to do is go down the course and go for it, and I'll do well." But it hadn't gone well.

The easy thing was to blame the skis. Rossignol tech rep Scott Shaver comes over to take Eva's race skis from her, and in frustration she lights into him. "The tails hung up! They didn't come around. I had to put so much energy into getting them around!" She recoils at the sound of her own whining and recovers her natural girlish voice. "I don't know what to do. Lately, I haven't even had to think about GS. But this just felt like a different event." Shaver is momentarily speechless then defends himself, saying the skis were prepared the way he always prepares them.

"Sometimes these things happen," he says, doing his best to soothe. "You gotta just forget it. It's done." There's another run to come. But Eva isn't ready to be mollified. She thinks maybe the skis are too sharp and wants to go out early before the second run and test her other race skis, to see if a switch is warranted.

"You saw it," she says to a bystander, as if gathering evidence. "I couldn't turn 'em!"

Sitting on the bumper of an official U.S. Ski Team Subaru, Eva's thick black curls hide interior clouds even as a stream of racers in harlequin colors and mostly high spirits flows around her. A delicate piece of braided gold on her left wrist contrasts with the solid muscle beneath her burgundy race suit. She glowers up the course. McKinney comes by, having skied a run almost as disappointing as Eva's, and puts an arm around her protégé's shoulder.

"I hate this," Eva mutters from within her cloud. She is near tears.

So what's the big deal? One bad run in a race that is really only important to the provincial USA racing community? But to see it that way is to greatly misjudge the fire in Ms. Twardokens.

Sandy Caligore, a writer and long-time follower of the World Cup, says, "E.T. takes this seriously. Oh, yeah. Every race, every time she steps into the starting gate." And then he adds, "She has always been one of the most technically proficient skiers on the team. And she has always been a pretty emotional racer, happy or sad after a run or a race. You can definitely see it on her face."

The fierce pride, and the technical prowess, are gifts from Eva's parents, Polish immigrants George and Halina Twardokens, who are ski instructors and, in George's case, a professor of kinesiology and biomechanics. George starred on the Polish national fencing team that travelled to Philadelphia in 1958 for that sport's World Championships. Unbeknownst to his teammates, he and Halina had a plan. While he was in the States she would travel to Copenhagen, and, with precision timing, they would defect simultaneously.

George won a bronze medal in saber. Then, as the last man due to get on the airplane, he turned around, defected to the U.S. But back in Poland Halina's trip had been delayed. She was trapped, hounded by the KGB, her attempts to leave the country denied for three years. "Finally," she says now, "I got lucky. They let me go." And she joined George in the U.S.

The family moved west, to Reno. George and Halina taught skiing at Mt. Rose, and George took a position at the University of Nevada at Reno. He has authored distinguished papers on the mechanics of skiing and is a technical advisor to the Professional Ski Instructors of America. On the slopes he is easy to spot for his elegant skiing style and his trademark white, snap-brim cap.

Eva was a prodigy, compact and preternaturally balanced, like a gymnast, winning races by five and six seconds as a 12-year-old. She joined the U.S. Team at 16. Growing up, George says, "It was carved turns for breakfast and avalement for dinner. We were very serious students of technique." Eva absorbed it the way some kids know every major leaguer's batting average.

But it is Halina to whom Eva owes her deep skiing skills. When their only child was three, her parents decided that just one of them should instruct her; otherwise they would bicker over methodology. And it was Halina, a downhiller back home in the High Tatras, who became Eva's mentor. "I'm super close to my mom," Eva says. "My dad… sometimes if I'm having a hard time with something new, he'll have some wisdom. But it's my mom… she's my best friend."

George, in fact, wondered if his obsession with technical detail might be holding Eva back. "There was a notion," he told me on the phone, "that she was too perfect – over coached. There is enough theory to suggest that conscious competence slows you down."

Eva, sitting, sagging there on the Subaru bumper, looks as if she could use her mom right now. Shaver has taken her skis off to the tuning bench. Women's Team head coach Bill Gunesch comes by and leans in close. Inside the tent of his arms, Eva cries, briefly and silently, while he talks.

She is both a woman and a child. Mostly, the woman prevails: physically mature, articulate, and poised. She is a star – albeit a step below the very top-echelon stars, the Maria Wallisers and Tamara McKinneys – and she carries herself accordingly. Sometimes though, like now, she seems a little girl whose meteoric rise has foreshortened – certainly changed the nature of – childhood. Junior National Freestyle Champion at age 12. U.S. Junior Skier of the Year in 1982-83, at 18. High school diploma by correspondence. National GS champion in 1985. And that moment on the podium at the Bormio Worlds. Eva already has a serious past to live up to. And the burden of even greater potential. No one doubts that she is technically prepared to assume the role of a champion. The question is: Is she emotionally ready?

Halina blames Eva's relatively lackluster finishes over the last two years on her daughter's "sensitivity." (She ended up 24th and 39th overall on the World Cup following her stunning 16th place overall at the conclusion of her rookie season.) After a good start to the 1986 tour, Eva's favorite race skis were stolen, and she never quite recovered top form. This year, a disqualification in an early slalom – unjust, as it turned out – seemed to have a similar effect. Halina believes Eva has simply been "out of luck."

"Out of commitment," George says, diverging from his wife. He believes that all great champions, from the Mahre brothers to Stenmark to Girardelli, "have been problems for their coaches… They have a personal commitment; they take matters into their own hands." He lambastes the U.S. team, which he says coddles the racers. "They say, 'You just lay back and we will take care of everything.'" But now George believes Eva is ready to take matters into her own hands, ready to make this commitment.

After the crying, things begin to go better. Injured teammate Diann Roffe ambles by with a hey-what-do-you-say-you-can-do-it-kid kind of upbeat pep talk. Recently retired U.S. teamer Christin Cooper swoops past on a break from her gig as TV commentator and gives the Twardokens tresses a friendly ruffle. Bootman Chris Poletis appears out of nowhere with a peanut butter and jelly sandwich and a 7-Up. "How'd you know?" Eva croons, allowing herself a smile.

Equipment reps float about like bees, stopping now and then to lay their wares on deserving racers, the newer flowers who haven't signed with anybody yet. Eva is paid by Rossignol, Marker bindings, Nordica boots, and Park City Resort. It's a good enough living that she recently bought herself a new Saab 9000. Her appreciation for precision, high-speed driving is well known within the team. Her father says, half-mockingly, "It's a scandal. No kid should earn more than a full professor!"

The game among the Subaru bumper loungers is go get E.T. to laugh. Jeff Callahan, a K2 tuner with the women's tour last year, succeeds where others fail. He snitches a pair of crutches from little Amy Livran (broken tib-fib) and hauls his considerable bulk across the snow, revealing a nice flair for slapstick. Eva protests, when she can finally speak, "Stop! You're making me cry!"

Up at the start for the second run, there are elaborate rituals to follow. Eva has already spent 20 minutes with Shaver jumping on one pair of skis for a few turns, switching to her training boards for comparison, then back on the race skis, and so on down the hill. Shaver slips dutifully along, lugging the extras. Eva is his top gun now that Tamara has switched from Rossignol to Dynamic, and he wants her to be happy.

In the roped-off ready area, Eva stomps around in baby-blue warm-ups, punching teammates tomboy-style on the shoulder. She takes a sip from a water bottle and settles into a meditative crouch, head between her knees. The girls are running "reverse 15," same as the World Cup, wherein the top 15 racers from the first run reverse order for the second. Eva is up sixth.

She takes her poles and begins a trance-like walkabout, bouncing like a boxer and swinging her legs, one at a time fore and aft, pendulum style, to stay warm. When the second racer is in the gate, Eva strips down to her racing tights and steps into her skis, the bindings having been opened and boot soles cleaned of snow by Shaver and his screw driver. For the final minute before her number is called she crouches on her heels, arms around knees, eyes closed, skiing the course in her mind. She is out of the start like a wave exploding on a reef.

The rest is pure liquid speed – "a little bit on the edge," as Conan Reuprecter would have it – but mostly right smack in the magic zone where everything works. It is a run George Twardokens would have described, had he seen it, as "full of beauty and relaxation and quality of turns." The way he and Halina taught her to be on skis.

Eva's second run sounds different than her first. There is no chattering; her edges are like knives carving soap. She still grunts, but this time down it is punctuation for a rhythm that matches perfectly the one imagined by the course setter. Swish, ungh. Swish swish, ungh. Parry. Thrust. Swish.

It is the fastest run of the afternoon – by far. "Extraterrestrial," you might say. Faster by almost a second than Armstrong, the 1984 Olympic gold medalist, who holds on, barely, for the win. Eva gives her a high five at the finish line. When Armstrong checks the scoreboard and sees Eva's time, she shakes her apple-red cheeks and says simply, "Awesome."

E.T. is on a cloud now. Her combined time puts her in third place. (Beth "Mad Pup" Madsen, standing fourth after the first run, snatches silver with a fine second run of her own.) Given the horrors of that first run, it's almost as good as a win. She accepts a kiss on both cheeks from team Alpine Director Harald Schoenhaar, who mock-scolds, "See! You can do it!"

Eva sighs, eyes dancing under still-serious brows. She is radiant. Conan sneaks up and lifts her off the snow in a bear hug, saying, "See! Eh? Eh? Eh?"

Now the television and radio crews are after her with questions about the phenomenal run. ("I tried to get angry, to get even.") About the Olympics next winter in Calgary. ("In the back of my mind I'd like to bring home something special.") And so on. It's getting cold, the sun is behind the ridge, but Eva doesn't mind, bathing in the warm congratulations. She doesn't even mind when a woman carrying little glass bottles summons her for the mandatory drug test.

Nearly lost in the hubbub is Scott Shaver, who wants to exchange Eva's race skis for the training pair, the ones she will carry to the podium. There, in the last of the Colorado light, bouquets of flowers will be presented, and medals draped around necks. And there will be cheers and boxes of Swiss chocolates. The top three racers will hoist their skis high amid the cameras' whirr.

Off to the side Harald Schoenhaar reflects, "You know, Phil Mahre said you have to learn to ski technically, mechanically. But at the top it's a psychological game."

When Shaver gets a chance to make the ski switch he tells Eva quietly, "They were identical to the way I've always tuned them. I didn't change a thing. These," he says, chastely patting Eva's talented quads, "were working."

# Letter to My Girls

Dear Cloe and Cecily,

I have always tried to encourage you, to be positive about the things that you could do, the things that you want to do. You are both fine young athletes. You could be exceptionally good at anything you set your minds to. You feel this, too, I think.

But now, after a trip to Aspen to write about the first post-Olympic women's World Cup race, I have a request. Please, my babies, do not become World Cup ski racers.

Sure, these women are the best. They are paid handsomely. They make their edges hold on glass mountains. And when they're not under race-day pressure they free-ski like the wind, like they wish gravity were even more potent than it is.

But in Aspen I stood and watched the violence that can accompany such beauty. First down Friday's downhill course was the young Swiss Beatrice Gafner, a new star on a team of 1980s supernovas. She sailed through the mid-air turn leading to Aztec, clung to the steeps there and rocketed into the banked, multiple g-force Airplane Turn. Off the lip at Strawpile doing sixty-plus and heading for the big right-hand sweep around Norway Island. There she set her edge and plunged toward the finish. Only three more gates to go.

But the course was much faster than it had been the day before in practice. A blustery cold front had moved in overnight turning the snow to granite, and Gafner was carrying terrific speed. A mid-turn compression, like a "Road Damage" dip on a freeway at 70 mph, threw her back on her tails. Her body twisted and she went down, bounced once, hard, and slammed into the orange-netted fence. All in a sickening split second.

Emergency people scurried to where she lay limp on the snow. The call went out to put a hold on the course. Radios crackled: "Hold! Hold!" But the next racer, Vreni Schneider, also of Switzerland and flush from winning two gold medals in Calgary, was already on course. Despite the existence of two "yellow zones" en route to stop a skier in just this eventuality, no one stopped Schneider.

She came flying off Summer Road onto Strawpile and set up for the Norway Island turn on exactly the same line Gafner had taken. The Swiss are nothing if not precise. Schneider set her edge, seemed to see Gafner inert on the snow ahead and hit the compression all at the same time. Shoved back on her heels by the same giant hand, she somehow managed to fling herself around Gafner's body and into the fence just ten feet beyond.

Later, after the race had been called off, a pretty-faced ESPN reporter would stand at this spot and point to the gashes in the fencing left by bodies and skis.

This time, officials managed to secure a hold. Gafner required a sled, injuries unknown. Schneider was up, but only on one foot, a damaged knee suspended tensely below.

Meanwhile, it had begun to snow. The fifth starter was Maria Walliser, World Cup overall champion for Switzerland in 1986 and 1987, a heroine at home, almost unfairly blessed with athleticism and a photogenic beauty. In her red and yellow, skin-tight "Suisse" suit, Walliser hit what coaches were already calling the "Swiss corner compression" and went down, too, as if she'd been shot, as if someone had pulled the lever on the trap door. Spectators recoiled in horror as she crushed the same fence, back first then arms and legs and skis and poles all in a jumble.

After a long moment, during which she seemed certainly to be dead, Walliser stood up, an abrasion slash across her left cheek and (damn!) favoring a knee, arms around the shoulders of two men. Then her gaze went blank, and she passed out in their arms.

After another couple of racers, the event was cancelled. The storm had settled in, visibility was shot. Later, the Swiss coach talked with the press. He held the course and the course setter blameless. Marginal visibility and pilot error, he said, had caused all three crashes. All three women had suffered multiple injuries, and all were out for the rest of the season.

ESPN, as might be expected, made the most of the dramatic footage on its taped broadcast later that night. In his intro, color man Bob Beattie cackled and teased the TV audience about the gore to come. Then he acted as if: Hey, that's ski racing and that's horrible, but let's take a look at that again. And again. And one more time: slow motion bodies hurtling through air, contorting hideously on impact, bouncing back off the fence like discarded dolls. Every repeat a punch to the solar plexus.

I'm sorry, Cloe and Cecily, if it seems that I want to limit your bright horizons. You're both tremendous skiers. You could be top ski racers if you set your sights. I just don't think I could live through it if it was my own flesh and blood I was watching.

# Christmas Tree

When I was growing up we bought our Christmas trees at a tree lot like everybody else. They smelled piney or fir-y and they got pitch on your hands, but we didn't really see them as alive somehow; they were another ornament, a rack for ornaments, in the living room.

When I was in college at Berkeley, Governor Ronald Reagan said, in pooh-poohing a proposed Redwoods National Park, "You see one redwood, you've seen them all." That astonishing statement, combined with the teachings of the fledgling environmental movement, made it seem imperative (to a young firebrand) to save, if not hug, every tree possible. What moral justification could there be to cut a living evergreen for mere decoration?

During the years I taught skiing, Christmas itself changed. It was our busiest work time of the year. No days off. No lounging around the tree on Christmas morning. On the slopes, we helped vacationers celebrate their holidays. Inside, it was a briefer, quieter, more intimate season. We hung a few balls on a potted plant or cut a single bough from a robust tree nearby.

With the coming of my own kids, though, things changed again. The Christmas tree was back. When Cloe was old enough to walk, we skied in a few yards off the highway south of Telluride and cut the scraggliest little tree we could find. Didn't matter what it looked like, it was a treasure that lit her up like a candle.

As she got older, the questions became more complicated. Not the questions, the answers. We still went into the woods for a tree, but Cloe asked things like, "Daddy, is the tree suffering?" (as I lay on my side in the snow working the saw). Or, "Daddy, is it glad to be picked for our Christmas tree?"

I didn't have the answers. Instead I proffered the rationale that we only cut crowded little trees, trees that very likely wouldn't survive the competition for light and space in the forest. She seemed to accept this, or at least to weigh the idea against her sympathy and the need we all felt to do this thing to our living room.

Now both daughters, Cloe and Cecily, are involved in the selecting and bringing home of the tree. We have struck a kind of uneasy deal with ourselves and turned it, in self-defense, into a ritual. It seemed the best way to go.

In the morning, we pop up a big batch of popcorn. Then we sit around the table stringing the paper-light flowers on needle and thread. It's a delicate operation. Those that break you eat. We pack the results carefully into anorak pouch pockets. We do the same with fresh cranberries. We load skis in the pickup and head up East Dallas Creek Road until snow makes further wheeled progress impossible.

It's December, and cold, so we rub hard blue wax on our ski bases and ascend slowly through the oak brush and aspens. Deer and elk tracks crisscross the path. Cecily scrunches down over a set of tiny foot-and-tail prints – a mouse, we decide. A creature stirring.

As we climb higher a few spruce mix in with the aspens. Then it's all spruce, a dark green sea of evergreen timber.

Our chosen tree is jammed up against a big Engelmann spruce. It has no branches on that side. I dig snow from around its trunk and get the keyhole saw out of my pack. Cloe asks again, "Do you think it's in pain?" I say probably not; I hope not. I say I think that pain as we know it requires a brain, and that this tree's spirit will certainly not be affected by something as temporal as a saw.

Then we get out the strings of popcorn and cranberries, so white and so red, and drape them around another little tree nearby, a stronger, fuller one with a good chance of reaching the sky.

This is part of the deal. We decorate a little piece of the forest, sing it a song, and imagine the feast for the birds and squirrels when they happen upon these marvelous foods.

On the way back down the girls are ecstatic. Our skis glide at the slightest encouragement. Behind me the tree glides too, the tips of its upturned branches sweeping the snow like a broom. The world is spinning under us, as it should.

Back home the tree looks bigger, more regal. It has brought some forest magic into the house. Its life is ebbing, but it is the center of the celebration now, and it stiffens to hold the weight of tradition. More popcorn strings. And cranberry strings. And lights. Necklaces of silver and gold beads. Painted wooden bangles and glass balls from Ellen's family, and from mine. A cotton angel on top.

Our tree, for all our mixed emotions at taking it, is a genuine centerpiece, a symbol of the season. Under its sparkling adornment it is loved as a piece of the planet's beauty – fleeting, ethereal. In it is the zipping by of years, of childhoods, of weekends when we can ski together into the forest. The transience of forests themselves. Life and death. Moral choices. Taking and giving.

The ritual, complete with its questions, brings us closer to what is precious and true.

# My Girls On Boards

For a while, when my two teenage daughters took up snowboarding, they needed me again. Tall, strapping kids, they had become very good if somewhat indifferent skiers. Definitely out of the nest. Rarely did we ski together. More often they went up to the mountain with friends. Even more likely, midwinter basketball lured them to faraway gyms to party with their peers. Ellen and I never pushed them to ski, though we did start them young, first in a pack on my back, then on their own two feet. Cloe was fearless. Cecily liked the security of the leash for a while. When she started snowplow cruising on her own, she kept the thumb of one glove in her mouth until it was soaked through. Ellen and I just hoped that our love for the sport would rub off. But maybe, we were forced to think now, the kids were moving in different directions.

Then came snowboarding. Without any prompting from us, the girls asked to try it. The first day flung them back to beginnerdom again. The aftermath was hard for a father to look at. Cecily's knees were the size of grapefruits. Cloe, who claims she doesn't bruise easily, could have starred in "How the Leopard Got His Spots." The wrist guards, which seemed like a good idea at the rental shop in the morning, inflicted their own abrasive tortures. Both girls were beat up, wet and exhausted in an utterly new way.

But behind the glazed looks, something had clicked. Some flicker of graceful possibility had insinuated itself in their subconscious. As soon as they could walk normally again, they wanted to try it a second time.

Now they were tilting awkwardly on the easiest terrain, testing the unusual sensations of riding sideways, like a surfer, and with their feet locked in place: no stepping, no walking, no catching your balance with a quick shuffle. No poles! "Ambulatorily challenged" is a phrase I've heard from unimpressed two-plankers.

But the girls worked at it tenaciously, refusing offers to go in for a rest, their eyes steely with resolve. They figured out how to weight the front foot at the beginning of a turn, then to slide the tail into a direction change. How to tip up on their toes for turns to the front side and then back on their heels for edging turns the other way.

Meanwhile, I cruised alongside regally on two skis, feet free and edges dicing, a Zen master to their Grasshoppers. At those slow speeds and on that baby-smooth snow I merely toyed with gravity, while for the girls every turn meant grappling with the relative Titans of acceleration, friction, and balance. They encouraged me to take off and ski elsewhere, if I liked. They insisted they were getting along fine despite the occasional mystery biff and the inevitable seat-of-the-pants pondering. But I didn't want to leave. I was having fun. They were my babies again, on a fast learning curve, yes, but needing my help, my benevolent patience and encouragement.

It wasn't as if I had no sympathy. I had been a beginner on the board once myself, back in 1986 when snowboards still had fins on them. I was getting the hang of it, too, after a morning lesson and an afternoon solo at Purgatory, one of the first Colorado areas to allow boarding. But at the end of that long day, a failure of nerve at speed led to a cartwheeling denouement and a badly sprained ankle, an ankle that warns me to this day of approaching low-pressure systems. I haven't been back on a board since. But that didn't mean I wasn't pulling for the girls to break through on the wide ride.

It happened all of a sudden. After a few days, Cloe could go anywhere but the steep moguls. She could slow it down to a walk, with delicate slips and swivels, and she began ripping big turns, cranking the board way up on its side and carving those deeply etched, semicircular lines, clean as a Picasso sketch.

Cecily has taken a little longer. But on our most recent day out together she began passing me, knees bent, hands out like a storyteller hushing a crowd, riding up on the edge, pressing into the curves, flowing from one arc directly into the next. Both girls have a new sparkle in their eyes, feline and delighted.

I am resigned to the fact that they will soon pass their father in other ways, including technical chops and ridge-walking strength. This will happen. Just as it happened to my father when I was a teenager. We had a deal, my father and I, that on the day I surpassed him on skis, he would buy me a whole boysenberry pie, a particular favorite of mine, and a rarity in Southern California. The day came; I think I was 13. And on the drive home from Mammoth Mountain, in a diner in one of the little towns strung along the backside of the Sierra – Bishop or Independence or maybe it was Big Pine – there was my pie, bursting with sweet berries, as was my dad, with quiet pride.

Not long ago, I feared I'd lost my girls, that the snow-sliding bond we'd shared since they were little was crumbling. And I knew it was in their minds, too, when in her high school graduation speech last June, Cloe thanked, among other people and things dear to her, her snowboard. "I had lost interest," she told the audience, "in the thing that my dad loved and so wanted me to love – gliding over the snow… [then] I started snowboarding this last season… One powder day I was flying down Gold Hill, smiling all the way, and I think I discovered that love of gliding my dad feels when he skis."

I don't know what sort of pie the girls like best. They can have any kind they want. I'm more than happy to pay up. Thank you, snowboards. Thank you, thank you.

# The Dakar of the Snow

One of my teammates, Vermonter Greg Vautour, leaned in close. He had to shout to be heard over the wind. "They want us to ski 7,000 vertical feet, as fast as we can, without stopping, in a whiteout, in avalanche conditions."

All true. Wind tore at the summit of the Aiguille Rouge, the Red Needle, above Les Arcs, where we stood waiting for our start number to be called. Wind-born snow raced along at boot-top level, like a rip tide, to be deposited on some lee slope probably already loaded and aching to slide.

Through the fog we could barely make out blips of team colors in line ahead of us. There was the red and silver belonging to alpine daredevil Jean Marc Boivin and his team from Les Carroz. There were the North Face yellows of Franz Vogler's defending champions from Oberstdorf, and the optical reds and blues of the team from Le Corbier La Toussuire led by dashing French World Cup star Jean Noël Augert. The all-women's team from Meribel/Axion2 in their classy one-piece whites tended to vanish completely, then reappear as ghostly shadows in the swirling snow. We were all, God willing, about to ski from the point of the Needle, at 10,584 feet, down to where the snow ran out, in the mud and cow shit at the farming village of Le Pré.

The they to whom Vautour referred were the organizers of this, the second, the 1987 edition of the Raid Blanc. It's a weeklong ski mountaineering race stitching together swaths of the Italian, Swiss and French Alps. This was Day Five, and the French appetite for *extrême* had not been satiated in the least.

"The White Raid" is the brainchild of Thierry Sabine, a man who, ten years ago, thought it might be fun to race 7,000 miles from Paris to Dakar, Senegal, across the Sahara. The so-called Paris/Dakar has since become the ultimate 20-day, camera-ready challenge for international Mad Max bikers and all-terrain machiners. Thierry is no longer with us; his helicopter hit a dune last year, making him the fifteenth Paris/Dakar fatality in nine years. His father, Gilbert Sabine, has carried on. Sabine père has insisted that the Raid be considered the "Dakar of the Snow."

The application form we filled out touted the event as "a new ski, a total ski, a liberating of the tops of the most massive Alps, with fantastic ups and downs, carefully selected for their sportive character and the beauty of the traverse." It also said, somewhat poignantly, that it would be "a rally which crowns the courage and endurance, the spirit of the team and the surpassing of yourself, qualities that Thierry had always wanted to put first."

The surpassing of yourself. Hmmm, I thought, standing sideways to the wind. Is this even possible?

The race is run rally-style. Each day there are two or three timed specials – some uphill with skins, some up-and-downhill, some on-piste, many off. Some nights are spent in hotel rooms. We stayed one night in the four-story Refugio Teodulo, at 10,900 feet, on the Italian hip of the Matterhorn. One night we were to sleep high on Mont Blanc, in "igloos" built by the French army. But that didn't happen when a blizzard prevented the soldiers from reaching the site.

We were "L'équipe Américaine, Smugglers Notch," the first and only American team in a field of 38, from all over Europe. The official starter usually mispronounced the name of our sponsoring ski area to where it sounded more like "Smoocher's Nutz… trois, deux, un, Go!"

"I sink we cannot win ze Raid," said our wry, wiry, French guide, James Merel, who grew up in the Haute Savoie town of Bourg St. Maurice. James smokes unfiltered Turkish cigarettes and likes to say, "No problem," even in the direst circumstance. Like now, in this whiteout. "But if nobody falls," he added, "maybe we can be funny."

He meant we could have fun. We knew what he meant. Every team of five had to have a French certified guide. Vautour, a 34-year-old veteran ski instructor from Vermont, had met James a couple of years before on a ski vacation to Les Arcs. And so it was to Greg that James wrote last November: "I have a very great thing to propose you for these winter… It is one week ski, Le Raid Blanc… Do you want to do one American team with me? It is very expensive, but you can be sponsoring because it is a very big run in Europe."

It was indeed expensive; the entry fee alone worked out to about $1,000 per skier. But Vautour put the whole package together – sponsorship, uniforms, airplanes, buses. The same tidiness showed in his skiing. His technique is impeccable, Eastern-ice precise, as befits a Smugs native. His dad used to be the mountain manager.

Greg's boyhood buddy Paul Abare, also 34, is a race coach at Smuggler's, a solid, powerful skier whom James entrusted with the sweeper position. Should any of us fall or need help Paul would be able to pick up the pieces. The Catcher in the Rime.

Our resident cowboy, and weakest skiing link (he would be the first to agree) was Kip, née Henry Tonking, a college friend of the Vermonters and a last-minute fill-in. He flew in from Reno, where he evaluates mining claims in the Nevada desert. Kip scared everybody by falling and dislocating his shoulder on the very first day as we worked our way around the blue-ice crevasses of the Breithorn Glacier above Zermatt. But he popped the shoulder back in himself and quickly regained his mustachioed, Marlboro-man grin. James liked to keep Kip close, under his wing in second position, where he could yell, "Go, Henri! Come on, Henri!"

Each team had to have a journalist. Greg had cold-called me in the fall, after reading a few of my pieces in *Powder* magazine. I was the oldest team member by four years and the only one with a wife and kids. I'd done a fair amount of backcountry skiing in the Rockies, but nothing as radical and competitive as the Raid. This matter of hurrying on very big mountains in extreme conditions worried me. Back home, when things got serious, we slowed down.

Journalists, particularly sports journalists, are not well regarded in France. And the journalist was often the albatross on these teams. After the run to Zermatt on Day One, I asked a friendly fellow on the Deux Alpes team how they'd fared. "Oh, okay," he said with a shrug, "except for ze fucking journalist!" Some ambitious teams abandoned their journalists after the first day, preferring to take the two hour and thirty minute penalty in hopes of making up the time, with a leaner four-man squad, in the days to come. There would be *abandons* for other reasons, too; they were announced each evening: split lips, broken bones, plain exhaustion.

I thought I might have ended our team's chance for a decent overall finish on only the second special of the Raid. Following the Breithorn-to-Zermatt ski, we'd regrouped for what was essentially a long groomed-snow downhill to Cervinia. (Two border crossings already, Italy to Switzerland and back.) I hadn't needed to be reminded that this was the Plateau Rosa, the site of the infamous Kilometro Lanciato, or Flying Kilometer. This was the pitch where, in 1964, spectators had watched a man nearly torn in half in a cartwheeling fall at 100 mph. And it was the place, that same year, where Steve McKinney had pierced the buffeting air to set a new world record speed of 117.640 mph.

I myself was content to hold a loose tuck at maybe 45-50 mph, while keeping my teammates in sight. The vast, treeless terrain was backlit silver by a powerful afternoon sun. Out of the glare a spectator appeared in my line. He must have been trying to cross the course. I edged left to slice around him, but he juked that way, too. His eyes grew wide as I hurled myself the other way, headfirst, out of control and pointing straight for a gaping hole at the side of the piste. A crevasse.

I hit the ground hard and slid over the edge. My life didn't exactly flash before my eyes. Instead, I recalled a scene from the day before, when our insurance was double-checked and we were fitted with those permanent, plastic hospital I.D. bracelets. I imagined a medic examining my wrist at the bottom of the crevasse, *"l'équipe Smoocher's Nutz."*

Once I was over the lip, I could see it wasn't a crevasse after all, but a ten-foot-deep wind trough. My fear turned to anger, and I popped back up screaming: *"Merde! Putain! Vas te faire foutre!"* It occurred to me I'd never been more eloquent in French. Never mind that we were in Italy. Paul, the sweeper, helped corral my gear, cocked my bindings for me – I was still yelling – and we were off again.

I thought I'd blown it for the team, for our chance at a decent overall finish. We weren't the Mahre brothers; we knew that. But we had hope. The celebrity superstar teams would be out of reach, but we had thought we might at least not embarrass ourselves. As it happened, Le Raid was long enough, the chances to succeed and fail so numerous, that when we reached Day Five in Les Arcs we were right about where we deserved to be, in the middle of the pack in 17th place. We had even developed a little rivalry with a team of young hotheads from the resort of Piau Engaly, in the French Pyrenees. One of them dropped a helmet on my head, without apology, as we rode a bus through the Mont Blanc tunnel. Another one skied wildly, dangerously, across Paul's tips in the tight woods near the end of another special. "*Je m'excuse,*" the boy mumbled at the finish line, but Paul was having none of it. "No!" he shouted. "You're not excused!"

Piau started just ahead of us on the Aiguille Rouge, in conditions race organizers were calling *limite d'extrême.* The wind was so violent they had to close the tram behind us. True mountaineering test or pure foolishness? The question became moot in the starting gate. The only way out was to ski down. "No problem!" James said, rallying the troops. He knew this route like the bases of his well-worn Rossignols. This is where we would distance ourselves from Piau, he said. No problem.

The first half-mile ran over the Glacier du Varet. It was not steep, but glazed with a treacherous wind crust – like strips of bacon, I later thought – with vertical striations of rippled fat and lean – a tougher, supportable crust here and a breakable one there. Bodies were strewn everywhere. We all fell, even James. But we bounced up each time with little loss of time or gear.

In the gloaming we were passing people, passing whole teams. Then we shot, skier's right, through a notch in the wind-whipped ridge, and onto the lee side. Snow sifted out of the howling air, fell to earth by the ton. We still couldn't see, but James never slowed down. He skied like a man who needed to get home. (He was in fact going to see his girlfriend, Brigitte, that evening.) We did our best to keep up the red-white-and-blue duckling line.

Out front, James skied the slabby, hip-deep powder the way he skied everything, with big, round, imperturbable arcs. The amazing thing was that Kip was right there with him, matching power with power, however crude, right there on his tails. To my left Greg was a rolling ball of smoke, just an occasional gloved fist or pole basket protruding. Paul floated unseen behind me.

Something happened on this run, something that made our aching quads and shivering worry fly away. In the absence of sight, we somehow found our balance by feel, by proprioception alone, and locked on. It wasn't the same old find-it and lose-it and find-it-again balance that is a standard feature of most long descents. This one stayed pure as a laser beam. On a featureless canvas I gauged speed by the feel of the snow hitting my face. I wasn't thinking technically; I wasn't carving or banking, skidding, or unweighting. Instead, I was following a path somehow already known to me and to my long, giant-slalom feet.

Call it flow. Call it skiing "out of yourself." (The surpassing of the self?) Falling down the rabbit hole – whatever inadequate term you can come up with. It lasted all the way to the stone barns of Le Pré. No stops. Twenty-four minutes, six seconds. The lactic-acid pain was there but muted, like a memory of pain. Piau Engaly finished a full five minutes back of us.

There would be one more day of racing, with a long, morning skin up the Aiguille Grive. At the top we had to punch steps through a vertical cornice before switching to downhill mode. It was in many ways the most beautiful traverse of the Raid, through slanting light and feathery snow as the latest storm departed. Most of the tension had gone out of the air. We could hear yodeling up ahead.

There were banquets. (When in France…) On one table – it might have been the table of World Cup icons Fabienne Serrat, or Patrick Russel, or the Raid's winners, Augert's team from Le Corbier La Toussuire – the centerpiece was a full-sized sheep made of cauliflower.

My favorite meal, though, was the supper we were served by the hut mistress at the Refugio Teodulo. It was the night after my brush with the "crevasse." The hut stank of sweat, and we would sleep, all 190 of us (minus the abandons), with our backpacks as pillows, six to a shelf. But the dinner was sublime, served in shifts at long wooden tables. Maybe it tasted so good because I hadn't died. Maybe it was because we were innocents abroad, crossing borders of all kinds, feeling, after months of built-up uncertainty, that we might belong. Maybe it was just that we were hungry and the food was really good: fresh pasta with a simple red sauce, hard cheese, chunks of crusty bread and sweet butter. When Maria asked if we wanted more and brought out steaming second helpings, I fell irretrievably in love.

# Sugar Shacks

An unpaved road rolls east out of Stowe, Vermont, across rounded Green Mountain hills. Mud squishes beneath my tires. Sugar maples line the route, their bare crowns scratching an overcast sky, their straight, gray trunks tapped and hung with sap buckets like galvanized earrings. There is a sugarhouse on the left, steam billowing from open vents in the roof. A hand-carved sign reads: "Paul E. Percy Vermont Maple Syrup." I stop the car and walk up to the shack.

"Mr. Percy?"

"That's what my wife calls me when ah'm late for dinnah."

It's April, and Mr. Percy is in the midst of his 56th sugaring season. He slowly extends a hand, big and warm. A bucket of clear, watery sap hangs on a faux maple trunk "growing" out of the floor. "This tree runs real good," he says, his words deadpan, his eyes mischievous. The fake tree is a bit of Vermont humor, not unlike the sap buckets you may see gracing a telephone pole or two anywhere along Route 100 this time of year.

The raw sap in Percy's bucket tastes only faintly sweet, nothing like the sticky syrup it will become after it boils down. It tastes the way the woods smell in spring here, still covered with snow but sharp with the musty, secret scent of new growth.

Up the road at the Stowe Ski Resort, crews from the Mount Mansfield Ski Club prepare the Nose Dive trail for the 56th running of the Sugar Slalom, a season-ending tradition since 1939. One part rite of spring and two parts serious FIS points race, the Sugar Slalom boasts a storied winners list, including Olympians Bobby and Barbara Ann Cochran and local hero

Billy Kidd, who first took the boys division in 1958, then went on to garner America's first men's alpine Olympic medal in 1964, a silver in the slalom. It is also a semi-serious grudge match race for U.S. Ski Association Masters, including former U.S. Team members. All of the racers, from spindly juniors who barely fill out their speed suits to crunchy old Woodchucks, look forward to the finish-line tradition "sugar-on-snow," in which maple syrup, hot from the pan, is poured over mounds of snow, where it turns instantly to chewy-sweet maple candy.

When the sap begins to flow, usually in early March, farmwives in this still-rural land send their husbands out of doors for a season that may last only five or six weeks but one that may net them a couple thousand dollars, money that can mean the difference between breaking even and ending the year in a financial hole. Other Vermonters haul a little sap and boil enough syrup for family needs. Doug Lewis, a local downhiller who won a World Championships bronze in 1985, remembers sugaring as a boy. "We'd boil down a few buckets in somebody's kitchen. I recall we wrecked a lot of kitchens. All that steam just destroys wallpaper."

It takes about 40 gallons of sap to produce one gallon of syrup. The rest goes up in maple steam. Percy's sugarhouse smells like pancake breakfast all day long. One of the biggest producers in this part of Vermont, he sold 4,200 gallons of syrup last year. He figures he's got about 200 acres in his sugarbush, supporting 24,000 taps. "If the moose aren't wandering in there," he says ruefully. "When they wanter, they'll take down anything."

Instead of dripping into buckets the old-fashioned way, Percy's taps feed a maze of delicate tubing, strung like spider webs from tree to tree. Sap is pumped to holding tanks and finally to the evaporators in the sugarhouse. When the days are warm and the nights cold, the sap runs freely and Percy and his crew may work around the clock. Like milk, sap can't be stored for more than a day or so. Once naturally occurring bacteria start multiplying, the sap yields a darker, lower-quality syrup. "If the sap comes in cold and fast," says Percy, "and you boil it right away, the bacteria doesn't have a chance to grow and you get light-colored syrup. Late in the season, when the temperatures get warm and the trees start to bud, you can't but make a dark syrup. People say it has a buddy taste."

But there is more to getting a quality syrup than weather luck and sleep deprivation. Sugarmaking is an art, and good sugarers like Percy are alchemists, transforming one thing into something else far more valuable. They juggle precise flow rates, densities, temperatures, and sugar content. Percy even gives the phase of the moon a role in the recipe. There's an inexplicable element to sugarmaking, a sixth sense, a gift, like condensing language from prose to poetry.

The windowsills at Percy's are lined with sample bottles, one from each batch of syrup this year. Backlit against a gray sky, their colors range from honey yellow to weak tea, officially: Vermont Fancy, to Grade A Medium Amber, to Grade A Dark Amber, to Grade B. Even Dark Amber is lighter than Aunt Jemima's Rich Maple, for instance, which contains only four percent maple syrup. "All the real sugarmakers will tell you the lighter color is the best," says Percy, who prefers the "delicate" flavor of Fancy. "I don't know a one who'll tell ya different."

Percy drains some proto-syrup from the boiling pan into a tin cup and floats a hydrometer in the center, to test specific gravity, his movements so sure they appear off-hand. A ball-peen hammer in a back pocket tugs his pants down below his plaid shirt. "So, you're a skier," he says conspiratorially. "You may not believe this, but I used to beat Billy Kidd. He moved here from Burlington in the seventh grade, and I used to beat him." Kidd apparently bears no hard feelings and retains a native Vermonter's craving for maple syrup, in spite of his having lived in Colorado for the past 26 years. Each spring he has gallons of Percy's syrup delivered to his Steamboat Springs home.

A few miles west of Percy's tap-line operation, on the other side of Stowe, the Trapp Family Lodge is sugaring again in the old way, taps hammered into each tree dripping sap into individual buckets. Johannes Von Trapp, 57, the youngest son of the singing Von Trapps, used to sugar these trees as a boy, but for the past 40 years, as the hotel and cross-country skiing business has grown, the sap has gone untapped. Now, deep in the woods behind the lodge, sweet steam chortles from a new sugarhouse. Von Trapp and his sugarmaker, Jonathan Pryor, who is a good 20 years Paul Percy's junior, have resurrected some of Vermont's "traditional arts," including ice harvesting, cheese making, and maple sugaring. Lodge guests are invited to participate – or simply watch, and marvel.

The best way to get to the sugarhouse is on cross-country skis down the Sugar Chute Trail, part of Trapp's extensive Nordic trail system. These maples are immense, spreading their crowns 70 feet in the air. Many are more than 100 years old and can support three or four buckets each. Pryor steers a sleigh pulled by a big Belgian horse down through the gaps between trees, stopping to empty buckets of sap into a tank on the sled.

He is a dapper man in creased woodsman's wool. He enjoys an audience, and he often has one leaning over the railings of the sugarhouse gallery. Today he tells a skiing family about Benjamin Franklin's plan to develop maple sugar as the standard sweetener for the colonies. "He wanted to get us off our dependence on West Indian molasses, which was controlled by the English," he says. Alas, like old Ben's nomination of the wild turkey as the national bird, the maple sugar idea didn't fly.

Pryor not only knows his history, he's a connoisseur of traditional sugaring methods. With his assistant, Corey, down below chucking rounds of spruce and birch into the crackling-hot "arch," he stirs the thickening liquid as it flows from one corner of the dining table-size pan to another. Occasionally surface foam threatens to boil over, and Pryor dangles a piece of uncured pork fat over the pan – oil on troubled waters. But you don't want too many drippings. A sensitive palate will detect a bacon-y taste in the syrup. Steam engulfs the room. Now and then Pryor disappears completely in the mist. "Standing over the boiling pan all day," his voice emerges from the cloud, "I have crystallized sugar in my eyebrows when I go home."

As the sap nears the consistence of syrup, Pryor scoops it with a wooden ladle and pours it back, looking for "sheeting" as it falls. For backup, he checks a cupful with a syrup thermometer. "Seven!" he calls out excitedly. It's like a birth. "Seven [degrees above boiling]! We're syruping off now, Corey!" He opens the spigot and a stream of gold pours into a stainless steel can.

"Yup, they [the trees] are running real fast and real sweet right now. About 2.6 percent sugar. It can be down as low as one percent." Every sugaring season, like every ski season, is different. Sometimes spring arrives all at once, the trees bud, and the sap turns cloudy, "woody" tasting, and stops flowing abruptly. Sometimes spring comes in fits and starts, like this year, warm then cold again, and the sap flows and flows. The sugarmaker, like the skier, plies his trade on the whims of the weather, expectant, humble, open to the magic.

After filtering and grading – this batch rates Medium Amber – Pryor hands out paper cups of still-warm syrup. The visiting kids lean over the railing and beg for more. "Please, oh please!"

Stowe's Sugar Slalom and the onset of mud season tend to overlap on the northern Vermont calendar. Some years the race is held on less than optimal snow conditions, as this note from the April 1956 edition of *Mount Mansfield Skiing* attests: "… short course or long, complete cover or no (six feet of powder in the woods to two feet of trout stream in the center of the Corridor), the Sugar Slalom will be run in a spirit of friendly competition (meaning grim determination), and fun (meaning fun)."

This year there is a ton of snow. The extra moisture has been good for the sap run. More snow falls on race day, April 14, tumbling through a fog so thick it's as if the whole mountain were a steaming sugarhouse.

The racing surface is soft on top, icy beneath. Approximately 400 juniors from around New England have braved two runs on the Corridor (upper Nose Dive) slalom course. Another 81 Masters have survived the same monster ruts. Former U.S. Teamers Tyler Palmer and Marilyn Cochran Brown win the men's and women's Masters titles. There are also guys in purple wigs who finish 10 seconds out. All mill about the finish area. Everyone is waiting for sugar-on-snow.

Stowe's closet-sized, trailside sugarhouse is sheeted in tin. Porcupines ate most of the wood. Inside, sugarmakers Grizz and Fidel hold court, alternately stoking the fire and stirring the boil. Grizz has done this, he thinks, every Sugar Slalom for the last 36 years, but he's not quite sure because of the gin-and-tonics ceremonially consumed this day. Fidel yells good-naturedly at a bunch of kids in racing suits: "Out! We'll never get a boil if you don't close that DOOR!"

At last, Fidel emerges with a saucepan of thickened syrup and dribbles it down raised troughs of snow, Jackson Pollock-style. Racers of all stripes flock like pigeons to the treat: prepubescent boys whose tights hang like puppy skin; lissome academy girls who wear their hair in braids like Andrea Mead Lawrence; grinning 40-somethings who can't – don't want to – let go of this feeling. All wield wooden Popsicle sticks to scoop up the congealed, caramel-colored goo. Out come platters of cake doughnuts and fat pickle wedges. The combination sounds crazy, but it works: tart and juicy, crumbly cake, snow-chilled, chewy nectar. A combo like spring itself, with its mess of endings and promises, sweet and bittersweet.

# Let Bode Be

Bode Miller doesn't want to be a hero or a heretic. And yet that is what we – the media and an incurious public – insist he be.

One or the other. Ski god or goat. It's all so black and white, especially in an Olympic year. The other athletes, Bode's fellow ski racers, know better. But here in our living rooms and on our sports pages, you're either a winner, or you're a loser. You either get that gold medal predicted for you by TIME magazine, or you've failed. No nuance. No appreciation for just how stunning an achievement it is to finish fifth in an Olympic downhill, eleven hundredths of a second off the podium. No. No shades of gray allowed. Just "disappointment" and "failure."

The media pieces about Bode, and indeed about all of the U.S. Team, read like report cards from chastising nuns. (The exception this Olympiad, in Turin, is Ted Ligety, who claimed a surprise gold in the alpine combined.) Daron Ralves "falls short." Bode "blows shot at gold." Julia Mancuso's "run of mediocrity." Lindsey Vonn's "struggles." (Apparently, if you take a horrific fall in training then get up out of your hospital bed to race, your sins can be commuted to "struggles.")

Just today, following Bode's "latest gaff" in the giant slalom (an unforgivable sixth), I read that he has but "one shot at redemption" – Saturday's final slalom.

Redemption? What is this, the Spanish Inquisition? No athlete expects the Spanish Inquisition. Least of all a "Live Free or Die" iconoclast. New Hampshire-ite Miller has tried to tell us what he is about. He has wrestled with the words – he is no Robert Frost – but he has honestly tried to convey what for him is a simple quest: to go as fast as is humanly possible on a pair of skis. Not to win, he's always been clear about this. But rather to make his skis carve lines that have never been carved before and then try, like a rodeo cowboy, to stay aboard those flashing skis, to simultaneously drive and ride them for as long as he can.

If he wins, fine. If he doesn't, his quest is no worse for the effort. In fact, every run, successful or not, adds to what Bode refers to as "the knowledge." His is a gift of physical imagination. He's looking for the edge of the possible, nuzzling up to it, and then pushing through it. Bode reserves the right to his own definition of grace.

His legacy will be in extending the boundaries of skiing, arguably a greater achievement than bringing home the hardware, though he has done plenty of that over the years. Everybody on the World Cup circuit, the yearlong "White Circus," which Bode has won, twice, knows this. Everybody who has raced against him, including everybody at these 2006 Games, knows that when Bode taps into the magic and rides it to the bell, nobody can touch him. Nobody can come close. He's an idol in the Alps, where people understand ski racing. Over there, they appreciate what he does without all the messy expectation.

Over here, we figure he owes us. With our quadrennial awareness of alpine skiing all artificially pumped up by NBC et al, he's got to be the favorite. He's got our flag on his back – he owes it to us. He must justify the celebrity we thrust upon him. He must ratify our sense of national superiority: "USA! USA!"

The commentators say: Couldn't Bode just throttle back a little bit, say to 80 or 90 percent, finish these runs, and win a medal? He could, but Bode doesn't work that way. His life has never worked that way. We love the up-close-and-personal bit about having grown up in a house his parents built, without running water or electricity, out in the wilds of New Hampshire. It's an easy cliché, like Lincoln and his log cabin.

But the real importance of this upbringing is lost on us. Bode's parents were serious back-to-the-landers, back in the 1970s when doing your own thing carried the weight of religion. These people were not dabbling at country living. They were seriously committed to independence, to self-sufficiency, and a kind of adventurous, radical freedom. A young Bode absorbed these values with every bracing trip to the outhouse, every round of firewood split and fed into the woodstove.

As a skier, he has never bent to the desires of his coaches, unless he figured their suggestions advanced his agenda. He's been a handful from the start. The cussedness is a part of his brilliance. He is one of only five skiers in World Cup history to win in all five disciplines – downhill, super-G, giant slalom, slalom, and combined. This has been enough to keep him on the team, enough to make him without question one of the two or three greatest male skiers America has produced, along with Dick Durrance, Buddy Werner, and maybe Phil Mahre. Although Phil loses points in my mind for carping last year, even as Bode wrapped up the overall World Cup title: "He needs to finish more races." Phil Mahre, as great as he was, will not be remembered for redefining the possible.

Bode's work, his exploration of skiing's outer limits, requires joy. As he told an Italian newspaper the other day, "Sport is an act of freedom . . . [It] was born clean and would remain so if it was about just competing for the fun of it. But the media and the public corrupt it because of the pressure they create."

The weight of expectation, and what sometimes seems to be willful misunderstanding, have taken their toll. Bode's father Woody looks and sees that his son is not happy. "Fame is like a poison," Bode told the same Italian reporter. "I used to have a better life when I was nobody."

This is sad. And it is at least partly our doing. We want Bode to be perfect, and triumphant. But few celebrities and even fewer athletes thrive in the unreality under the microscope, and Bode may not be one of them.

He deserves not our disappointment but our admiration. He's a quintessential American: brilliantly innovative, a touch immature, candid to a fault, unbound by the preconceptions of others, confronting his gift on his own terms.

You can't force magic; it has to come to you. These days in Turin, the magic is having a hard time finding an unhappy Bode Miller.

# Life of Velocity

*"'Que serac, serac'... We said that one night camped under a hanging ice block, wondering if it was going to fall on us."*

In the end, it wasn't Mount Everest ice, or thin air, or even a fall on skis at 130 mph that killed Steve McKinney. It was a drunk.

In the early morning hours of November 10, 1990, McKinney, 37, the greatest speed skier of all time, was sleeping in the back seat of his disabled Volkswagen Rabbit off the shoulder of Interstate 5 south of Sacramento, when an intoxicated driver slammed into the rear of the car, crushing him. So passive a death was the final paradox in a turbulent life of speed, a life that McKinney once said was a "search for peace at the very heart of movement."

McKinney was born two months prematurely, in 1953, when his mother, an amateur jockey, fell off a horse that "went crazy and crashed into a wall." Francis McKinney raised her eight children on a ranch outside Reno, Nevada. She schooled them at home, and she taught them to ski on the slopes of Mt. Rose above Lake Tahoe. Steve's baby sister Tamara was the first American to win a World Cup overall title, in 1983.

At 17, he was invited to join the U.S. Ski Team. A potentially brilliant downhiller, his volatile energy clashed with Ski Team stricture, and he left, or was asked to leave, in 1974. With his blond hair flowing over his shoulders, he instead studied Buddhism and taught himself to rock climb, and to fly hang gliders. At six-three and a ropey 190 pounds, he had the cat-like athleticism that would just as soon jump off a roof as wait for a ladder.

But he wasn't superhuman. In 1973, a 100-foot fall while climbing in the Sierras left him in a body cast and temporarily out of commission. That spring, on a whim, he traveled to Italy, to the venerable Kilometro Lanciato, the "Flying Kilometer" speed track above Cervinia. He even skied a few tentative runs in his cast, and the experience set the competitive course for the rest of his life. He'd found his calling.

He went back to Italy the next spring and set a new speed record of 113.6 mph after being, in his words, "launched into a beautiful, weird flight" down the Plateau Rosa glacier. He held his wind-piercing tuck through the vibrations and the doubts better than anyone before him, the very embodiment of Zen "non-action within action." Rumor spread that the record had been set on acid.

McKinney set more records on the tracks at Portillo, Chile, in 1977 and 1978, at Cervinia again in 1978, and at Les Arcs, France, in 1982. The run that established McKinney's permanent place in the pantheon was the one at Portillo in 1978. In it, he roared through the 200 kilometer-per-hour (124 mph) "wall," a statistically mythical speed, not unlike the sound barrier in the 1940s.

After that McKinney became something like a mythical character himself. The astonishing feats continued – climbing to over 25,000 feet on a new route on Mt. Everest, without porters or bottled oxygen; hang gliding from 21,500 feet off Everest's West Ridge. But for all his stupendous acts, friends said McKinney was often distant and angry. Human imperfection ate at him. Half-hearted commitment made him mad. Telluride's Marti Martin-Kuntz, a long-time friend and a fellow speed skier, said, "This lion leaps out of him and wants to tear things apart." The humor was darker. The blue eyes flashed beneath raptor brows.

Lately, though, some said he had mellowed. He was back climbing again after a helicopter crash in the Andes, in 1987, had left him with a partially dysfunctional arm. And he was enjoying raising his five-year-old son, Stephan. In 1992, had he lived, he would have seen his dream of speed skiing as an Olympic sport realized, on the Les Arcs track on which he set his last record, in 1982. He had plans to return to Everest and ski from the summit.

Mellowed, perhaps. But not often at peace. "You always lose it in society," he told me once, referring to himself. "So you have to go back, do it again.

Up in those high couloirs I have my talks with God. On that speed run, there is that little flash of peace. Clean, smooth, white… It's a cleansing deal."

I have a cardboard file box at home that I decorated, years ago on its top surface, with a black-and-white photo of McKinney, cut, I think, from the pages of *Mountain Gazette*. It must be a *gelande* contest – a big jump on alpine equipment. He's wearing a bib number. And he is way up in the air (the photographer has caught him "above" the treetops), perfectly balanced, feet and skis together, hands calmly at his sides, body straight and tilted forward like a hood ornament on a supremely confident, mid-century sedan. That was the thing that got me, that chest-out ability to completely possess his momentum, whether through the air or on the snow. He was comfortable there in what for mere mortals would be death-defying extremity. Not casual. Not showy either. But comfortably godlike, to a point just shy of insouciance.

Other athletes' bodies crouch in a language of desperate effort. Steve McKinney's spoke of soaring.

# PART III

# Powder Epiphanies

# Largemouth Bass

We were waiting for Dick Bass. That was normal.

Waiting for Richard D. Bass, the perpetually late, never-say-no, friend-to-legions human magnet. Whirlwind of positive energy, Texas oil tycoon, builder of the Snowbird Resort in Utah, conceiver of the seven-summits project, first man to climb the highest mountain on all seven continents, and at that time (1985) the oldest man (he was 55) to have climbed Everest. Life was a feast too big even for his prodigious appetites. We waited because he was constantly suffering, he would tell you in his raspy Dallas drawl, from "the tyranny of the urgent."

Cramming too much in, or trying to cram in more than the hard rules of time and distance will allow, was Dick Bass's m.o. So why would it be any different here in Switzerland in the winter of 1986 as a contingent of Snowbird people gathered at the Grand Hotel Zermatterhof to cement a newly engaged sister-resort relationship – Zermatt and Snowbird?

The banquet was due to start in two hours. The folks from the Zermatt tourist office had already visited Utah, earlier that winter, with an appropriately angular, 400-pound chunk of the Matterhorn as a gift. Bass was supposed to present the Americans' return offering, a set of exquisite Navajo sand paintings. The rest of the Snowbird group had been in Switzerland for three days. But Bass still had not arrived, and the snow that had been pounding the high valleys of the Rhône River for 24 hours showed no sign of letting up.

Then, suddenly, there he was bursting through the lobby doors. "Pedro! How are ya, buddy? [I had been invited along as a member of the Fourth

Estate, if indeed an assignment from *Powder* magazine qualified.] Yeah, we made it! I haven't slept in three nights. I was givin' a speech in Pebble Beach – I give speeches now! Ha-ha! And the limo broke down so we had to thumb. Missed the plane in San Francisco then caught one outta San Jose, but that put us late into Frankfurt. Missed the train, so we took a plane to Geneva where they lost our skis and... Hoopie! Amigo!" Bass greeted Snowbird vice president of mountain operations Kent Hoopingarner.

When during the formal dinner it was Bass's turn to speak, he apologized in advance for his tendency to hold forth, referring to himself with a chuckle as Largemouth Bass. "Most of you know I have big lungs from talkin' so much. That's how I trained for Everest. Ha-ha!" When Bass laughed it was a big, square-mouthed grin, eyes squinting nearly shut à la Teddy Roosevelt, minus the glasses.

He stood up and raised a glass across the table to Emil Perren, a local Zermatter guide, a mountain of a man, albeit slowed with age. "I lost my climbin' virginity on the Matterhorn in 1949," Bass began. "It's every schoolboy's vision of the Alps – and that's where my heart will always be." His eyes brimmed with tears. "Emil, remember when we climbed the mountain (Bass was 19) an' the snow went out from under me. And my heart went into my throat. I was gone. Sayonara. But your brother-in-law, Theodore, burrowed in an' saved me. Here's this bright-eyed flatlander from Dallas, Texas, hangin' on the end of a rope! . . Don't worry, I won't talk all night."

On and on the stories flowed. Stories about his plans for Snowbird beyond the skiing. "I'm a dreamer; dreams have always sustained me." Dreams of a Snowbird Center for Human Understanding – literature, painting, opera! It would be "dedicated to the development of the body, mind, and spirit." Bass said these things, and they didn't sound corny. His enthusiasm was pure, contagious.

The emotion rose in his eyes again. "Let me tell you somethin' Kazantzakis [*Zorba the Greek*] said: 'By believing passionately enough in that which does not exist, we create.' Now, that could be the motto of Snowbird. I'm goin' to create the finest ski resort in the world. I know it...

"Up on the ridge of Everest, I slipped once, an' only a little patch of soft snow saved me from eternity in a crevasse. I said to myself, God is savin' me for a higher purpose. An' that's when I had the idea for the Snowbird Center. Negative thoughts drain you. An' fear just takes your strength right now! I see it as a renaissance thing – the forward and upward thrust of humanity."

His knee was bopping under the white tablecloth. The coffee was finished. And the brandy. "So anyway, it's 7,000 feet down one way, 8,000 down the other way. I told myself, you slip you're jiggered boy, your life is suckered..."

The headwaiter had to come, finally, to kick us out of the dining room. It was past midnight. And Bass was still talking.

Dick Bass died on Sunday, July 26, 2015, of pulmonary fibrosis. He was 85. He died at home in University Park, outside Dallas, in an 11,000-square-foot house crammed with art. He was fond of Robert Service: "To scorn all strife, and view all life/With the curious eyes of a child..." Marching up Mount Elbrus, the fourth of his seven summits, Bass recited Kipling's *Gunga Din* to his ropemates, in its entirety, from memory.

He came to my cabin in the Colorado high country once. He owned a piece of land nearby. "Pedro," he said, "one of these years I'm gonna build me a cabin like this an' put my feet up on the porch an' write poetry!"

He never did it. He liked to say, "If you never stop, you can't get stuck!" Stopping long enough to put his feet up wasn't in his genes.

Back in Zermatt, the snow continued without a break. All that night avalanches poured off the cliffs, burying the only road up from Visp, cutting off the train. "We're interlodged!" Bass crowed in the morning, referring to the condition at Snowbird when slide danger is so high guests are required to stay inside the lodges. "Say, Zermatt an' Snowbird have more in common than I thought! But it is half important that I get to Frankfurt for an 11 a.m. plane tomorrow. I have to make a weddin' – one of Marian's kids – in Dallas. I don't know if the marriage counselor could smooth that one over!" Marian was the second of his three marriages.

The thing was, no one was coming in or going out. The valley was officially closed. But, as Lauren Talgo from Snowbird's marketing department told me, "The worst mistake anyone can make is to say to Dick, 'No, that's impossible. You can't do that.'"

And sure enough, by mid-morning, Bass had commandeered a helicopter and, in limited visibility, was winging his way toward the next improbable deadline.

# Tears in the Snow

Arnie Wilson looked up and saw the love of his life, Lucy Dicker, sliding down the couloir toward him.

She bounced off the rocks where the chute made a dogleg but kept on sliding and tumbling until she was almost upon him. Without thinking, Arnie dove at Lucy in what he described in his book, *Tears In The Snow*, as "a rugby tackle." Somehow he held on, and the two of them careened another thousand feet down the slope.

Lucy's skis were gone. Arnie's were soon ripped away, too. Bumps tossed them into the air together. Glacier ice tore through Arnie's ski jacket and stripped the flesh from his arm. A final jolt flung them apart, despite Arnie's desperate grip.

When they had stopped sliding, Arnie scrambled to Lucy's side. She appeared to be staring at him but didn't respond to his entreaties. And then he saw the blood bubbling out of her left ear.

This was on April 6, 1995, above La Grave, France. It had been less than four months since the two of them had completed an audacious lark. They'd skied every day of calendar year 1994 on an around-the-world junket: 365 days, 240 resorts, five continents, 13 countries, 18 time zones and 109,000 miles by plane, train and Russian pickup truck.

It was a huge media coup. Arnie was the skiing correspondent for London's *Financial Times* newspaper, to which he sent 50 dispatches during the trip. Lucy was the director of Touralp, a French tourism company based in London. She was French, maiden name Richaud, with a mane of auburn hair and, as Arnie wrote, "a smile to melt glaciers." The two had been together scarcely more than a year. She was 40, he was 10 years older.

With their travel and media connections, they garnered sponsorships from clothing company Degre 7, *Snow+Rock* magazine, Avis, and American Airlines. Ski The Summit, the marketing arm of the four ski areas in Colorado's Summit County, gave them $25,000 cash.

I met them by chance in Big Sky, Montana, early in their quest. I was on some kind of press trip, and they were there: in and out, wined and dined, ski a few thousand vertical feet, and off they went to the next ski area, the next day in the string. But it was clear, even in that brief encounter, that they were charming, bright people, a little amazed by their own mad scheme, and very much in the first blush of love.

I ran into Arnie years later in Telluride, where he was skiing with another Brit, Tom Herbst. In typical whirlwind Arnie fashion, he and Herbst were off later that afternoon for Purgatory Resort a couple of hours away by car. And then… I've forgotten where.

It was the first time we'd crossed paths since Lucy's death. He told me he'd since married, and he was now editor of *Ski+board*, the quarterly journal of Ski Club Great Britain. I told him how sorry I was about Lucy. He thanked me and said with his eyes that he had not gotten over her still.

I found *Tears In The Snow* on the bookshelf and re-read it. It is full of raw ache and a kind of stunned, unpolished storytelling. Understandably so. Right up front Arnie wrote, "I was planning to write this book with Lucy. Then when I lost her, she became the book."

It was going to be a triumphal – maybe just a bit tongue-in-cheek (how could it not be?) – recounting of their outlandish Guinness Book accomplishment. How they managed to keep the streak intact through the entire year, with a little help from the International Date Line, and despite numerous close calls: having to hike up a dirty patch of snow at sunset in Manali, India, after nearly 24 hours of travel from Europe; skiing in the rain and the dark on a Chilean volcano; sneaking in a run at the indoor Ski Dome in Tokyo to check off yet another day; skiing by the light of snowmobile headlights at 4 a.m. on the closed slopes at Mammoth Mountain before catching the next ride.

And the book does visit these stories, along with the stresses and humor the trip engendered. But, at heart, it is about an all-too-brief love affair and its horrific end. Of course. It had to be. The fall haunted Arnie's dreams as he was writing. Sometimes he replayed it from his perspective: helpless, watching, impotent. Sometimes in the dream he was inside Lucy's body as she smashed into the rocks.

Arnie's revelations are unselfconscious to the point of embarrassment. Not his, the reader's. He wrote that he couldn't bear to keep Lucy's bloody ski suit. But he also couldn't bear to part with her underwear, which he keeps inside a cushion at home in London. He wrote, "All I wanted to do is tell her I love her. And say goodbye. Two things I couldn't do when she died so suddenly."

# L'Espace Killy

At one point the road leading to the modern ski resort of Méribel squeezes down to a single, very narrow lane where two stone barns, built centuries before the automobile, nearly touch. I stopped the car to take a picture and met Alice Fraissard and her friend Marie, strong, middle-aged farm ladies in flower-print dresses. Later in the spring, when the snow has melted, they will move their cows up on the *alpages*, the high, treeless meadows of these French Alps, meadows that were presently occupied by cavorting skiers. I asked them what they thought of the Olympic Games coming next February to their valley and to other high mountain valleys in the *département* of Savoie.

"*C'est pas grande chose,*" said Marie – it's no big deal. "It's upped everybody's taxes, but it's already brought more tourists, who also help pay."

"Meanwhile," Alice chimed in with a wry smile, "Jean-Claude Killy is getting rich from this."

Killy is the dashing ski legend who won all three alpine gold medals at Grenoble in 1968, the second time France hosted the Winter Olympics. (The first was at Chamonix, a few valleys to the north, in 1924 – the first-ever Winter Games.) Native son Killy, then just 24, came through despite terrific pressure and ascended beyond hero to near godlike status in France. He played a key role in convincing the International Olympic Committee to award the 1992 Games to his home region. Then he set about dividing the spoils, spreading the venues among 13 different mountain towns with Albertville, a small industrial city of 20,000 residents at the edge of the peaks, as the nominal center. Killy critics, whose scoldings are always tinged with respect, point out that naturally Val d'Isère, the great man's hometown, gleaned the ultimate prize, the staging of the men's downhill events.

One can't miss seeing preparations for the Games: cranes hoisting up an athletes' village in the ancient hot springs town of Brides-les-Bains; the laying of pipe for artificial snow-making at Méribel (just in case); putting the finishing touches on the state-of-the-art bobsled and luge track, right next to 500-year-old farmhouses, at La Plagne. And everywhere roadwork, widening and straightening, tunnel building, and repaving.

It's a huge infusion of modernity for a region that was the last puzzle piece added to the map of modern France. The feudal Duchy of Savoy had been around since the 11th century, more or less independent of its neighbors, France, Italy, and Switzerland. When, in 1860, Savoie and Haute-Savoie were annexed, by peaceful plebiscite, to France, the last Duke, Victor Emmanuel II, moved east and became King of Italy. Savoyards feel French for the most part, but they remain devoted to their vertiginous kingdom, to a particularly hearty food and drink, and to their claim (barely arguable, in my view) of the best skiing on the planet.

Take Les Trois Vallées, home to Courchevel, Méribel, and Val Thorens. The resort connects three valleys (really four) to create the biggest one-ticket ski area in France, maybe the world. Two hundred lifts – from drag lifts to gondolas ("eggs," the French call them) to swooping, 180-passenger *téléphériques* – an uphill capacity of 200,000 skiers per hour, spread like a web over 100 square miles. The entire lift-served acreage of Colorado doesn't add up to half that.

Méribel is the middle valley of the three, where the hockey tournament and the women's alpine events will be staged. It is a new (postwar) ski station, but completely devoted to indigenous architecture. Chalet-style buildings of wood and stone with low-angle, slate-covered roofs dot the forested hillside like shepherds' huts. I stayed in one overlooking an ultra-modern gondola terminal but took my meals at a series of restaurants and cafés that recall a time when the people of this parish spent snowy days baking bread in communal ovens.

At the Café Les Glaciers the proprietress brought me two-handled bowls of coffee with steamed milk in a separate pitcher and crusty fresh bread from the bakery next door. At the bar, local ski instructors – farmers and carpenters in the summer – stood in their primary-red École du Ski Français uniforms fortifying themselves with red wine and small cups of strong black coffee.

You want one of these instructors to accompany you skiing, if for no other reason than to learn your way around the daunting terrain. It's not so much the difficulty as the vastness. Méribel alone is many times the size of Vail, but you will want to travel over to Courchevel to the east and to Les Menuires/ Val Thorens on the west. Getting from one end to the other of this grand domain can take all day.

My ski school guide, Eric Boulanger, and I struck off on skis promptly one morning for Val Thorens, the highest of the stations, and were only a little late arriving for lunch. On the way we had ridden three gondolas and three or four chairlifts, and we skied about 15 miles of smooth spring snow that compared to the velvety feel of "certain wines," as Eric put it. His skiing style was as elegant as his simile.

Lunch, as always in France, even on a mountainside, was an unhurried celebration of tasteful refueling, faces tilted to the sun. I had the *salade des bergers,* the shepherd's salad, a Savoie staple, with butter lettuce, thick bacon, walnuts, cheese, and egg, accompanied (appropriately) by a dry white Chignon from Chambery, the lowlands capital of Savoie. Below us the land dropped away in treeless folds of snow and rock washed in shady, watercolor blues and pale, sunlit pinks. The word Savoie comes from the Latin for fir forest. From the tops of these mountains, the forest is very far down, 9,000 vertical feet down. Ninety percent of the skiing is above timberline. Way off below our lunch deck, skiers traced their lines in miniature, "*comme des fourmis,*" Eric said, like ants.

After a last, tiny glass of *génépi,* the local digestif, we worked our way back to Méribel with a descent along the way into the Belleville Valley and Les Menuires, where the men's slalom competition will be set among the "purpose-built" high-rises there. Once we'd regained the ridge at Tougnete, we carved down the women's alpine courses, off the Roc de Fer. At the lazy pace we assumed, the terrain was not scary, but rather a kind of fabulous roller coaster ride of treeless mounds and broad banked gullies.

I would have needed months to sample all of the skiing within the Olympic sphere. There wasn't time enough. I wouldn't, for example, get over to the old forested village of Les Saisies, where the biathlon and cross-country tracks will be set. Nor did I get a chance to check out the high-altitude Les Arcs site for speed skiing, a demonstration sport making its first-ever appearance at the Games. But I couldn't not visit Val d'Isère, aka *L'Espace Killy*, Killy's World.

Right away, entering Val's rocky stronghold, you see the Face de Bellevarde, the forbidding north face on which the men's downhill course twists its way through couloirs and pillars of golden rock right down to the edge of town. One way to get up there is via the Funival, a funicular railway whose tracks disappear into a tunnel inside the mountain.

I took supper that night at the Brasserie des Sports, a place that would probably be dubbed a "sports bar" in this country, except that there were no televisions, only red-and-white-checked tablecloths and walls full of trophies and black-and-white photographs of Killy: Killy in his fierce crouch on a race course; Killy smiling with the mayor; Killy posing with rugby and car-racing friends. (One doesn't see many pictures of school-age Killy. His mother abandoned the family when he was seven, and he quit high school at 15 to ski.) I couldn't help but recall the one time I'd seen Jean-Claude in person, at Bear Valley in 1974, when I was teaching skiing there and the great one was racing the pro circuit. It snowed a bunch the day before the race, which didn't bode well for the kind of hard, icy track racers prefer. In fact, by the end of Saturday's dual format slalom – which Killy won – the ruts around the control gates were hip deep. But on Friday, with no gates set and the storm pouring out of the sky, I watched Killy free-ski the powder. Straight down. He skied Grizzly Basin straight. No turns. Down the steepest, most desperate part of that high Sierra rock. Tall and loose and bolt upright, as if his relationship to gravity was different than everyone else's. I suppose it was.

I skied alone the next afternoon, without a guide. Val d'Isère is nearly as vast as Les Trois Vallées, but I felt the itch to explore on my own. I struck out to the east over hill and dale toward the Italian border, toward the Glacier du Pissaillas and the farthest reaches of Val's enormous range.

There were few other skiers out this far, and after a couple of runs I began to recognize them. One was a snowboarder wearing a t-shirt that read: "Val d'Isère, The Powder and the Glory." Another was an older, subtler gentleman. He had on vintage gear, sixties-era leather boots and long, stiff skis. He had an elegant style that was right out of Killy's (and my) time. The books on technique called it *virage aval*, turn to the valley. With each pole plant he was opening a door and then slipping effortlessly across the threshold. I decided to follow him. Maybe he knew where the best snow was, that perfect sun-warmed corn that Eric Boulanger called *velour*.

The time was late enough I felt the need to angle back to the west, but my man was skiing ever farther east, away from civilization. Every time we came to a col or a pass where a decision had to be made, he opted to go skier's right, farther east. Could I get back to a lift? Or even to a road in the valley? I didn't know, but I stuck with him, at a distance, out of a perverse faith.

Just when I thought we would both be lost forever beyond the last *alpages*, he found it, a series of exquisite, wave-like troughs, their curving sides facing directly into the sun. Our timing was just right; the snow surface had melted down about an inch. The feeling was like floating through the invincible part of a flying dream.

I lost my man somehow in the narrow, shadowed streets of Le Fornet, a satellite village that is the last plowed-road outpost above Val d'Isère. So I didn't get a chance to thank him. I'd missed the day's last tram, too. (Tiny Le Fornet, population, what, 100 people? has its own tram!) But there was a bus, a clean, new, free shuttle back to town. How fine was that! As I settled into a seat I thought of something else Marie, my unconcerned Méribel farm lady, had said: "*La France est très civilisée, n'est-ce pas?*"

# The Games are Already Won

I CRY WATCHING THE WONDER YEARS. And horse races. (Thoroughbreds will run hard enough to burst their own hearts.) So, when an 11-year-old girl in a snow-white and red Savoyard dress stood alone in the center of the Opening Ceremonies stadium in front of Jean-Claude Killy, and the President of France, and nearly 33,000 people and let go a dove of peace, I was a basket case. But then (it gets better) she rose into the air on an invisible lift and sang *La Marseillaise* in a high, pure voice while the last pink blush of alpenglow drained from the peaks behind me.

Jugglers came up magically out of the floor, and acrobats, and stilt-walkers, and trampolinists, and in-line skaters, and bungee jumpers, in a Fellini-like six-ring circus – all of them whirling in concentric circles as if they were the gyroscope at the center of the planet. And why not? In a just world, Albertville, Department of Savoie, Rhône-Alpes Region, France, should be the center of the universe for this Olympic fortnight 1992.

The world as we knew it four years ago in Calgary has fundamentally changed. Into the stadium and around the circle marched teams from a united Germany (!), from the newly independent Baltic states, teams representing Croatia and Slovenia (loud cheers), as well as one for what was left of Yugoslavia (conspicuous quiet). The once monolithic Soviet team, renamed the Unified Team (EUN), included pairs figure skaters from Lithuania and Ukraine who wore jackets with the old CCCP initials circled and lined through. The loudest roar was reserved, of course, for the French, looking like foil-suited astronauts. But the second biggest cheer erupted for one of the smallest teams: two black African downhillers, one carrying the flag and one walking behind, from the former French colony of Senegal.

The Americans were welcomed warmly, even raucously, and it is fitting, I suppose, that an American sporting export gave these ceremonies their most participatory element. One little wave began innocuously enough during the introductions but soon swelled to tsunami proportions. Round it went with a deafening roar, just as it might have at Dodger Stadium or Madison Square Garden. At first, none of the dignitaries in their special box would join in. But, ultimately, the energy was impossible to resist, and Killy, whose charisma almost single-handedly brought these Games to Savoie, Francois Mitterand, Princess Anne of England, and even (finally) Dan and Marilyn Quayle, stood and lifted their arms with the passing surge.

Surely, these were the most televised Games in history. CBS bet the farm. In France, Eurosport, the continent's answer to ESPN, beamed 24-hour coverage in three languages. There were screens everywhere: in endless rows in the press rooms; outside, 15 feet tall beside the race courses (in case you can't see Swiss downhiller Chantal Bournissen's dimples from where you are); screens even on the media buses I rode to events spread around the ancient duchy of Savoie.

I asked a hockey writer from Philadelphia if he was planning to attend the first U.S. game, against Italy, and he said he might. Or he might just stay in the pressroom 100 feet away, with the sounds of the crowd throbbing through the wall, and watch it on TV. I probably wouldn't have cried watching the Opening Ceremonies on a screen, but then again I might have.

Even Killy admits the men's downhill course was designed with TV in mind. It knifes right through the photogenic cliffs of La Face de Bellevarde. It hangs like a serpentine, red-safety-net dragon on the mountain wall above Val d'Isère's ancient stone village. It is so steep the TV cameras can pick up almost the entire course from the finish area. This made for wonderful viewing for on-site spectators, too. But the spooky terrain dictated a turny course, in order to keep speeds down, and the pure downhillers, the gliders, were not happy. Pure downhillers never enjoy being forced to moderate their speed.

AJ Kitt is a pure downhiller. But America's top hope worked hard during training to improve his turns. On race day, in front of a crowd that swarmed over the hill like a rock concert, such accomplished turners as Marc Girardelli (LUX) and Paul Accola (SUI) missed gates and did not finish the twisting beast. (One of the Senegalese did finish, much relieved, 22 seconds out of a medal.) A man near me in the finish area said, "I can see why Kitt's mother can't stand to watch this stuff."

When AJ's start was announced, his name was pronounced, as it would be, phonetically in French, "Ah Gee Keet." And much like the big, curly-headed kid from Rochester, New York, it was kind of an Ah, Gee run – good enough for ninth place.

The weight of *toute la France* that day rode on Franck Piccard's slender shoulders. Not only was he France's only downhill medal hope, he is a local boy, born in Albertville and reared in Les Saisies, the Savoie village where the cross-country events were being staged. The pressure on Piccard must have been immense, but not on a par, surely, with the weight Killy felt, in 1968, when he was *expected* to win gold in all three disciplines. France is a more fatalistic athletic nation today.

So, when Piccard, the twenty-third starter, whipped down the course second only to the granite-chinned Austrian Patrick Ortlieb, everybody went nuts. Piccard emerged from his self-made cloud of dust along the finish rail blowing kisses. The celebrations in Val d'Isère and Les Saisies lasted all night. (I watched them, yes, on TV.) The next morning there were eight inches of fresh snow on La Face de Bellevarde, threatening the combined downhill and the sanity of Games organizers. But for the time being, Killy's controversial course and the fragile French esteem were riding high. As one newspaper reported the morning after: "The Games are already won!"

If these are the TV Games nonpareil, they are also the autobus Games. I'm riding in one right now, on my way up the Isère Valley to Tignes for the freestyle moguls finals. It will be a two-hour journey from my billet in La Tania (part of Les Trois Vallées complex) down steep, forested hillsides to the medieval town of Moutiers, where there is no snow, and back up the Isère River to where snow is piled six-feet deep on slate-roofed chalets. My autobus is one of an army of nearly identical rolling living rooms recruited for the fortnight from tour companies all over France. This one is a Renault (what else) with more glass than your basic commercial greenhouse and so long it needs the entire road edge-to-edge to make the hairpins at the head of the canyon. The French government spent billions widening these curves and adding lanes all over the Savoie. They had to. Otherwise just two of these houseboats meeting in the wrong place at the wrong time could bring the whole transportation network to a halt.

The magic buses have taken me to sights and sounds I never knew existed. At La Plagne I learned that it is not possible to see a bobsled coming. It is there and gone before you can squeeze the camera trigger. Listening to a ski jumper in the air at Courchevel, I decided, is like having someone blow in your ear. The Japanese are the quietest knifing by overhead. It must have to do with jujitsu, or Zen, because the fabric in the suits is all the same stuff by regulation. Whenever someone launches a particularly long flight, officials grab him at the finish and check his "verification of material." They do the same at the alpine races. All ski suits must meet FIS permeability standards. Different materials, different weaves, affect aerodynamic efficiency – drag and lift. Permeability, it turns out, is a matter of fairness.

No one grabbed Austrian Hubert Strolz at the finish of his race in Val d'Isère. In fact, the defending Olympic champion in alpine combined never made it to the finish line. Leading by a mile after the downhill and the first run of slalom (his advantage was 4 seconds, as good as a mile), and needing only to stand up through his second run of slalom, Hubert leaned in and missed the third-to-last gate. It was a duffer's turn, lazy and disastrous, one with which every weekend skier could identify. A very human error on the biggest of stages.

Perhaps most human of all, and most honest, was a comment Killy made as the first week drew to a close. Asked in a press briefing if he would consider organizing another Olympic spectacle some day, he replied, "No, never. The first time around was a privilege. The second time would be suicide."

Killy had said during the lead up to February – both to pump up his homeland and as a not-so-subtle jab at Olympic venues of the recent past – that these Games would be in the mountains, of the snow. After the men's downhill opened the fortnight on a blazing blue note, we had more stormy weather than clear. As week two opened, Nordic combined jumpers sailed through a spitting mist. That night in Albertville (for the pairs freestyle skating finals) I found the streets glistening with reflected light in a way that made the homely, industrial town of 20,000 prettier than it really is.

So hard and warm was the snowfall on Thursday, the moguls finals appeared to be contested on the far side of a gossamer curtain. French weathermen described it as *chutes de neige incessantes*. French "Bad Boy of the Bumps" Edgar Grospiron missed a turn in practice and slipped unceremoniously to a stop. Instead of refocusing, dropping his head and shutting the world out as so many of the competitors do, he stood on top of a mogul and directed the huge crowd in a cheer, using his ski pole as a baton to incite a rolling thunder. Then, with eyes (seeing eyes?) painted on the knees of his ski pants, he rode that energy, rode through the downpouring snow, right through to the gold medal.

Following behind the snow, wind raged across the treeless ridgelines, blowing Monday's women's super-G into Tuesday. But Tuesday dawned still and cold in the high mountains with temperatures around zero and skies the bluebird color of the Italian team uniforms. Or maybe it was the color of King Harald's eyes, though I didn't get close enough to the Norwegian sovereign, who was in the stands at Val d'Isère, to verify his Paul Newman rating.

His Highness was abroad to cheer his athletes' remarkable medal harvest – as usual, the Norwegians could have used a combine – but inevitably, it seemed, this day was to be an Italian day. Gold number one came in the women's super-G, contested on the slopes of Méribel. I didn't see it in person; I watched live on TV from the Val d'Isère press center. (My reservations about "the television Games" were constantly tempered by my gratefulness to the tube. Due to the distances between venues, I was never able to personally witness more than two events in any one day, and often just one. If it weren't for the TV, I'd have been more in the dark about things Olympique than my kids at home. In fact, when we talked on the phone, they were telling *me* about the cross-country racers slobbering on their chins and falling down in heaps at the finish line.)

By chance that morning I'd positioned myself in the center of the Italian press corps, who (like me, watching the tele) oohed politely at Frenchwoman Carole Merle's aggression and at Austrian Katja Seizinger's graceful strength.

But they went all Vesuvius when 21-year-old countrywoman Deborah Compagnoni sliced onto the course, and they kept screaming ("*Grandi! Grandi!*") with each passing gate. Her run was indeed grand, surgical even, much cleaner and closer to the gates than anyone before her, and the time reflected it. She finished 1.41 seconds ahead of second-place Merle, another time zone at this level of racing. The Italian journalists slapped each other with their gloves, jumped up and down, hugged one another, hugged me. Then we all stormed outside to watch, in the flesh, their Alberto in his attempt at an historic giant slalom double.

Historic in that no Olympic alpine skier had ever repeated, four years later, as gold medalist. The flamboyant Tomba had won both the slalom and the giant slalom in Calgary and was a favorite again this time. He certainly hadn't lost his bravado, insisting to the media that the host city should rename itself "Albertoville." He was also quoted as saying: "I used to have a wild time with three women until 5 a.m., but now I am getting older. In the Olympic village here I will live it up with five women, but only until 3 a.m." That boast may have been apocryphal, but such was La Bomba's mystique, it could have been true, and it no doubt got into the heads of his competition.

They were not going to hand him the win, however. Four-time World Cup overall champ Marc Girardelli skied both runs about as well as a giant slalom can be skied. His skis snapped back and forth across the fall line as if on rubber bands, shooting thin, ruler-ed contrails to the sides. He was masterful. (Cruelly for the recreational observer, the GS at this level is the most beautiful of ski races. Cruel because unlike the blur of downhill or the quick-quick slash of slalom, the turns look doable, understandable in a visceral, on-your-best-day sort of way. When, in reality, they are the most difficult to master turns of all the disciplines, requiring iron-thighed strength and a silky touch at big speeds.)

Everything Girardelli had done well, Tomba did better. He led after the first run by .13 seconds. Then, in the second run, as the last racer down and trailing by .2 seconds at the intermediate point, Alberto slipped into another gear, at once attacking and caressing, his torso oak-solid while his feet danced an elfin nimbleness. He won going away. "*Bravissimo, Alberto! Bravissimo!*" Silver medalist Girardelli, knowing better than anyone what he had just seen, moved quickly to embrace his rival.

How suddenly the fates reverse. Compagnoni, called "Tombagnoni" for her Alberto-like style on the snow, was queen of all she surveyed – until the first run of the women's GS the following day. In one sickening moment, she sat back mid-turn, veered off the course and snapped the anterior cruciate ligament in her left knee. Her tears flowed as much from anger as from pain. The next morning, in her hospital bed, Compagnoni held court before a somber Italian press, she in a brace and wan Madonna smile, they whispering questions like a bunch of bereft uncles. One day the gift, the next it's taken away.

Tomba went to visit her in the clinic, on skis, from Les Menuires, where the men's slalom would be contested, over to Méribel. The rumor was he got lost on the return trip, so vast and white is the Trois Vallées sea. He had one more event, in which he would attempt the unprecedented double double – to repeat as champion in both tech races.

He could have won the slalom easily, too, but he had (for him) a horrible, mechanical, first run; his time was well down the list. During the long break between runs he shaved clean his two-week-old beard. On the way back up the Pomalift he smoked a cigarette. Then in the start shack an assistant handed him a dainty cup of espresso, which he downed in one sip. Breaking the wand this time, he was a bull, the very definition of momentum. He found that calm at the center of action where the poles seemed to fall down in advance of his arrival. No one came close to his second-run time. But it was not quite enough, in aggregate, to unseat the first-run leader, Finn Christian Jagge (NOR), who held on, barely, for the gold. Afterward, Tomba said he was thrilled with silver. He didn't have a silver medal; now he did! And he put a coda on the day, and on his legend, by hoisting the last-place racer, a hapless Costa Rican who finished an eternal 2.5 minutes behind the winning time, onto his broad shoulders and parading around the finish corral, everyone present delirious with the gesture and the joy evident in both men.

American rookie Julie Parisien experienced a kind of reverse-Tomba in the final alpine event of these Games. She won the first run of slalom, on talent and timing so immaculate her turns assumed a lilting, rock-a-bye rhythm.

But, because this was the Olympics and the field is extra broad (see Team Costa Rica above), she had to endure a three and a half hour wait between runs, and then start last in the reverse-15 format. I thought I might melt from the tension.

When she was finally on course again, and the micro mistakes began to add up and we knew she probably would not hold onto a medal, that part of it – the race for gold, for supremacy over the others – suddenly wasn't all that important. What was important was the public attempt at something so outrageously difficult, the communion of effort and skill, the beauty of it shining through.

The women talk sometimes about "giving too much" in a ski race. Maybe that's what happened to Julie Parisien. (Her heart looked to be breaking by the end.) But when they do that, I am the one on the receiving end; I am the winner, gifted and grateful. And likely as not brimming over.

# Late Storm

A LATE-SEASON STORM ROLLS THROUGH, a big one, the day after the Telluride ski area closes. A cruel irony? A classic bit of ski-bum lore? It has nevertheless happened an unlikely number of times since we moved to this part of the world.

In fact, the first example we knew about was in the spring of 1976, before we left California for southwest Colorado, before we'd set eyes on Telluride or its mountain. We saw the storm documented on screen, in the silent, unedited rushes of a 16mm film our friend Lito Tejada-Flores was making.

Lito had been commissioned by Telluride's original ski-area developer, Joe Zoline, to do a promotional film for his fledgling ski area, just then completing its fourth season and struggling in the anonymity afforded a place 300 miles from Denver and an hour and a half from the nearest stoplight.

I don't recall how Lito and Zoline connected. Lito was not exactly a well-known filmmaker. He was our ski-teaching buddy at the small but intellectually potent Bear Valley ski area, in the Sierra north of Yosemite. Not famous, perhaps, but his 1969 documentary *Fitz Roy: First Ascent of the South-West Buttress*, had won the Grand Prize at the Trento Mountain Film Festival. And we knew our friend to be a prodigiously creative man, as a writer, photographer, inventor of fonts, and practitioner of the slow-dog noodle.

Lito came back to Bear Valley breathless from his trip to Telluride that April of 1976. He had arrived in Colorado just as the ski area was shutting down for the season. He'd missed the lifts, but he was there for the big postseason storm.

In his Bear Valley cabin, Lito threaded the film through the clicking, flickering projector, dimmed the lights, and the living room wall lit up with a seemingly static image: the horizontal line of a cornice separating blue sky above and an unbroken field of powder below.

"I'm thinking of having pan pipes in the background here," Lito said. He may even have put an LP of the breathy South American flutes on the turntable. (Lito's father was from Bolivia.)

The image didn't change and didn't change, and then it did. In slow motion, a red-sweatered skier burst through the cornice from the back, coming straight at us, landing, eventually, in a thigh-deep custard of windblown snow.

The skier was fellow Bear Valley instructor Ragnar Håkonsen, an athletic, photogenic Norwegian who had made the trip with Lito. Ragnar drove his skis in deep (long, straight skis), his legs compressed then extended, again and again, like an accordion, as bricks of dense snow flew off the wave in front of him and up into the cloudless sky.

This was Mammoth Slide, when it was just an avalanche path, before it became a named ski run. They had ridden a snowcat to the top, courtesy of Joe Zoline, just for the filming. It was wild, hypnotic, fantasy footage.

Lito next trained his camera on downtown Telluride. Then, as now, closing day signaled the beginning of off-season and the streets were empty. Only back then, with a population under 700, with no Mountain Village and no airport, empty was really empty.

Ragnar donned cross-country skis and strode effortlessly down the unshoveled sidewalks of Colorado Avenue. A foot of fresh snow balanced on delicate iron railings and on chairs left out in the storm.

He floated past the mining-era Floradora Saloon, past the Sheridan Opera House, with its sign, "Picture Show Every Evening, Admission 10 and 15 Cents," painted right on the brick wall. And below those were the words Bath House, and an arrow pointing to the basement, a steamy downstairs refuge already well-known to newcomers as a place to get warm, to get naked. The town's steep-roofed Victorians seemed asleep under white blankets, seemed put to sleep as if by a spell, like Brigadoon, in no particular hurry to wake up.

Lito raved about other aspects of the town, the surprising civilization he'd found sprouting from the decay, where mining was dying and skiing ascendant. "Two bakeries!" he said, as we watched Ragnar glide through the frame. "Two newspapers!" The hoary, hundred-year-old *Telluride Times* and a utopian upstart whose name I forget. "A movie theater!" in the old Opera House.

None of which would astonish a denizen of an established ski town like Stowe or Aspen. But to us, it did sound amazing. Little Bear Valley, population 150, had none of those things.

Lito didn't stay around in Telluride to film the snow melting. He kept his camera eye on the blinding white slopes and softly buried streets.

He wanted to go back, he said as the projector stopped. He wanted to move there, at least for a while, to this slowly awakening place transformed, gentled, disguised (but not really; surely this was the real Telluride?) by a blast of April snow.

It didn't take him long to convince the rest of us that we should join him.

# Powder Epiphanies

Shouldn't you have to wait years for that defining powder skiing experience? Put in your time? Dream it? Suffer for it?

It took me 20 years, the last five skiing a hundred days a season, to find it. It took that long for the alchemy to work, for the weather luck to kick in, for me to link enough deep-snow turns in a row, for the magic to take over.

My daughter Cloe, who turned 19 last February, did it in five days.

It had been a dry Christmas and we had modest hopes as the two of us set out, on December 31st, for a five-day, father-daughter loop around northern Colorado. We weren't looking for epiphanies.

The storm arrived that night. By the afternoon of the 1st, we found ourselves traversing into Sun Down Bowl at Vail, angling through a foot of new snow. Cloe biffed on her first turn, when the spoon-like nose of her snowboard scooped too deep into the marshmallow creme. Down in the gully near the end of the run, she nosedived again, this time stopping upright like a stick jammed in the sand. Feet strapped down, snow up to her knees, she couldn't budge.

In wasn't long before Cloe adjusted her stance back on the board, shifted her emphasis from driving hard with the front foot – as she had learned to do on the hardpack – to steering more with the back foot, using it like a rudder in the deep. To stay afloat, she realized, she had to manage the attitude of the board under the snow. She was riding a wing; she had to find trim. That was epiphany number one.

The next day brought more new snow, a complete fresh blanket. "Crazy," Cloe kept saying from inside her neck gaiter. "Dad, this is crazy." The turns accumulated.

I noticed on one lift ride that Cloe's anorak had ripped along the side seam. It might have been torn by an errant branch in the Yonder trees, or perhaps it simply exploded during one of her exuberant, head-over-heels tumbles. "Doesn't matter," she said at the top. "Gotta keep going." She sensed rather than understood the possibilities. She did stop long enough for me to patch her up with strips of duct tape, a true powder skier's fashion accessory. So young, I thought as we dropped into China Bowl again, to have earned those stripes.

Snowflakes swirled like asteroids at warp speed in our headlights on the way to Steamboat Springs that night. They never let up during our two days of weaving Steamboat's famous trees. Powder epiphanies two and three occurred there. First, Cloe realized that out in the open, on the trails, all was cottage cheese: snow, sky, up, down, bump or smooth. While in the trees, underneath the aspen canopy on Shadows, say, or Closet, the wind quieted, the slim trunks defined the pitch ahead, and the muted light gave definition to pillows of new snow.

Next, she made a deal with the unforgiving bark. "I figured it out," she announced with glee, halfway down one run. "I just look at the spaces between the trees and not at the trees themselves." It was a cliché I'd thought too trite to mention, or not yet anyway. And there it was, out of the mouths of babes. "Crazy," Cloe said, her confidence growing with each lap.

We became woods creatures, snowshoe hares on long, fiberglass feet. Snow poured from the sky until it was thigh deep, then waist deep. On our second Steamboat day, Cloe said, "I'm so in the habit now of just putting my hip into any big pile of snow. I don't know if I'll be able to go back to snow that makes noise."

It seemed nearly criminal to leave, but we had every reason to believe that our last stop, at Winter Park, would be just as good. It turned out to be even better. Avalanches had closed the highway from Denver. The only people skiing were locals and the few lucky ones, like us, who had driven in from the west. Storm totals on Friday morning showed 68 inches since the first of the week. The giant moguls of Mary Jane were muffled under six feet of frosted flakes.

Cloe learned to smooth through those steep bumps by balancing the considerable pull of gravity with the resistance of the deep snow. Firm legs, then soft. Pressing down into it, then skimming the surface. Gaining control by letting go.

She was right there on the threshold of powder Zen, learning not to fight it, finding out (as Dolores LaChapelle wrote in *Deep Powder Snow: 40 Years of Ecstatic Skiing, Avalanches, and Earth Wisdom*) about "turning the self over to the snow."

In The Jane's dense evergreens, we practiced good tree-skiing protocol: always keeping each other in sight, leapfrogging, spotting each other. I could practically see Cloe's mind working, eyes wide behind her goggles, as she cast her gaze well down the hill, gauging, projecting, planning her moves.

Once, in the glades above Golden Spike, we careened to a stop practically on top of one another. We burst out laughing. The energy of our sudden halt had left us face-to-face, buried up to our armpits. "Oh please, oh please," Cloe pleaded. "Just one more day!"

That's the final powder epiphany: addiction. Nothing else in skiing will ever be as good. Cloe had stolen fire from the gods. I was proud and a little fearful. I remembered my conversation with the woman at the ticket window that morning. When I had said, "Two for today, myself and my daughter," she had asked (a reasonable question), "One adult and one child?"

"No," I had answered, flummoxed by the sound of my own words, "She's all grown up now."

# Fat Skis, Dad, and Me

Dad has this dream. Not an all-encompassing "I-have-a-dream" dream. Just a garden-variety sleeping dream. He's had it since he was a coast-dwelling teenager teaching himself to ski at Big Bear, in the San Bernardino Mountains east of Los Angeles. He still has the dream on occasion at age 71.

"Although now it's harder to get to the skiing part," he told me as we dangled on a chairlift above the slopes at Steamboat, Colorado. "There are frustrating delays, forgotten things. You know how dreams go. But when I do get to the skiing, it's always the same: I'm flying through deep snow, and it's completely effortless."

Over a lifetime devoted to work and family, Dad's off-again on-again skiing reality had brought him close to experiencing the dream a couple of times. But those moments were fleeting glimpses, and they had happened on two-dimensional groomed surfaces. The real thing, that out-of-body buoyance in three-dimensional snow, that feeling of being poured down a mountainside, had remained out of reach.

I wanted to make that dream happen for him. He introduced me to skiing, to what became my passion and later my livelihood. I knew this feeling. I'd lived it. I wanted to give it to him gift wrapped, perfect, effortless. Plus, I figured I'd get a good story out of it.

As a regular contributor to *SKI* magazine I had the wherewithal to create what I hoped would be the ideal setup. I arranged for a couple of warm-up days on the slopes at Steamboat. Then I called Jupiter Jones of Steamboat Powder Cats to reserve two seats on his cat in early March, when the weather records said we'd have the best chance for fresh snow. I asked Jupiter about fat skis for Dad. He said he had a spare pair, and he said it was true what everybody was saying: on the wide platform of the "fat boys" his customers found it a lot easier to get around in powder. They didn't fall as much, they didn't get as tired, and they felt as if they were really doing it, linking turns in a way that was both ecstatic and respectful of the wild, white terrain on Buffalo Pass.

Dad would claim, rightly, that he never attained more than intermediate skiing skills. And he hadn't skied much in the past few years. But I was positive he could do it. He is an athlete from a family of athletes. There are home movies of him as a boy in the 1930s balanced on a wooden circus ball. In college he roamed the hot corner and batted cleanup on the baseball team. My optimism was further colored by my own blooming love affair with fat skis. ("Try these," fellow ski tester Dick Dorworth had said, handing me a pair of early Völkl fatties, "they'll subtract 10 years from your skiing age!") And I was still in the thrall of memories from the 1950s, of an upright, bareheaded man on the slopes at Mammoth Mountain, seemingly in full command of the forces involved, while I, at age seven or eight, hustled up and down the rope tow wanting so much to be him.

I didn't properly take into account how different our worlds had become. I lived at high elevation in Colorado, eagerly anticipating the arrival of each new snowstorm. He drove the Gordian knot of Southern California freeways, his appointed post on the State Transportation Commission coda to a career in governmental relations. I delighted in the frictionless glide of the right ski wax. He thrilled at increased use of car-pool lanes. I thought I was doing something nice for my dad. He thought he was doing something important for me. I didn't see that I was setting us both up for failure.

We spent the first two days coursing some of Steamboat's mellow, lift-served terrain.

"The backcountry is going to be silky!" I enthused as we rode a quad chair through conifers plastered as white as Dad's hair.

"I wonder what the poor people are doing today," Dad joked, deflecting nerves, sidestepping expectations. He hadn't skied in more than a year. A planned warm-up trip to Tahoe earlier in the season had been canceled. He was a little shaky, his balance precarious, and he had to stop and catch his breath every so often in the middle of a run. But run by run he felt better, started finding his legs under him. He said he wished we had more time to acclimate, and I concurred, but the schedule was set and the next day we were off in the cat.

There were nine other skiers with us in Jupiter's snow jalopy: two Aussie couples traveling together, a couple from the island of Jersey in the English Channel, an orthopedic surgeon, a printer, a sport shop manager. Everybody but the sport shop guy was on fat skis: Völkl Rangers, RD Coyotes, Wolf Cold Smokes. I brought my K2 Big Kahunas. Jupiter handed Dad a pair of 180-cm, superwide Dynamics. All of them are descendants of the Atomic Powder Plus, the progenitor of the fat "revolution" beginning in the late 1980s when snowboards opened so many eyes to the advantages of a wide ride, especially in three-dimensional snow.

The one nonconformist, the shop manager, was a Steamboat local. He brought along slim telemark boards and leather boots, and he skied superbly, genuflecting into the belly of each turn before bounding up and scissoring through the weight change. He made it look easy, but there was a deep well of technique there underneath years of wild-snow experience.

Jupiter gave a lesson at the top of the first run, hopefully named Success. "Just go straight for a while up here where it's flat," he said. "Get a little speed and then bounce. Don't worry about turning. Pounce down into the snow and back up, heavy and light, heavy and light. Then after a while use the spring in your skis and the resilience of the snow to bounce up, get light, and turn the skis slightly. Okay? Here we go."

The snow before us was unmarked and soft but not the trademarked "champagne powder" Steamboat is proudest of. Wind during the most recent storm had pressed the snow into a consistency more like unsifted flour than that of goose feathers. Dad started into the slope tentatively, like a man wading into a swift river. The bouncing thing didn't seem to be happening for him, and as the pitch rolled over and got steeper – when turns became necessary – his weight shifted back onto his heels and he reverted to a stepping christie, one foot and then the other tracing twin tracks in the settled powder. The fat boys did their job, though. Even with all his weight on one foot, Dad remained afloat. He could steer (compared to skinny skis, the fatties are like power steering on a car) and thus control his speed.

He didn't fall, and down at the pickup he admitted a cautious optimism, borrowing from the Twelve Steppers: "Well, one turn at a time."

In the cat on the slow grind back to the top, Jupiter kept it light, a talent with which he is preternaturally gifted. It seemed his friend Warren Miller, of the annual ski films, had come to shoot some footage on a day very much like this one: still air, clear, with views half way to Utah. Miller filmed a run on Buffalo Mountain that we were about to ski, Jupiter recalled, but when the sequence showed on the big screen that fall, Miller's voice-over crooned: "Here I am on my favorite run in the world, China Bowl at Vail." Jupiter laughed at the memory. What was he to do but change the name of his run to "China Bowl"?

Dad didn't fall on China Bowl. In fact, he didn't fall until after lunch, on our sixth run, when "jelly legs" finally sabotaged his wide-track swooping. One crash led to another. He was really pooped and sat out the day's two last runs. As he clambered into the cab (Bonus! He got to ride in the cab with the cat driver.), I said, "Hey, Dad, you were floating!" But he wasn't buying it. "No. Not really," he replied, grim jawed. He was disappointed in his performance. He hadn't come through for all concerned. Perhaps tomorrow would be better.

The next day we were joined by *SKI*'s photographer. I felt guilty about subjecting Dad to the added pressure of picture taking. God knows he didn't need more pressure. Not that he was skiing badly. The individual turns were coming, but the flow down the fall line, that thing that takes the most faith, the most time to learn, eluded him. His face showed only determination. I found our roles completely reversed from my early skiing years. Now I was the father and he was the child. I wished him simple fun, but I couldn't will it to happen. I didn't know whether to talk or not, whether to hang with him or leave him alone, whether to explicate technique or just shut up, let it go, let him ski.

I did try giving him one tip that had worked for me when I struggled in powder as a ski school apprentice. It's related to Jupiter's bouncing idea but more cerebral and, I hoped, more holistic. I tried to get Dad to focus on the heavy and light phases in a turn.

When the skis are down deep in the snow, go with it, I said. Let your weight slump down onto both feet, as if you were landing a small jump, from one step up, into sand. Then, from the heavy bottom of the arc, there will be a natural (Newtonian) reaction toward lightness. Use that lightness, the rebound from bent skis, to redirect into a new turn. Don't squander the lightness, I said; it goes by quickly. Seize each one, and they become the links in the alpha-wave chain known as rhythm. It was a lot to process, but it was the best I could come up with.

Two or three times that afternoon in the expansive meadows above Soda Creek, Dad linked 'em. His crescent tracks remained long waves, but the rhythm was there: the belly of one turn (deeply shadowed blue) leading to the lightly sketched crown of the next. They were continuous S's – no straight lines. Gazing back, Dad still was not convinced, but he knew he was closer. He would tell me later that the "bliss was beginning to overtake the stress." He allowed himself a smile.

When the photographer was not shooting I cut loose myself once in a while. My pleasure marinated in the sheepish sense that the skiing was so sublimely easy on the Big Kahunas. Where on skinny skis I would have been drawing careful marks, figuratively biting a lip like a kid working to keep the crayon inside the lines, on these big, surfy platforms I was Picasso sketching fast and loose on a fresh sheet of white. I could skim and shade and etch the terrain in ways I couldn't have imagined before the new skis.

It was not effortless. Scores of judgments and adjustments, many of them unconscious, went into every one of my turns, reflexive now after decades of practice. I thought about the way Dad had taught me to drive a car when I was 15: so smooth and seamless and anticipatory that a drink on the dashboard would never spill, a sleeping passenger would not wake.

It took me years to appreciate how he managed to drive like that. And at last I realized how foolish it had been to think Dad could instantly – even with the help of a brilliant new tool – achieve a dreamlike breakthrough on skis. I had tried to manufacture an epiphany. And, worse, I had failed as an instructor.

On the last run of the day, the photographer asked me to jump a wind wave, land as close to him as I could and still manage to miss the trio of young spruce below him. My fat boys could do nothing for my form in the air. I grazed a wing on landing and straddled the third tree, which was a good foot taller than I. In snow-plastered repose at the crash site I pondered the fact that, like many people, I have occasional flying dreams.

When Dad and I had been home for a while – he in California, me in Colorado – and our respective memories had distilled, I wrote him to apologize for confusing his occasional dreams with my daily practice. He wrote back that he was sorry he hadn't taken the whole thing more lightly. He continued: "Given enough uninterrupted time on skis I still believe I could get to a level of bliss that surely is out there. Yes, I would love to try again next winter."

# Go Down Easy

My girls couldn't believe that I actually kissed another woman. My wife kept the thing in perspective. Mostly. It happened, after all, on the little screen, and I had been acting. The director made me do it.

The woman had a mane of red hair. We were standing in the snow at sunset after having skied together across the hills outside her Sierra cabin. We wore leather boots and free-heel skis and tailored woolens that would have looked right on Claudette Colbert and Gary Cooper. The year was supposed to be 1943 or thereabouts, and we were saying goodbye before I shipped out to war.

All of this emerged from the fertile imagination of Gary Burden, a Ridgway, Colorado, neighbor in the 1980s. Burden had a line of platinum record albums on his garage wall, albums for which he had done the cover design, albums by Jackson Browne, The Doors, Joni Mitchell, Crosby, Stills & Nash, and Neil Young's *Rust Never Sleeps*, which he also produced.

By 1985, Burden had become interested in directing music videos. MTV and VH1 were taking off, and the art form combined his love of music and facility with images. Burden and his buddy Dan Fogelberg decided to work together on a video for "Go Down Easy," a haunting ballad on Fogey's *High Country Snows* release. Fogelberg was and still is an enthusiastic skier. He keeps a house within powder-morning striking distance of Wolf Creek in southern Colorado, even shows up unannounced some nights, with his guitar, at the Mud Pub in Pagosa Springs. Burden had an idea for the "Go Down Easy" script that would link the lyrics with Fogey's ski-passion and the sport's romantic pre-war era.

The song, written by Jay Bolotin, starts out: "Linda lost a lover in the early part of autumn/And she moved out to the country hoping all would be forgotten..." and proceeds to show how, below the surface of Linda's peaceful mountain life – chopping firewood, making jewelry – memory inevitably intrudes on her attempts at intimacy. "...Her friends are sometimes lovers/ Though there'll always be another/She thinks about when nighttime lays on down."

Burden came up with a backstory to Linda's sadness and an ingenious way to connect Fogelberg to it.

We see a figure striding on cross-country skis toward the camera. It's Fogelberg in contemporary dress. A storm is brewing. But as wind-blown snow threatens to envelope him, he comes upon an abandoned cabin. He breaks in, builds a fire and discovers a packet of old, sepia-toned photographs and letters. By firelight, he scans the pictures, imagining the story they tell, and lip syncs the words: "The last time that I saw her/She was making sure the winter/Wouldn't come through that old door frame/Where the door is several inches from the ground,/The cold hard ground..."

Fogelberg conjures the young lovers and the cabin in its prime. (Location scouts had found a perfect site off Echo Summit near South Lake Tahoe.) The couple link telemark turns, figure eights, like hearts carved on a tree trunk, down a nearby hill. They fall into one another's arms, laughing.

Penelope Street, a pioneer freestyler, tele skier and Sun Valley native, played Linda. She also brought the costumes, authentic ski outfits – honey-colored wooden skis, wool pants, poles with baskets the size of LPs – from the days when Sun Valley was the first great, and oh-so-fashionable ski destination. Burden tapped me to play the young man, drafted into the service and not long afterward killed in action.

In the video, Fogelberg imagines Linda alone on the cabin porch having received the devastating news. The camera zooms in to reveal a tear coursing her cheek. Fogey sings the chorus: "And it's hard to go down easy/And it's hard to keep from crying/And it's hard to lose a lover in the early part of autumn." The scene required several takes, and every time Penny came though with real tears. I was moved. We were all moved. "It's easy," she said, pricking the movie-magic bubble and smearing her makeup. "I just think about someone mistreating an animal, and that makes me cry."

There's a party scene where Linda shies away from the revelry. ("She sits down to the table/With her friends and several others/And she tries real hard to never be alone.") And a scene in which she imagines her lover (me) in bed, and when she turns again to look, he's vanished.

My copy of the video was lost years ago. I loaned it to an editor who wanted to see it, and it somehow disappeared from his desk. So, my memory of the final, six-minute product is as hazy as the smoke in Fogey's fireside scenes. We never could get the damper to work right. Fogelberg about suffocated, but the gauzy effect looked great on film.

I do remember that for those couple of days Penny really became Linda, and a part of me was really sorry to have died. I also remember the cinematographer, L.A. Johnson, saying "Never better! Never better!" after each shot. And the time he ordered my nose hairs trimmed in a scene that was photographed through a screen door.

Friends reported for years afterward that they'd catch the video now and then on VH1. (It was way too tame for MTV.) The whole thing seems like a dream now. Like a brief, long-ago encounter, à la *The Bridges of Madison County*, one that memory doubts really happened. A cinematic illusion that nevertheless left indelible tracks.

# A Heartbeat Away

Cynics have suggested that candidate George H. W. Bush picked Indiana Senator Dan Quayle as his running mate to discourage any thought of assassinating the president. To those folks, I submit the following, told as gospel truth by a skier who was there.

So, the storyteller begins, the Vice President Quayles are in Vail at Christmastime for a little skiing and merrymaking. Every year the Vail ski patrol hosts a potluck at its mountaintop headquarters. A couple of patrolmen live up there in an adjoining apartment. They bake the turkey and ask their friends to bring side salads, desserts, etc. A few patrollers have been assigned to the Vice President's on-mountain security detail, along with the Secret Service, and they thought, or one of them thought, it would be polite to invite Mr. Quayle to the party.

Perhaps to their surprise, he shows up, having arranged a ride from the base on a snowmobile. He doesn't bring food, which is understandable. But he has brought, by way of gifts, some enameled, White House cuff links and tie tacks.

Dinner has already commenced, and the Vice President sees that everyone is serving up his or her holiday feast on paper plates. As this is not very vice-presidential, he slips into the kitchen and pulls a more suitable plate out of the dishwasher.

The evening progresses, Mr. Quayle takes his leave, and straddles the snowmobile behind his driver. The assembled mountain people, most of whom will ski down in starlight later, are left to contemplate the meaning of his visit.

One patrolman says to a second, "Well, it isn't every day the Vice President of the United States comes and eats your pot luck."

To which the second patroller answers, "No, and it isn't every day the Vice President of the United States comes and eats pot luck off your dog's dish."

# Today's 10th

Master Sgt. Billy Cole's team digs in for the night at 11,800 feet, just below the summit of Ptarmigan Hill. It is Day One of a five-day Tactical Procedures/Skills Exercise in central Colorado's Gore Range. Cole and his seven mountain troopers drop their 80-lb. "rucks," step out of their camouflage-white skis and commence digging shelters in the snow.

The men curse a sugary January snowpack. "This is soup!" they shout, employing an oft-used and versatile disparagement. Every shelter turns out different. Capt. Jeremie Oates, an Aspen native and former junior racer, fashions an underground shelf with a fragile snow roof, just enough room for him and his sleeping bag. Radioman J.T. Winborn covers his straightforward trench with a poncho. "Look at those guys!" Billy Cole calls out, pointing at photographer Tim Hancock and me fussing with our EMS tent. "They haven't even had class, and already they've got a sheltah!"

The accent is Bridgewater, Mass. The attitude is pure "Car Talk" guys – preternaturally delighted. Cole's eyes and nose crinkle up together when he smiles. He is the NCOIC, the non-commissioned officer in charge, the leader by example, the teacher. His shelter has an elaborate overhang constructed of interwoven fir branches, skis and poles. "Check it out!" he crows, his crew-cut fin of white-blond hair punching the air. "My don't-ask-don't-tell condo!"

After a dinner of beef stew (RATION, COLD WEATHER NO. 1-B), we stand around a bonfire as the temperature drops to 0° F. "If this was tactical," the 40-year-old Cole says, referring to a more realistic type of exercise that might involve night moves, bad guys, and blank ammunition, "we wouldn't have a fire." But… As it is, the mesmerizing flames and easy camaraderie add warmth to a sober game. These men are an elite fighting force, part of the Army 10th Special Forces Group (Airborne), proud inheritors of the mantle "ski troops," once worn by the World War II-era 10th Mountain Division.

Despite the informality, this is in fact combat training. Experience counts. Stories are important. Dodging smoke and sparks, Cole tells about an arctic training mission he participated in, with the Brits and the Norwegians, when under live fire they purposely drove their snowmobiles into holes chopped in the sea ice to practice cold water survival skills. And of the time last winter when his car was bombed in Serb-held Bosnia. Oates recalls that his great uncle George served in the 87th Infantry Regiment, which trained, along with the 85th and 86th (the three regiments together comprising the 10th Mountain Division) at Camp Hale, no more than a long day's ski from where we are camped this night.

The 10th, as every skier should know, brought together America's first generation of mountaineers – "college boys to cowboys," as they were collectively described at the time – to fight Hitler's formidable alpine troops. The instructor corps at Camp Hale during the winters of 1943 and 1944 reads like a skiing Who's Who: Sun Valley ski school director Friedl Pfeifer; Dartmouth coach and Swiss world champion Walter Prager; Stowe's Kerr Sparks; Alta's Sverre Engen; racing and jumping champions Robert Livermore, Toni Matt, and Torger Tokle; Teton guide Paul Petzoldt; Sierra backcountry pioneer David Brower; and ski filmmaker John Jay, to name just a few.

The ski sport was in its infancy then, so gear for the "ski army" came from unlikely places. American ski manufacturers could supply only some of the 20,000 seven-foot skis needed. So, prewar propeller factories and furniture makers supplied the rest. Poles came from the Orvis and Montague fly rod companies. Climbing skins were fashioned by handbag and girdle manufacturers. 10th teams tested everything from freeze-dried foods to new-fangled nylon climbing ropes. They helped develop the Weasel, a forerunner of the ski-area snow cat. They drove mules to haul their howitzers and experimented with shooting down avalanches, a deadly effective tactic used by Austrian and Italian mountain troops stalemated in the Dolomites during World War I.

In December 1944, the division shipped out for Italy, and by February 1945 they were pressing the German "Gothic Line" in the Apennines Mountains. A few advance patrols went out on skis, but it had been a warm winter; for the most part, the snow was gone. Nevertheless, the division's overall fitness and mountaineering skills showed, as 10th companies scaled an icy cliff on Riva Ridge, catching the defending Germans by surprise and opening the way north. The rout was on, though weeks of fierce fighting remained. By war's end, the 10th had suffered the heaviest casualties per combat day of any American division in the southern theater. Almost 1,000 men were killed, and nearly half of the 10,000-man force was wounded. But on May 2, the German army in Italy, with their backs to the Alps, surrendered. A month later victorious ski troops liberated an Axis warehouse full of skis and held a downhill race on the snowfields of Mount Mangart.

To a man, 10th veterans today talk of the unit as "a fraternity, a brotherhood." They sang bawdy songs and became fast friends. "We had a philosophy to helping each other," says Pfeifer in the 1996 documentary *Fire On The Mountain*. "That's the main thing in the mountains." When the brothers in arms came home, they revolutionized the ski world. Bob Parker, Pete Seibert and Bill "Sarge" Brown invented Vail. Pfeifer and Fritz Benedict resurrected ghost-town Aspen. Larry Jump started A-Basin. Bill Healy imagined Mount Bachelor. And so on. Parker says in the film that "our mountain training gave us two things, an unusual work ethic and, two, we knew we could do almost anything… in terms of physical effort and mental effort. Obstacles didn't seem particularly difficult to us."

By Seibert's reckoning, 2,000 men of the 10th went into some aspect of the ski business. In skiing's golden age – the post-war period through the 1960s – 10th alumni founded, managed or ran the ski schools of no fewer than 62 American resorts.

One almost never hears these men identified by rank. The 10th was an informal and egalitarian outfit. The same holds true for Billy Cole's Special Forces Group. When I first met him, Cole pulled me into his room with a warm handshake, then filled my palm with a cold beer. We were at the Sunlight Mountain Resort near Glenwood Springs, Colorado. It was early

January, and Cole and his team of ski instructors were conducting alpine ski training. By day, 136 soldiers in camouflage Gore-Tex stormed the chairlifts. The evenings were given over to drinking beer, playing pool, and staying in touch with battalion headquarters at Fort Carson.

Capt. Oates was in the room with Cole that afternoon, as was J.T. Winborn and Chief Warrant Officer Steve Hoffa, who at 40, is looking to retire soon. "There's a bar with my name on it in Telluride," he told me. Oates, 28, was the youngest man and the only officer present. I never got used to Cole and the other enlisted men addressing Oates as "sir." They did it out of habit and respect for the institution, though their military and life experience far outweighed the kid's. Up in the mountains, I never did see anyone salute.

The 10th Group is not your regular army. The average age is a mature 33. Most of the men have families. They've all volunteered at least three times to get here: once into the service, then again into Airborne ("We've been known to jump at night from 35,000 feet and drift 40 miles if there is heavy anti-aircraft fire at the LZ," Cole told me matter-of-factly), and a third time into the rigorous qualifying school for Special Forces, the Green Berets of Vietnam, John Wayne, and Sgt. Barry Sadler fame.

"I'm a teacher," Chief Hoffa told me on a chairlift ride, blue eyes scanning his own history, "not a Rambo. Not a Terminator. I've been to some hellholes I can't tell you about, but..." And he went silent. The crest the group wears features a Trojan horse, the classical symbol of stealth. As "quiet professionals" and masters of "unconventional warfare," these guys have been on some missions about which they are not at liberty to speak. At least not to a writer. "I will tell you," Hoffa said, "that if you wake up one day and hear that somebody whacked Saddam Hussein – it was us."

The secrecy goes back to the Special Force's origins in the OSS, the Office of Strategic Services, which sent non-uniformed soldiers behind enemy lines during WWII. As the Cold War heated up, the U.S. Army in 1952 created the 10th Special Forces Group to "conduct partisan warfare behind Red Army lines in the event of a Soviet invasion of Europe." Early volunteers included refugees from behind the Iron Curtain who brought valuable language and cultural skills. Today, Green Berets are expected to be conversant in at least one foreign language. In 10th Group, those languages are likely to be Russian, Polish, or Serbian.

With the winding down of the Cold War, 10th Group's assignments have evolved. Billy Cole's team spent time in northern Iraq after the Gulf War, feeding Kurds and enforcing the northern no-fly zone. "That kind of stuff makes you feel good," Cole says. The threat of fighting in the snowy north (read: Warsaw or Moscow) has abated. But there is still a commitment to skiing as one of many wild-terrain skills, and these guys take to the task with gusto.

Some of the skiers at Sunlight came in pretty raw. A young Texas recruit staggered away from Defiance, one of Sunlight's toughest double diamonds, coated from head to toe with powder. "I saw the sign at the top there that said 'Experts Only.' But our instructor, Sgt. Torrens, told us that was for civilians only."

Chided a teammate, "You look like a frozen pickle, man!"

Many of the instructors got their ski training in Germany where 1st Battalion is stationed. Cole skis in the self-described "Iron Cross position," with hands out to the side and feet glued together, skis clacking through wedeln-inspired turns. Capt. Oates, as one would expect of a racer, steps dynamically from edge to edge. He is arguably the finest skier in the bunch, but compared to the older guys, he lacks teaching experience. Early in the week, he led his class down Defiance, where one of his men fractured both bones in his lower leg.

This is not a common injury anymore on civilian slopes. But, in fact, there were two such breaks at Sunlight in five days. (Cole put off several ski dates with me in order to check in on his wounded at the hospital in Glenwood Springs.) One reason for the accidents, I'm convinced, was the soldiers' gear: not as primitive, certainly, as the war-surplus, white-painted gear that flooded the market and allowed so many Americans to start skiing in the 1950s, but seriously behind the times. The skis, from Karhu and Erik, were long, stiff and straight. The Lowa boots were low-cut lace-up models. And their Army-issue alpine-touring bindings were several generations behind what Silvretta currently has on the market. The only really up-to-date pieces of the kit were the purple climbing skins from Ascension Enterprises.

Capt. Paul "Doc" Crowl, a Jimmy Stewart lookalike who grew up skiing at Lake Arrowhead in Southern California, put me on the gear for an afternoon. I felt a direct connection to the past. You had to stand right on the bottoms of your feet; there was no support from the boots, no room for error. It was reminiscent, as Doc Crowl said, of "your first experience on skis when you were four."

It seemed so incongruous, that the finest army in the world would issue 25-year-old technology to its best and brightest. The rationale I heard from the guys was that one, the Army is not out to create stylish skiers but simply efficient ones; and two, the 10th Group follows the lead of the German mountain troops with whom they train. And the Germans are "just now" starting to look at newer skis and bindings. Whatever the reasons – and some of the men told me unofficially that the labyrinthine military bureaucracy and its current, down-sized mindset are chiefly to blame – no one complained about the gear, and everyone made up in enthusiasm what they lacked in high-tech turn shapes.

It snowed every day we were at Sunlight, making for soft landings, and there were a lot of them. The neophytes crashed and hooted their way down the bumps. Or banked big, unsteady arcs on the groomed, much like the Camp Hale trainees pictured in *Fire On The Mountain*, one balance glitch from frozen pickledom. The good skiers, including Oates and Cole, flexed forward on their skis, looking like Friedl in '44, finessing turns with considerable skill and not a lot of ankle support.

Following the Thursday final skills test – uphill stem; downhill stem; open parallel/medium-radius turns; closed parallel/rhythmic turns; aggressive skiing in mixed difficult terrain – it was time to party. Beer flowed freely downstairs at the Sunlight Mountain Inn, as did a wicked, clear firewater in a duct-taped plastic bottle brought over from Bosnia. Billy Cole presented a new American flag to Pierre and Gretchen DuBois, the Inn's owners, saying, "I noticed you have an American flag up theyah. And it's soup! I think you need to bring it down, send up a new one."

Awards were handed out, and farewells said. The army was reassigning Jeremie Oates to NATO headquarters in Brussels. Belly Cole expected to be sent again to Bosnia on a de-mining mission. Big men with close-cropped heads and muscles bulging under their shirts hugged each other and occasionally wiped away tears.

I huddled for a while with battalion commander Col. Tom Rendall, telling him I thought some of today's fatter skis could really help his men, especially with packs on in the backcountry. He said he'd look into it. Around 2:30 a.m. a call went up for the singing of "The Ballad of the Green Berets," Barry Sadler's Vietnam-era hymn to "fighting men who jump and die… Silver wings upon their chests/These are men, America's best…" None other than the colonel himself stood and belted it out. Billy Cole, sloshed as we all were, put a burly arm around my shoulder and said, "Just write that we're a bunch of nahmal guys, working hahd, doing our best."

Somewhere between Ptarmigan Hill and Sugarloaf Peak, on the way to the next RON (Remain Overnight) site, photographer Hancock and I decide to leave C Company and head back to civilization. We've been traversing single file across the face of a massive, windblown ridge, well above timberline. Five miles and 3,000 feet down to the west is the abandoned site at Camp Hale. A few remnant foundations and a small monument there attest to the heroics of the 10th Mountain Division. Beyond Camp Hale is the alpine jumble of the Swatch Range. At the north end sits Vail, which was an isolated sheep ranch in the 1940s. To the south is Aspen, where men of the 10th went on weekends to unwind for a dollar a night at the Hotel Jerome and to which they returned after the war, as Fritz Benedict said, "with a sense of purpose born of survival."

Billy Cole's team is wearing their nylon "overwhites," M4 automatic rifles either slung across chests or strapped to already heavy packs. But for the modern weaponry, they could be right out of one of those black-and-white photographs from 1944. The pace is deliberate, the snow alternately wind-pressed and rotten: soup. Tip over in this stuff and you either need a hand getting up, or you need to be incredibly strong and stubborn. I see instances of both.

"What a beautiful day, huh?" sings out Master Sgt. Billy Cole. "I'd enjoy it even more if my ruck weighed about 20 pounds less." He'd enjoy it no matter what. When you've nearly been blown up in service to your country, cold-weather training in Colorado is a lark.

We say goodbye, wish one another well. I'm thinking about Bosnia. Or maybe it'll be Kosovo or Iraq next. Cole is thinking about the Vermont bed-and-breakfast he and his wife hope to run when he finally retires.

It feels as if I'm sending family into harm's way. Immensely competent family, yes, but as 10th Mountain veteran Earl Clark says in the movie, "War is still war, and men must die." As I ski away, I'm aware of the 10th Group coin in my pocket. Cole gave it to me at the Sunlight party. It has solid, silver-dollar heft. Every ski trooper carries one.

On one side is the Trojan horse. On the other I read the time-honored mountaineers' greeting, "Berg Heil," and the words "The Best."

# David Light

David Fishback was a runner. Tall and whippet thin, he ran track in high school in Northern California. He may have run middle-distance events in college, too, I don't remember for sure. But that's the kind of energy he had. Either he was lying in the sun browning his sinewy limbs and his balding, James Taylor-esque pate, or he was racing ahead on some project, big strides powered by an extra-fast motor, elbows pumping, torso angled forward as if leaning into a wind.

Other carpenters I'd worked with said things like, "Close enough for government work," or, "You'll never see it from my house." Rationalizing imperfect work drove David up the wall. He was a super perfectionist, all the more so because three of the four houses we built together in the late 1970s were his designs as well.

He wasn't a trained architect. He was a self-made, self-proclaimed, Renaissance man: artist, carpenter, musician, poet, fly fisherman, mogul skier, environmentalist, seer. An early proponent of solar, he built Telluride's first "envelope house," wherein warm air collected by the greenhouse circulated up over and then back under the living space to the greenhouse again, creating a self-driving warming cycle. All of his buildings had greenhouses, including his own place up Alder Creek, which also featured a giant crib of river rock in the crawl space for thermal mass. I cut the spruce beams for two of David's greenhouses, under his watchful eye. "Measure twice, cut once," he'd repeat sagely.

At home, David played guitar and wrote songs. He was thinking about cutting a record. To the job site, he'd bring tapes of new music he'd discovered, late-period Fleetwood Mac ("Tusk"), early-period Police ("Every Breath You Take," "Canary In a Coal Mine"). Every morning, he'd arrive at the job site with fresh sketches, new ideas, a new way to solve some building problem. We wondered if he ever slept. He was a good boss, albeit restless and intense. We were fairly paid, generously even. He saw his crews as friends and his friends as co-conspirators in this urgent business of life.

Along about the third or fourth house, he married a beautiful girl with straight blond hair down to her waist. But it didn't last. And things began to go downhill. We failed to notice at first.

Then one winter he showed me a poem he'd written called "Recipe." In it he detailed the precise mix of drugs he preferred to craft a successful day. Begin with a line of coke first thing in the morning. Add mushrooms and weed on the ski hill. Cans of Coors Light stashed in the snow. More coke. And, finally, a tiny Halcyon tablet for getting to sleep at night. Repeat. Benefitting from all this alchemy, or so he thought, David drew sweet mogul lines on Lift Six, lines whose steep troughs bounced him left and right in an alpha-wave dream. No thought, just perfect reaction.

We all smoked pot fairly regularly in those days, and a brewski after work was de rigueur. But as habits changed for some, either because of new responsibilities or evolving body chemistries, for David the search for chemical balance got more and more desperate.

One night after Ellen and I had moved with our two girls down mountain to Ridgway, David came pounding at our front door. It was four o'clock in the morning. "I need your sledgehammer," he demanded, wild-eyed. He'd left one of his cars in Ridgway, but it was locked, he didn't have the keys, and there was a Halcyon tablet in the glove compartment he was pretty sure. He had to have it, had to break in and get it. He desperately needed to sleep. Otherwise, he pleaded, he was going to die. "You've gotta help me, Peter. I'm dying!"

I was frightened for him and talked him into going with me to the emergency room at Montrose Hospital where they held him over in the psych ward for a couple of days. The diagnosis came back, either from Montrose or from Pueblo, where David was committed for a time to the state mental hospital. Bipolar, they said, manic-depressive. Which made sense.

David knew it, of course. Knew something was wrong. But he didn't want to believe it, refused to believe it. He wrote hallucinatory, paranoid letters during his stay in Pueblo, Cuckoo's Nest stuff about doctors trying to poison him. He foiled them by clamping the pills under his tongue and pretending to swallow. They wanted to steal his power, take over his mind. And he wasn't going to let them.

I guess for some manic-depressives the highs are so high that life on lithium feels like depression, like walking underwater. Rather than provide a kind of even-keeled stability, which is what it's supposed to give you, it feels nearly as oppressive as the depths of a natural cycle. This, I assume, is the way David saw it. He steadfastly refused lithium. I think he believed, or convinced himself, that the manic, creative times represented his natural state, and he just had to learn to control the gift, to use it in such a way that the dark side never got a toehold. But, of course, things didn't work out that way.

He'd call us from the Santa Cruz Mountains, where he'd gone after his welcome in Telluride had worn thin, with amazing stories of how he'd finally figured it all out. He'd designed the "master template" for solving all of the world's problems. He'd changed his name to David Light. And now he was heading out across the desert to see a certain Native American mystic who was helping him, and vice versa, along the journey.

Or he'd call from France. The most fabulous string of coincidences! Women at Charles de Gaulle Airport see his power aura and take him home for days of cosmic sex then introduce him to gallery owners in Paris where he will show his new-process photography which is already selling for big bucks to corporate clients in the States but right now he is in Chamonix where he just hiked up this 5,000-foot couloir with his magic Head Outback skis and it avalanched on him on the way back down but he rode it out…!

And then we wouldn't hear anything – maybe a terse postcard – for three, four, five, six months, while the depression sucked him down. During these periods a brother helped get him jobs building decks in the redwood canyons east of Santa Cruz. But over time the jobs were harder to come by and harder to complete. It wasn't a physical problem; he kept himself in shape. He admitted to sometimes being a step away from living on the street.

The next call might come from Mount Shasta or from Ashland, Oregon.

He'd "revolutionized" ski teaching and was now coaching the ski school there on how to ski moguls. He had these one-ounce skate skis. He could skate up 3,000-4,000 vertical feet in an hour. He'd skied 80 million vertical feet in the backcountry. The numbers spiraled upward the deeper the madness became.

He was back into music again and eating raw walnuts. Raw walnuts allowed him to sleep for 36 hours straight. He was working on a "global level" now, on the internet, and making a movie. He was becoming a wine connoisseur and developing technology for video conferencing. He was designing CD covers that were "more unusual and psychedelic than anything that has ever been seen." He was going to play guitar with Sting tomorrow night.

We could only nod over the phone and hope that a small percentage of these wonderments were true. Or, failing that, that their imagining made him genuinely, if temporarily, happy.

Finally, down in Taos, David couldn't outrun the dark side any more and took his own life. Typical of David, he was fastidious about it. He wrote a letter to the sheriff explaining what he was going to do and when. He included his brother's phone number in Santa Cruz. He even left some money to cover the phone call. Then he ran a hose from the exhaust pipe of his Toyota pickup into the camper on the back and crawled in and lay down to sleep.

I think of David every time I ski a nice mogul line, every time I put a saw blade to a piece of lumber, every time I hear "Canary In a Coal Mine." Every time I drive by a house we built across the river. And I wonder about the bloody luck of the universe.

# Otto Pilot

OTTO FREI STOOD LEANING ON HIS POLES at the top of the Trockener Steg tram in Zermatt, a small gold triangle gleaming from his left earlobe, and what remains of his white hair swept back behind his ears as if by a fast ski descent.

He was smaller and balder than my wife, Ellen, remembered. But then it had been 27 years since she and her college roommate had ski-bummed at the Freihof Lodge in Turin, New York. Twenty-seven years since those winter weekends when they washed dishes ("we had to polish those glasses"), and cleaned guest rooms ("Otto was so frugal, we cleaned the bathrooms with cold water"), and ate "real skiers' breakfasts" (oatmeal, hard cheese on toast) in the kitchen with Ann before any of the guests were up. Twenty-seven years since Otto provided lift tickets and taught them to ski at nearby Snow Ridge. Otto is 65 now; Ellen is 48. Snow Ridge was a long time ago.

She was more than a little nervous. We had wanted for years to come along on one of the Freihof Ski Tours to the Alps, to reconnect with Ellen's old guru, and now we were finally doing it. Ellen fretted that I might not like Otto, worried that time might have worked some unknown sorcery on her memories, worried most of all that after so many years she might not measure up. She still felt that need to please that our first mentors inspire.

Otto emigrated in 1955, from Zug in central Switzerland, to Snow Ridge, a natural snow magnet in depressed pulpwood country north of Utica. He married Ann, whose family ran a Swiss bakery in Scarsdale, and ran the ski school with his boyhood friend, Rudy Kuersteiner. Together Otto and Ann turned a neat, white frame house in Turin into a North Country ski lodge.

Despite its small (500-foot) vertical, Snow Ridge produced some serious ski racing talent: Renie Cox, who placed ninth in slalom at the 1960 Squaw Valley Olympics; and Ken Phelps, who made the U.S. downhill team in 1966. Most years, snow poured down from lake-effect clouds over Lake Ontario, and ski-weekers filled the Freihof's 14 beds. Ellen remembered the excitement in the pit of her stomach when she arrived the first time, by bus, the snowbanks over her head.

Turin never quite took off as a ski destination, but Otto kept working in the ski business. He's been an examiner with the Professional Ski Instructors of America for 31 years and a fixture in Alps tours since the 1960s, leading strings of mostly American disciples down the pistes at Neustift, Engelberg, and Zermatt, among others.

For her part, Ellen went on to full PSIA certification and a 10-year teaching career out West. She became a glorious skier, technically precise, fluid, and subtle. Ann and Otto's kids grew up. Otto had a hip replaced. Our own kids sprouted into teenagers. We, the kids and I, had not met Otto, but through Ellen we knew a few of his very Swiss aphorisms. Things like: "There is no such thing as bad snow, only bad skiers." And, "You have to work hard to have a good time." The latter said with a wink while pouring pflümli from hand-painted bottles out of the cabinet.

Now, decades later, first run up on Trockener Steg, Ellen held her ski poles out for Otto to see. They are gold Scotts with metal ring baskets, the only poles I've ever seen her use. Otto had given them to her over a quarter century before. "Oh my god!" Otto flinched. "Get some new poles! At least get some new baskets, okay." Otto says "okay" at the end of almost every sentence.

The group took off with Otto in the lead. His rock-solid stance sent Ellen immediately back to clinics at Snow Ridge. "He used to have us pulling up practically out of our boots," she remembered, "launching out over our feet to get forward." She remembered his arms, elbows held wide like falcon wings partially folded in a dive. "We all tried to look like him." She remembered that when Otto said, "Follow me," it meant, in his strict paternalism, follow right on his tails, not two turns back or slightly off to the side, but right there gobbling his shadow. She remembered that, "with

Otto you didn't get a lot of compliments. He'd say, 'Ya, ya. Try it again, okay.'" What he admired in people were toughness and hard work. And the standards he set were very high.

After a brief stop, Otto looked at Ellen and said, "Come with me." He dropped into a tuck. She did the same, and they quickly outdistanced the group. Down they sped on a groomed piste that followed for miles the glacial folds at the foot of the Matterhorn. Otto banked high on his edge, wings spread, outside ski biting cleanly, throwing spray. Ellen stayed with him. Otto juked short, then long, set up for a big roll and absorbed the weightless transition. Ellen ghosted inches behind. At the bottom, they waited for the rest of us to catch up.

"You're skiing good," Otto told her.

Ellen smiled a slow, deep smile. Otto had never said that to her before. It meant a lot. No, it was the most important moment of the whole trip.

"You're skiing good."

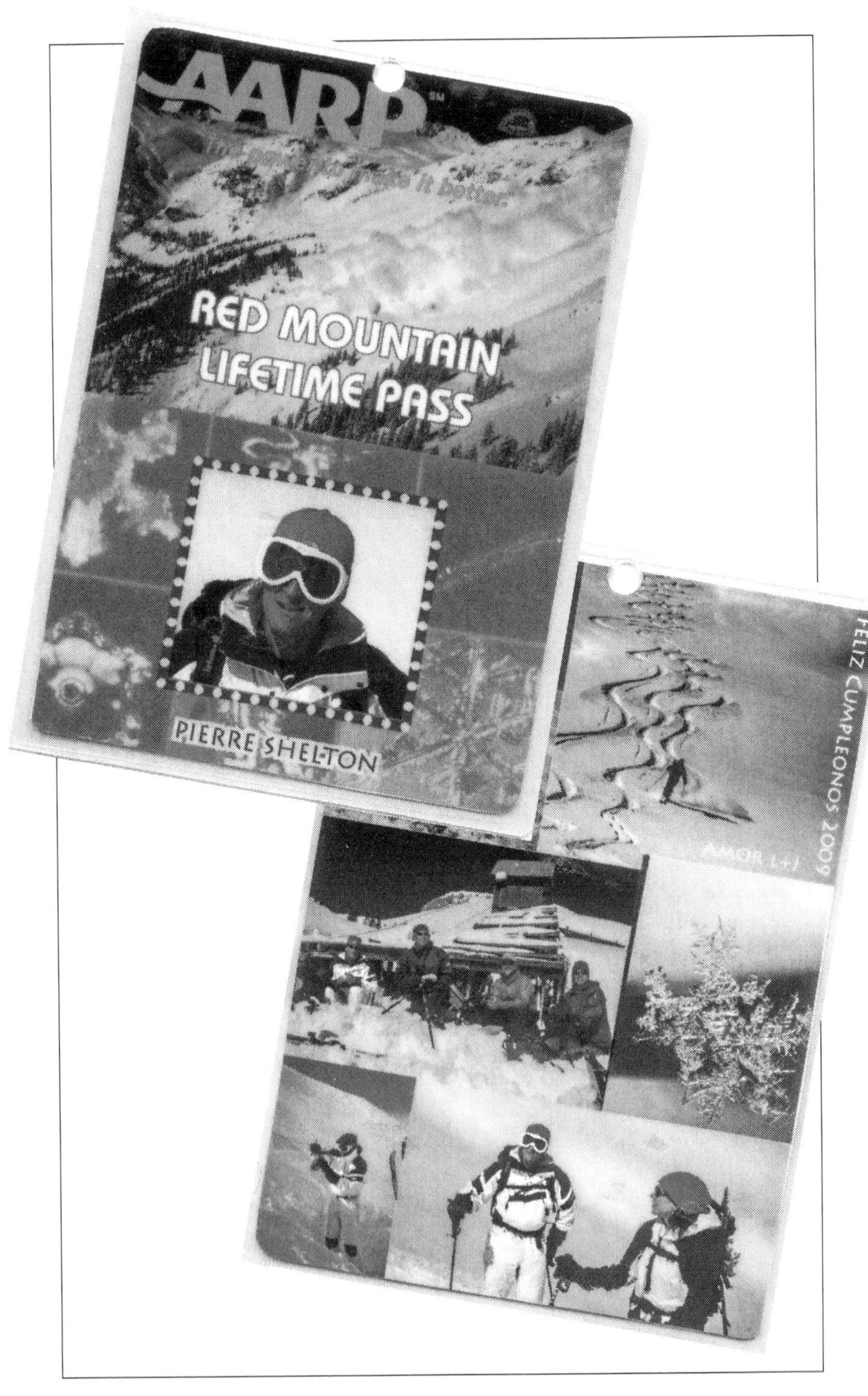
AARP
RED MOUNTAIN
LIFETIME PASS
PIERRE SHELTON
FELIZ CUMPLEONOS 2009

# PART IV

# ’Til We’re Buried

# High Route to Telluride

ELEVATION: 9,700 FEET. OPHIR, COLORADO. Population now: about 20 romantic mountain folk. Population in the early 1900s: something like 1,000 silver-crazed miners. The valley's steep, glaciated walls are dotted with abandoned mines. The clustered buildings of the town site – the ones that have avoided obliteration by avalanche – retain a weathered Victorian dignity.

It is June 15. Six a.m. The sun is about to ease up over the flank of North Lookout Peak, due east. We are headed right for it, four of us jammed into the pickup's front seat, skis in the back, grinding up the dirt road. Past the ruins of an old Nash Rambler, past the one-room Ophir schoolhouse, past the squat, log jail – a veteran of 80 winters and untold avalanches – and out onto the run-out zone.

With no flat ground anywhere in the valley, Ophir was built on the edge of the second biggest avalanche path in the state. Everyone looks left. Even Linde, who sits on Lito's lap and must twist awkwardly to see, looks north up the Spring Gulch slide. It has the classic hourglass shape: a gently sloping, fan-shaped deposition zone at the bottom leading up to a narrow-waisted track through the cliffs and on up to glistening ridgeline bowls at 13,000 feet, a half mile across and bristling with start zones. Smaller slides stop harmlessly well short of town. Big ones travel a mile or more and have been known to move houses. Many of the original buildings were constructed on runners, big timbers under their floor joists so that, sled-like, they might move with an avalanche rather than be crushed by it. Some houses have indeed been moved. Others have been flattened.

9,840 feet. Ophir cemetery on our left, at the up-valley edge of the fan. A slide earlier in the winter ground its thick-rivered way in among the gravestones. The remnant snow is hard as a rock: an eerie garden of white marble, frozen statues, sharp-cut ledges and walls, like an ancient devastated city, still radiating the immense energy that formed it.

Big slides are rare this time of year. The snowpack has stabilized, melted and refrozen many times over warm days and cold nights. We have come early to walk up on the frozen surface, then ski down the other side, on softening corn snow, into East Bear Creek Canyon all the way to Telluride, Ophir's sister city in the halcyon mining days, now reinventing itself as a resort town.

10,480 feet. Snowdrifts like pillows block the road. It is farther than we had expected to get and gives us a good start for the climb.

Preparations. Rocks under the wheels. David standing off to the side stretching, wheeling from side to side. Lito and Linde prepare their packs, strapping skis on, abandoning vests, restuffing them against the possibility of cold winds on top or a change in the weather, though the day begins without a cloud.

"I have wax."

"Good."

"Water?"

"Yup."

"Skis, boots, poles?"

"Skis, boots, poles."

In the predawn chill we set out, chanting our three-word checklist mantra.

10,600 feet. A half dozen trees are down across the road, blocking the way. We head uphill into the woods. The ground here is snow-free and soft underfoot. Ducking branches, we find ourselves nose to nose with the first green shoots of summer.

"My god, it's a giant asparagus tip!"

"Skunk cabbage."

"Corn lily."

"False hellebore."

It is too early and too cold to smell the earth, though we can imagine its sweetness.

10,700 feet. All of the trees in this aspen stand are down, or leaning, as if felled buy a tremendous wind. Walking on tree-trunk bridges, we finally make the open edge and behold the wind maker – another avalanche. The valley is a book of them. This one started near the ridgeline 2,000 feet above us, scoured a small bowl to bedrock and swept all the way across the river and up the opposite slope. The associated shock wave knocked down trees thirty yards into the woods on either side.

We move up the debris, walking on snow long since stopped, frozen into chunks like giant-curd cottage cheese, each chunk another stair step.

11,200 feet. Up over a treeline hump and into the upper basins. Suddenly the view is all white. There are no more trees, no colors – only shapes and their cool blue shadows. What in late summer, after the melt, we know to be precariously balanced scree fields are now sleek white waves and bowls, crystalline dunes that crunch beneath our boots.

11,400 feet. Left foot, right foot. It takes concentration to walk efficiently. The mind must be uncluttered to focus on the business at hand, to whit:

1) Staying upright. Walking on inclined snow with skis, lunch, water, shovel, emergency kit, cameras and extra clothes on your back requires a certain devotion to making each step the same, or at least to finishing each step in balance. Call it a balance dance.

2) Finding a pace. Lito is a firm believer in the snail approach to high-altitude walking. ("Watch me snail over this pass.") In which the pace is slow enough to allow complete recovery from one footfall to the next. On Denali in 1970, Lito was always the last to camp by at least 45 minutes. But, he is quick to add, he was the only member of the team not to develop some sort of high-altitude edema, the only cure for which is immediate retreat.

David, on the other hand, likes to sprint and wait – a metabolic preference, perhaps, or a psychological one. Linde and I are somewhere in between. We require a pace above snailing in order to concentrate, yet chug along deliberately enough to allow for long stretches without stopping. Finding my pace often means going too fast at first, then slowing down.

3) Keeping cool – and warm – enough. This is closely related to pace and the layers you wear. Staying cool keeps you dry, which makes it easier to stay warm when you stop. Getting cold in the mountains is scarier than avalanches. Becoming very cold, or hypothermic, makes you insensitive and dumb; you don't care much what happens. Perhaps it's not a terrible way to go – a little like nitrogen narcosis underwater. Picture the diver waltzing with the shark, ecstatic in his newfound freedom from breathing. Advanced hypothermia cases don't feel the cold. They just want to curl up in the snow and go to sleep.

But we're all walkers here, and focused. Because taking care is like taking your time. It makes things clear, and where we cannot afford to stumble, we don't. It gets us through.

12,000 feet. The bowl is huge. It looks vertical near the top. Our different paces have spread us out, each to his own breathing, heartbeat and careful placement of feet. We move, David thinks, watching us from his lead above, as if on another planet – adventurers with heavy magnetic feet.

13,000 feet. A small rock outcrop. David is sunning, marmot-like, as I arrive. Across the view to the south, west and east stretch endless snow-covered peaks. Some we know, some we guess at. Others are just whitecaps on the horizon.

Linde arrives, midriff exposed to help the heat escape. Lito snails up, occasionally knocking snow from his soles with a ski pole.

We will go the last pitch together. It is the steepest yet.

"How steep?"

David, with his carpenter's eye, guesses 42 degrees.

Lito says it's more like 30.

It feels like walking on a wall.

13,100 feet. The ridge, and suddenly another hemisphere opens to the north. Bridal Veil Basin drops away like a porcelain saucer. A receiving line of peaks marches north.

It is an easy walk to our left along the ridge to this unnamed summit.

13,432 feet. The top. We are at the intersection of two ridge systems. One runs east west and divides the Ophir valley from Telluride's upper basins. The other runs north south and divides Bridal Veil from East Bear Creek. From this spot, you could roll off into any of three drainages.

Instead, we sit and stare and eat. Ah, food, so often a perfunctory part of the day, assumes new meaning on a ski tour. The climb has emptied us, and the food – cheese and nuts, dried fruit, and David's beer – serves to anchor our lightheadedness while it refuels our bodies. Passing bags from hand to hand, the taking of food becomes a ritual, an integral part of this complicated 3D puzzle we are creating.

Waxing is another ritual. We rub on a coarse, soft yellow in strokes across the ski to break the suction of the wet snow. This also gives us a chance to feel our skis, to bend them like longbows and imagine their turns. Ah, the imagining. A few seconds of reverie behind closed eyes, in which the spirits are called upon to create great skiing. It's all there: the feel of the curves, the breathing of the body, extending and contracting, the lightness and weight, the resistance and the letting go.

Bindings click.

The first turn is a coming home.

13,100 feet. Stopped midway down the first steep pitch, I am surrounded by sliding snow. No, not an avalanche. There is a thin sun crust still unmelted on this northwest exposure, and it shatters where we ski, sliding along with us, tinkling madly like thousands of runaway chimes.

12,700 feet. A honey-coated marmot whistles and dives for his hole as we wing out onto the broad flat below the steep.

12,600 feet. We've come to the top of a whaleback knoll. In the distance we can see where our route will follow the creek course, twisting between narrow walls and out of sight. But the round nose of this knoll prevents us from seeing what is immediately below. The exposure is good. We know it will be steep, maybe very steep. We decide to ski it just as the sun takes a momentary powder behind one of the few afternoon puffball clouds. We wait.

David is dreaming of what he calls alpha-wave turns – identical short-radius arcs that transport him into a kind of peaceful brain-wave bliss. I am dreaming of what a fellow ski schooler has called alternate gravities, forces created by my own momentum, which will allow me to lean and bank, like a bobsled, against gully walls.

Who knows what Lito and Linde are thinking. They will entwine their tracks in figure eights of affection.

The sun comes. We go.

12,500 feet. I breathe in long, whooshing breaths, as if by matching sounds with the skis on the snow, I can ensure their continued response.

12,200 feet. We pull up as if spellbound, the only sound our collective breathing. The snow was perfect, a virginal sorbet. And by some trick of the day we were all set free at once on that knoll – freed from trying to ski, freed from thinking even, so that what came out was something akin to extemporaneous music, the score for which we leave behind as tracks.

11,200 feet. The harsh purity of the snowfields is now pierced by an occasional spruce. Ruby-crowned kinglets dart about the branches chatting purposefully. Here, too, is the splintered ruin of the Nellie Mine, the first sign of man's work since the diggings on the Ophir side. We're coming down.

10,800 feet. The Couloir, a 30-foot wide slot through the cliffs – the only way through. Vertical black walls block the sun and keep the snow icy, refrigerated. Bear Creek Falls roars offstage left, just out of sight. We ski one at a time, carefully. This is not the place to soar. Between my ski tips, I can see the Big Rock at the end of the dirt road up from Telluride – the end, most likely, of our skiable snow.

10,600 feet. Out of the couloir, relieved. Overhead, violet-green swallows ride updrafts along the cliff. Trickles of water and bits of ice from crevices above leap out into the sunlight, where they are briefly lit, like temporary diamonds, only to fall back into the shade and disappear at the base of the cliff.

On this last pitch above the Big Rock, we hip-hop old avalanche debris, lumpy by nature and further pocked with the melt holes of small rocks. Loosened by the day's thaw, they clatter from the cliffs above and light on the snow surface, where over time their warmth melts the snow around them, and they sink into cups of their own making. Dark pearls, pearls in reverse (they shrink in relation to their growing shells), they feed the melt process, hasten the day when they will be lowered gently to the talus below, one of a billion rock cousins, indistinguishable, pearls no more.

9,800 feet. Skiing right on the creek now. Its rush is only a vibration through the thick layer of avalanche-deposited snow. Spruce branches lie about on the surface. Bent willows point down-slide. It is the last tongue of winter, melting fast, pulling back up-canyon.

I pass several windows of creek noise where the snow has pulled away from the sides of big boulders. Water roars for a moment, then stops as I go by. The sense is like that of a child's game – hands-over-the-ears, opening and closing – at play with the sounds of the world.

9,600 feet. Open water. A water ouzel (American dipper) bobs on a rock midstream. Blink of white eyelids and he's off, wings beating furiously, inches above the water.

Walking is easy down the old wagon track. We are like rag dolls, hips loose and rolling; knees flip feet forward, plop, onto soft red dirt.

9,400 feet. First firs. A new spice in the evergreen perfume.

9,300 feet. Line of aspen change. Above: winter's bare finger branches. Below: a shimmering canvas of new green. Currants leaf. Rose hips bud. Birds gossip everywhere.

Dogs. Saws. Hammer's ring. The sounds of town are clear and busy – and welcome. Natural town sounds, they would be as foreign where we've been today as the snowy stillness would be among the streets and houses. The contrast is exquisite.

This is what we go for, I suppose. To trade our comfort for a little pain, our complacency for a little fear. To walk up in the shadows, ski down in brilliant sun. Hard snow turns to soft, winter into summer. Ophir to Telluride.

# The Accidental Bivouac

It was early winter, 1978 or 1979, when Davey O'Brien, late of Olympic Sports, proposed an overnight ski tour to Dunton Hot Springs.

Davey was one of Olympic's gear gurus back when the iconic Telluride shop occupied the Main Street corner next to the Floradora Saloon, back before the United States Olympic Committee, citing copyright infringement, made them change their name.

Davey had a heart condition. His grandfather and father had both died young. We were about the same age, 30 give or take. He didn't talk about it much, but he felt even then that he was living on borrowed time. He loved to ski. He loved the latest ski gear, and snow camping, and going light and pushing himself on new adventures.

So, he got a posse together, four of us, and told us about a fast-and-light tour he'd worked out on the map: from Woods Lake up over the shoulder of Wilson Peak and down the West Dolores River to Dunton, which in those days was closer to its ghost-town past than to the "rustic luxury" resort it has since become. It did have hot springs, and a bar, and it sounded like the perfect end point for a tour that would be mostly downhill.

I didn't know Davey well, but I liked him. I was new to Telluride and relatively new to backcountry skiing. I'd never been to Dunton. Jerry Greene, the town baker and an accomplished three-pinner, was on board. And our fourth was the new doctor in town, whose name escapes me now, perhaps because he didn't stick around long.

He was young and fit, and he had all the best skis and boots and parkas and stuff, and he wanted to come, so Davey said sure. We would go light:

bring sandwiches and snacks, no cooking gear, no tents to carry. The map showed an abandoned cabin on the Woods Lake side of the divide where we'd spend the night. There'd be a roof over our heads. And sure enough, after an afternoon of climbing we found it, right about treeline, grayed logs sagging back to the earth, and the whole thing missing enough teeth to allow the interior to fill with snow. That was OK. We tamped out flat spots for our pads and sleeping bags (Davey was the only one with a weatherproof bivvy sack in which to slip his bag) and spent a quiet, if cold, night watching the earth spin – stars appearing then vanishing as they crossed the inky slits between roof boards.

Before dark, we'd made a fire out in the snow and stood around its crackling warmth. Someone, maybe it was Davey, had brought a few cans of soda, Coke or Dr. Pepper. They tasted really good after our hike, until the doctor told us that all caffeine drinks were diuretics, that they ultimately cost you more fluid than you were taking in, and were therefore contributors to dehydration, which was, we knew, a contributing factor in hypothermia.

It turns out new research says this is not quite true – the diuretic part – unless you were to drink seven or eight cups of coffee, say. It was one of a few crucial things the good doctor got wrong.

Next morning we snailed up the treeless col between the Wilson massif, with its three sky-piercing fourteeners on our left, and the slightly less lofty Dolores Peaks on the right. At the top we stopped to scrape the climbing wax from our ski bases and cork in additional glide wax, ready for the long downhill run to Dunton.

The pitch ahead was south-facing, but it was early in the year, the sun was low in the sky, and there had been fresh snow recently, so the powder wasn't bad, a little crusty maybe, but skiable, even with our big packs and skinny touring skis.

Skiable for three members of the group, that is. It turned out the good doctor couldn't buy a turn. His uphill technique hadn't raised alarms; he'd gotten by on youth and strength. But on the descent his inexperience proved catastrophic. Every attempt at a telemark turn resulted in a head-over tumble. Then the exhausting recovery: everything snow-coated, limbs akimbo, skis buried, his pack like a sulking orangutan on his back.

We tried traversing him back and forth across the slope, but that wasn't much help; turns were required at either end. Attempts to teach him the standing kick turn – in deep snow, on the steep – failed. The day dragged. Without our noticing, the wind picked up and the sky went milky with cloud cover. By the time we reached the creek, buried along with its headwaters beaver ponds, it was already late afternoon. At least we judged it to be late afternoon. The sun had disappeared, and there were no shadows. The light had gone completely flat. Snow and sky, up and down, near and far were the same blank slate.

Still, Davey thought we had enough light to make it to Dunton.

It started to snow. Imperceptible ice needles at first, but then in bigger clumps falling through the gray-white air.

The way was downhill but just barely. We took turns breaking trail. Davey pushed the route most of the time. It was his "easy" overnight, his map, his idea. It wasn't his fault that the rookie hadn't told anyone that he couldn't turn his skis, or that time had slipped away from us on the steep descent from the ridge, time spent picking the doc up and dusting him off, talking him down – time we needed, as it turned out, to get down the river course while we could see.

Pretty soon it was dark. We got out the headlamps and kept slogging. I worried, when it was my turn to break trail, about falling through into the creek. The river meandered, mostly hidden, through its high valley. There were impenetrable willow thickets and occasional glimpses into black water – water windows in a concealing snow blanket.

Hearing the water, listening for it beyond the weak beams of our headlamps, became ultra important. I couldn't help thinking of Jack London and the short story "To Build a Fire." That poor schmuck had fallen through into a creek in Alaska when the temperature was 60 below. He knew that if he didn't build a fire in a matter of minutes, his legs would freeze solid, and he would die right there.

It wasn't nearly that cold for us that night with the snow curtain all around. It was cold, but not that cold. More than once we stopped to discuss our options. Davey was sure Dunton was just around the next bend. But it wasn't, even though we'd been plowing ahead for hours. The night was sapping our batteries, alkaline and otherwise. Our small pools of light dimmed to almost nothing. We could keep going, effectively blind, or we could stop and bivouac until daylight. We hadn't prepared for this. We were supposed to be drinking beer at the Dunton saloon. We had little food and no water. Was it riskier to plunge ahead, running on empty, but relatively warm with the effort? Or was it smarter to stop moving and hunker down until morning?

We felt ourselves getting stupid with fatigue. We decided to stop. We found a stand of young firs and dug in under their lower branches. The snow underfoot was too floury to build any kind of shelter, so we just burrowed down like inept bears and laid our bags out shoulder-to-shoulder, and crawled in fully dressed, boots and all.

Left to right, there was Davey snug in his yellow bivvy sack, snoring as soon as the nylon stopped rustling. Then there was the doctor in his purple mummy, suffering – if he suffered – in silence. On the other side of me Jerry started to shiver, an early sign of hypothermia.

Soon all of our bags had grown thick coats of white. Had anyone been there to notice, we would have disappeared completely, vanished into the storm.

I could hear Jerry's teeth chattering. The doctor's diuretics lecture from the day before clanged around in my head, but I had no water to give him. I did have some chocolate. And three or four times in the night I unzipped just enough to reach a square over toward Jerry's breathing hole. He took it gratefully, and the shaking stopped almost immediately, smoothed by sugar and fat on the tongue. The calm would last an hour or so, and then the quaking would commence again.

I felt a strange contentment, an unwarranted sort of peace. I didn't trust it. Snow avalanched off my bag every time I moved, but I felt somehow insulated from worry, even though I had a wife and baby daughter, and I thought about them often, back home in Telluride.

My nose was the only thing sticking out of the bag's hood, and it was numb with snow. I didn't think I slept, but at one point I opened my eyes and saw that the darkness had acquired a new, lighter shade.

I remember almost nothing of Dunton later that day. The car we had left, or the ride we had arranged, was there, obviously – we all made it home. Memory might have been affected by the flood of relief as we finally trudged in. Or maybe it was blunted by chagrin at our lack of preparedness, the weight, ultimately, of luck, the nightmare of what might have been.

I do think we shed our clothes and slipped into one of the hot pools. I have a vague recollection of being disappointed that the water wasn't hotter. And I do remember quite clearly the day I heard that Davey O'Brien had died. As he had predicted, his jinxed heart gave out a few years later. The news sent a chill down my bones.

# A Wedding of Opposites

CONSIDER THE POWER of a place you see almost every day year after year but have never been to. Such is the lure of the La Sal Mountains, a lonely island range in eastern Utah that stands as the visible edge of the universe for residents of western Colorado.

When I taught skiing at Telluride, the La Sals beckoned. It was fun to amaze ski classes with the fact that those white humps, like bird rocks well out to sea, were 100 miles away in the midst of the mysterious vastness known as canyon country. Sun-baked Moab is on the far side: outpost on the Santa Fe Trail, gateway to Arches and Canyonlands national parks, brief center of the boom-and-bust uranium mining industry, and mecca to Colorado River rafters and assorted desert rats. But it was the snow that got me. The highest peaks in the La Sals are 12,600 feet and more, with 2,000 to 3,000 feet above timberline. And no ski areas. No touring centers. No skiers at all, except for a maverick river outfitter who was rumored to make an occasional helicopter raid into the range. I chose to discount him. I preferred to think of the snow shining on the horizon as virgin, unexplored, at the edge of everyone's world, central to no one's.

Then last spring, with three friends who shared this long-distance fantasy of the La Sals, I decided to go to them, to climb Mt. Peale, the highest peak at 12,721 feet, and, if possible, ski from its summit. There were record snow depths in our own Colorado mountains that May. The home skiing continued to be great. But this would be a different kind of spring fare, a trip out to the shimmering mirage. A chance to give definition to long-time imaginings.

The drive west on Colorado routes 145 and 90 kept plunging downhill – through the San Miguel River Canyon, across the gently tilted grasslands of Wright's Mesa, past the decaying vanadium-mine ghost town of Vancorum, and on down into the hollow of the Paradox Valley. We were leaving the Rockies. The La Sals are not related to the mother chain. They are a laccolithic range, formed when rising lava bulged the rocks upward, lava that never found the surface. A half-dozen such incongruities pushed up out of the Colorado Plateau to become snowcapped islands above the red-rock desert. The La Sals are the highest, the queen laccolith.

We decided to approach from the east, even though Moab on the west side might afford more civilized access. Our decision was emotional rather than rational. We wanted to follow the line of sight along which we had so often daydreamed. It would have been more sensible to go into Moab first, learn what the locals do, maybe even track down Greg Williams and his helicopter. Might even offer us a ride to the top of Peale. But where would that leave us? Retracing other people's memories. No, we would preserve as much of the adventure as we could.

The jeep road gave way to uncrossable snowdrifts at 8,500 feet. Bobo parked at about noon in the sage near a stand of still-leafless aspen. Paul and I pulled the packs and skis down off the roof and began sorting gear. Jerry took the celebratory six-pack and buried it under a pyramid of snow. It was not yet hot – maybe 50 degrees – but the promise was there. In another month, the desert, even this high, relatively moist mountain shoulder above the desert, would be cooking. Now the walking was pleasant. Nights were still cold enough to freeze a good crust onto the snow. And the real melt-off was still waiting in the wings. We congratulated ourselves on our exquisite timing.

Soon it was time for skis and skins. The trail stiffened into a brisk climb through stands of big, white-barked aspens. Beautifully carved signatures, and some anatomically correct figure studies, adorned the trunks: *M. Sandia; J.M. Lovato; Coyote; Alieto Sandoval July 20/43*. Shepherds heading up to summer pasture. Far from hack graffiti, these delicate etchings (drawn with a sharp knife point?) were signatures, and yearnings, saying, "I was here."

The ghostly presence of the herders didn't detract from the wildness.

Instead, it gave it a new depth. In these mountains, the white blanket is like a kiss of sleep. No sheep or man had been here since last summer. Back in Colorado it is different. Recreation is, if anything, more feverish in winter. Snow is the product, skiing is the social norm. Here, we were rare birds in bright blue and red synthetic plumage, allowed (thanks to our skis) privileged entrance – easy, graceful travel. We were walking into a seldom-seen realm, beyond even the shepherd's ken. We were really alone.

Another mile up to a spring at 9,700 feet and we were nearing our objective, a little alpine valley between the rocky slopes of Mt. Peale and the sharp white crest of Mt. Tukuhnicivatz, Paiute for "Where the Sun Lingers." (I never did learn much about Mr. Peale, except that he was a surveyor, probably with the ubiquitous Hayden party in the late nineteenth century.) Then it was up to 10,100 feet, where we found a perfect campsite on a knoll above La Sal Creek, invisible under a solid four feet of snow. We were within sight of its source, a high arching basin near the ridgeline, and within easy striking distance of the peak.

We had time on our hands, so Bobo, the ex-Outward Bound taskmaster, suggested we build an igloo. Soulful shelter, man. Wilderness skills. Dig it.

I used a shovel to cut blocks out of the large-grained, well-bonded spring snowpack – "quarrying," Bobo called it – while Jerry and Paul worked the inside of the circle. "Tilt 'em in more. Rad lean! Rad lean! Otherwise it'll go up like a pyramid and you'll never be able to reach the top."

The blocks went up in a spiral, each one leaning radically in on its neighbor. Loose snow packed into the joints soon hardened into a surprisingly firm mortar. We dug a trench under the southern wall for the entrance. Like a beaver entering his lodge, you crawled up into the room from below. Cold air flows down and out. Body-warmed air stays trapped inside the translucent dome. Ingenious.

It was not pretty – too pointy, not enough "rad lean" – and only vaguely related to textbook Eskimo igloos. But it was home. The stove hissed outside. Cups of instant soup. Essence of chicken and noodles with lots of MSG. Fried bagels from Jerry's Telluride bakery, with butter and melted cheese, and Paul's homemade salsa. Plenty of hot brews steaming from mugs cupped in both hands.

The last pinks and plums of late light faded from the snowfields high on

Mt. Tuke. Long silences rolled out between sentences. Jerry, who is a fairly nervous person at home, what with the business (Baked In Telluride), the radio station (KOTO FM, low-power public radio, which he helped start), his job with the ski school, and various political embroilments (we worry about him sometimes) said, and I was inclined for the moment to agree, "There is no stress in the wilderness."

But there was stress the next day. Bobo's alarm did not wake us up at the appointed five o'clock hour and, worse, cloud cover had prevented the snow from freezing solid. All of a sudden there was some question about our making the summit and skiing where and when we wanted to.

We left camp in a vague gloom. Up through the last of the aspens and into a narrow band of stunted, timberline spruce. I wanted to keep skiing, to take advantage of the skins' gripping power and the skis' ability to spread our weight over the thin crust. But Bobo wanted to climb a rocky buttress *directissimo* to the summit. We were all experienced skiers and route finders. Too many cooks. I bit my tongue. Besides, Bobo already had his skis off and was moving onto the rock. Directissimo.

If it proved to be the fastest way, fine. We found ourselves in a fairly common and always uncomfortable situation: in a hurry on a mountain. The two don't mix well. On one hand, we faced the increasing danger of wet-snow avalanches as the day heated up. On the other hand, we had to fight the urge to rush; each of us had to maintain the discipline of one sure step at a time.

It didn't help matters that I was trying to take pictures. "Uh, hold it, guys. Just a sec. I want to get a shot looking down here. If you could just wait until I get ahead a little ways." And so on.

The going was slow on the clattering rock – safe but slow – and the morning wore on. The clouds burned off. The sun got hot, then a fierce wind arrived, and we were forced to stop and redress. The mountains that Bobo had referred to on the drive as a "mini range" were proving to be formidable.

Finally, after chopping steps in the last 300 feet of hard snow, we made the ridge and had our first sweeping view to the west. I was dumbfounded. Basically, I knew what to expect, and still I was dumbfounded. Moab's little irrigated splash of green valley was a clear but dizzying postage stamp 8,000 feet below us. There was the notch where the Colorado River came out of its canyon to intersect the valley momentarily before diving again between sheer rock walls. It was easy to see why 16th-century Spaniards forded the river here; everything else as far as the eye could see was an ocean of pinnacles, fins, labyrinths, spires, mesas, buttes, scarps, and gorges carved from varying shades of 150-million-year-old pink sandstone. With a little imagination we could pick out Delicate Arch in the Windows section of Arches National Park and Newspaper Rock to the south, where Indians of three different civilizations, beginning with the Anasazi, carved their messages in the rock. We could see the great wind-and-water-sculpted triangle between the Colorado and Green River canyons known as Island in the Sky. There was the Needles district of Canyonlands National Park, the Maze, and way out to the southwest in Arizona the bald crown of Navajo Mountain (another laccolith) hovering above Lake Powell. We had come to the edge of our world only to find a bigger, more mysterious one beyond.

We still had to get to the summit and look back whence we came. That was the goal, after all. We leaned against the wind for the final few hundred feet of cornice snow to the top where considerate souls who came before (in summer, no doubt) had piled stones into a sheltering wall. Once we sat down, all obsession fell away. There to the east was Colorado: Paradox, the San Juans, the West Elks, Grand Mesa. We found where Telluride would be, hidden in its box canyon. There Ridgway, where Paul, d/b/a Ascension Enterprises, makes climbing skins in his garage factory. Grand Junction about there. All appropriately Lilliputian, as the La Sals had always been before.

Jerry brought out his trusty portable radio and worked the antennae to find his beloved KOTO. Paul carved lunch out of hunks of cheese and bagels. Bobo read to us from the register, a battered mailbox in the rocks with "General Delivery, Mt. Peale, Utah" scratched on its face.

"Hey, listen to this: 'Melinda, sorry about last night at the dance. Richie, Moab.' Here's another one: 'After my daughter died I didn't know where to go.' Whoa. And another: 'Dos ojos. Gotcha. Coyote.'"

So many reasons to climb a mountain. At the moment ours seemed abstract and secondary to getting off it. Fast. One last sweep of the eye to take in all the highness we could, to revel for one more moment in that special singularity that comes with being the highest bump on the highest log around, reaching into the sky. The high feeling brought on a secondary wave of affection – for the mountain and for each other – one that would color our sightings of the La Sals long into the future. But the time for lingering had passed. We clicked into our three-pins and edged off.

Very carefully, for the summit ridge was narrow and frosted with ripples of hard sastrugi. Tricky skiing. A fall off either side would be disastrous. So we didn't fall. A card on the wall at what would soon become my favorite diner in Moab read: "Common sense is Instinct and enough of it is Genius!"

We found our gully, the headwaters of La Sal Creek. It was clean and smooth and dove like an ivory spout straight toward the igloo. The snow had become plenty saturated, but a few test turns convinced us we would be okay, as long as we kept moving.

The real skiing came as a great release – of stress, of expectations, and fantasies. Jerry was wrong, there is stress in the wilderness. But there is no stress in a perfect telemark turn. Bobo has such a stable, relaxed stance he looked like he was turning in his sleep. Swish, swish. He could have been the butler stepping lightly through the overripe corn. Jerry hung on the west-facing side of the trough. The pitch was steeper there and the snow a bit harder. Swish, swish, swish. Telemark shortswing with a knee-drop and a hop. Paul, the aging surfer, the gracefully aging surfer, used both sides of the snow dish to carve his high-speed cut-backs, sweeping up the sides until ebbing momentum forced him to stride, lean, and swoop back the other way, scooping up a bit of snow with his inside hand along the way as if he were patting the mountain. Good mountain.

In this way we made peace with ourselves. We felt graceful, free.

Back at the igloo, after a second lunch, we decided to break camp and head for Moab and the red sandstone world below. The day had reaffirmed our status as mountain people. Now it was time to flow down into the new place, to see about the desert with its blooming cottonwood and prickly pear, to relax and soak it all in. To ask the questions that were only now forming, now that we had come the long way over the snow.

# On Suspect Slopes

*Deep as the snow is,*
*Let me go as far as I can*
*Till I stumble and fall,*
*Viewing the white landscape.*
—Matsuo Basho (1644-94)

9 A.M. WOODSMOKE, SWEET CEDAR, swirls in the blue Ouray dawn. The whole town is in mid-winter shadow, steep rooflines and sleepy smoke beneath tall rock walls.

We knock and step into the warmth. David is almost ready. He spoons another mouthful of cereal, gulps coffee, searches for socks and a water bottle. There is an urgency to his movements, as there is to our waiting. New snow lies like a thick feather quilt on the ground, clings like lace to every twig of the aspen trees out the window. I feel a familiar hollow in my gut, even though I have just finished my own breakfast. It moves from my center out to fingers and toes and back again – anticipation like an electrical current in the blood. Silently, I am helping David streamline his movements, pushing his memory ("Lunch? Skins? Beacon?"), speeding his fingers as they lace high-top telemark boots.

10 a.m. On the road to Red Mountain Pass. There is no need to hurry. No one else is here to jump our powder lines. We will not likely see another soul all day. And yet there is this tug, this powder snow magnet, like a gravitational force, the attraction felt by our bodies to blankets of new crystal water.

Up to the highway crest at 11,018 feet. Past the old Idorado Mine works. Beneath the gun barrel of the East Riverside slide. (In avalanche country, they all have names.) Everyone onboard knows the story. How, on a snowy Sunday in March 1963, the Reverend Hudson and his daughters Amelia and Pauline were on their way to his pastorate in Silverton when the East Riverside exploded in white. A 20-ton snowplow working nearby was hurled backward; only a second plow kept it from sliding into the canyon. When the dust settled, there was a 30-foot wall of snow where the road had been. Seven days later they found the reverend's body 300 feet down the canyon. Six days after that, search crews located the twisted remains of the car and one daughter. The body of the second daughter finally melted out in May, 88 days later. We turn our transceivers on, still miles from the pass, just in case.

Rounding the last switchbacks, we rub holes in frosted-over windows and see that the ridgelines are only lightly scalloped. Not much wind ushered the storm through on its way east. This is good. The eagerness in my gut grows a little more specific as memory and imagination conspire to produce a vision of slow turns in flyaway snow.

But first, preparations. Stoic, bear-like Basho, an Akita named for the haiku poet, leaps off our backpacks and out of the pickup bed. He is no avalanche dog. He was bred to guard, not search. Once, in fact, when Basho was a youngster, Jerry risked his own neck to extricate him from a slide of the puppy's making. But he is a comfort somehow to have along, a loyal ski-day friend.

Skis and poles clatter to the ground. Skins are ripped open and their sticky sides smoothed onto ski bases. Clothing adjusted for the climb. Avalanche beacons double-checked. When we are ready, Tyler stands off to the side, switched to receive, and listens for the heartbeat ping, as one by one we ski past him, free heels clicking, pole baskets punching deep blue holes beside the track, thin air coming in long, strong draughts, striding out and up, past the weathered, golden boards of the Longfellow Mine, under the marmot cliffs, and around the shoulder of Quartzite Mountain.

12 noon. The saddle. Together at an unnamed dip in the ridge at 12,300 feet, 500 vertical above the last stunted trees. A rising breeze hustles spindrift, like grains of sand from great white dunes, across our path. Straight ahead is the northeast-facing bowl of Colorado Gulch and an

inviting rib, a flawless marble torso, stretched out from the shoulder where we stand to the toe of the basin below.

Side lit, the snow on the rib looks good – no, gorgeous – facets sparkling, Sirens calling. Jerry whips out his shovel and his saw as a matter of course and starts digging, plumes of snow flying over his shoulders, until he reaches ground. He smooths the pit wall with the shovel blade so it reads like a chart – a white-on-white layer cake – mute record of the season's accumulated storm cycles. Then he pokes the various layers with ungloved fists and fingers, testing density, feeling for weakness, like an internist probing a delicate pain. With the saw he isolates columns of snow then knocks them over, one by one, to gauge compression and shear strength. We peer at the grains he hands us. (In the air, snowflakes are crystals, buried in a snowpack, they are grains.) We spread them on the backs of our gloves, stare at them with magnifying lenses. Some, sifted from the newest layer, retain much of their delicate, six-armed magic. Mid-pack grains have lost their sharp points; some of them have bonded with neighbor grains in a delicate latticework. Near the ground the oldest grains are the biggest, the least cohesive, the most sugary. They have been altered by an incompletely understood process called temperature-gradient metamorphism. The biggest avalanches, the ones that run full depth, full track, can usually be blamed on these loose, faceted grains, this so-called "depth hoar."

But at last, for our little group, the weight of evidence and intuition – and the persuasive Siren song – say, Go. And we do, buttoned down, zipped up, anticipation thumping inside nylon cocoons. Jerry and Basho ease in first, still probing. Two test turns, jumping on the snow, trying to make it run. Then, tentatively, into the rhythm, skis slicing sine-wave oscillations, Basho forging a shoulder-high, straight-ahead ditch.

One at a time we go, watching each other like hawks, calling out encouragement and warning. I miss hearing the caution about the hollow pocket where the hill rolls over steeply midway. My skis break through to the rocks and I tumble forward in a blind white soup. But it is a lucky roll, ass directly over teakettle, and I am back on my feet without missing a beat, snow like smoke flying off my hands and head and out of my astonished mouth.

12:30 p.m. The mine. Jerry rummages in his pack for Basho's kibble.

Everybody faces south, into a feeble sun, sitting on skis or else on timbers protruding from the jumble of wood and tin that was once a silver mill. Sandwiches come out of waxed paper. Tubs of last night's rice. Bags of goodies from Linda's Bakery in Ridgway. Water bottles are partly frozen, but thermoses of honey-sweet tea steam from hand to hand.

What is this sweet glow, this inordinate satisfaction we feel as we sip and stare uphill, back up at the four (five, with the dog) sets of tracks? Each is a signature: Jerry's careful, machine waves; David's longer, deep-bellied telemark arcs; Tyler's brilliant, risky scribbling, now hovering, now punctuated with monstrous, laughing craters. Each ribbon is a history. There the stutter in an arc courtesy of stiffened wind ripples. There at the hip – the steepest section – where spray from one turn, rushing downslope, beat you to the platform for the next. There the subtle gully where the softest, deepest snow washed over your shoulder and you had to consciously raise the pole basket up and over the surface then down again into foam almost up to your fist.

The lunchtime reverie is short out of necessity. Despite the sun, we grow cold sitting still. It's time to move, skins retrieved from anorak pockets and reapplied to ski bases, time to climb up and out of the basin, to the west this time, to a different saddle on the route home.

1:30 p.m. The Powerline. Those old hardrock miners were a driven lot. One hundred and fifty-three of them died in snowslides in Ouray and San Juan counties between 1877 and 1985. Hundreds more were caught or buried and survived. (Not all avalanche stories are fatal. CDOT plow drivers tell about the man driving down at night to Ouray beneath the big icicles hanging off the Mother Cline. A chunk fell on his pickup and mashed the cab, preventing him from opening either door, or opening a window. He continued to town, and when he got there the poor guy sat in the middle of the road, honking his horn. And that's where the fire department had to come extricate him.)

Love of gold overcame the miners' loathing for snow, and now here is a remnant of their imperious practicality: a 40 foot-wide swath in the forest running straight as an arrow for 1,200 vertical feet, where power poles once marched across the terrain. Big trees, red-barked Engelmann spruce, some of them hundreds of years old, line the sides of the cut, casting shadows even on flat-light days, and guaranteeing – as far as such promises go on the Pass – shelter from the wind.

Tyler yelps like a coyote and bounds in first, nearly disappearing in his cloud. We see him best (the back of his head, a hand raised to the side) when he pops off hidden stumps – a human pinball bouncing off marshmallow bumpers.

My favorite line is down the skier's left side where saplings have moved out into the cut like children from under the skirts of their mothers. Their fuzzy tops make perfect slalom poles and force me into a reactive, surprise-filled line. When it's going well, I'm not making turns at all, I'm just aiming my whippy, floating feet through a controlled fall, touching down as necessary to absorb speed and redirect momentum. The mountain does the rest.

2:30 p.m. The Pass. Almost: there is one more pitch, with fewer than a dozen turns, right above where the car is parked, a pitch that has never, as far as I know, been named. It's just "the last pitch above the car."

Because of the cold, the snow here is just as silky as it was this morning, maybe a little settled under its own weight, but fine and quiet underfoot – just the soft hissing of crystals refilling the troughs behind us.

We stand for a minute at the road edge gazing back at tracks like intertwined DNA. Basho stumbles in. He's been up to his neck all day. His line is a tired canter straight through our fine etchings. He wants in the truck. His day in the white landscape is done.

# Promise Me This

Dear Son:

As near as I can imagine it, this is the way it happened. Five friends decided to leave the ski area boundary in search of powder snow. They walked in silent camaraderie for the better part of an hour, out away from the last chairlift and up the mountain's spine. There was fresh snow. After a three-week lull, a storm had blown through only two days before. The ridges on either side of their objective, the Little Rose chute, had been ripped almost bare of new snow. But in the center of the gully, where it narrowed and swept in one exquisite curving line to Prospect Basin below, the wind had deposited two to three feet of fine powder.

They knew that the ridge crests would offer the safest descents. The first skier took a ridge line in wind-scoured snow, but he drifted to his left, ever closer to the gully, where the texture underfoot was softer and deeper, where the skiing was more like floating in cream. The next skier in, the only one who wasn't wearing a rescue beacon, decided to jump right into the gully. I imagine his turns were cushioned by the soft snow, his mind tuned to a rhythmic, crystalline clarity.

Part way down the slide fractured behind him. The floor began to move, slowly at first in thick slabs like ice floes breaking up in the spring melt. Then it picked up speed, and he lost his footing. His friends shouted to him to swim, swim hard to stay on top of the rushing snow.

In a matter or seconds he had vanished down the spout. The tongue of the avalanche came to a stop a thousand vertical feet down and about 2,500 linear feet away in the basin. One friend took off to get help. The other three started looking, probing frantically with their ski poles, their own transmitter-receivers useless, guided only by flotsam: the tip of a ski here, a goggle on the surface there.

Twenty minutes later they found him buried about eighteen inches down. He wasn't breathing. They tried breathing for him even as the helicopter arrived and flew him to town. But he could not be revived. Twenty years old. Gone. Snuffed out.

Here is what I want you to promise me, Son. That you will stack the deck in your favor.

Promise me you will carry the gear, a transceiver, shovel, and probe poles, that you will learn how to use it, and that you won't go out with someone who doesn't have it.

Promise me that you will study what there is to learn. Learn about weather and snow crystals, about metamorphism and recrystallization, equitemperature strengthening and temperature-gradient weakening, about pillows and slabs and start zones and depth hoar, about bed surfaces and anchors, crusts and percolation. Learn how to dig a snow pit and how to interpret the layers, the snow history, revealed there. Learn about tidal effects and any other crazy theory that may just pull the snow down from under you.

Learn about your mountains. Learn the angles of the sun and the wind, what aspects the wind blows clean and where that snow comes to rest. Watch for patterns in storm and calm and the changing seasons within winter. Learn to read the scribblings of the weather on the land so that you will recognize their meaning in other mountains.

Promise me you'll go to school. Ski with some old-timers. Learn route finding and group protocol. Attend the avalanche seminar in Silverton or Jackson Hole, where, if nothing else, you'll rub shoulders with people who have lived a long time in the mountains. They may seem overly cautious to you, and they may answer too many questions, "We don't know." But go, and remember what they say.

Promise me you will not depend (not even secretly in the back of your mind) on the ski patrol to pull you out of trouble. Yes, they will try, if they can, if they believe they are not endangering other lives. But as Bill Sands, for five years the Telluride patrol director, said, "It takes so long [for us] to get out there and such a short time to die."

Also, it isn't their responsibility. Beyond the area boundaries, you are on your own. They have no more responsibility for you (in current patrol director Bill Mahoney's analogy) than if you got in your car and wrecked it half way down Keystone Hill.

Finally, promise me something you may not be able to promise. Promise to make mature decisions. Not to give up your beautiful, youthful exuberance, but to take your time at the top of a slope and weigh everything you know and feel. Especially feel. Admit what you don't know. As the American Avalanche Institute's Rod Newcomb likes to say, "All the avalanche experts are dead." Trust your intuition. There is so much we cannot know for sure.

Remember this: I'd like to ski with you when we are both old men. And this: We treasure skiing because of what it shows us of life.

Love, Dad

*[I wrote this letter to a 20-year-old son I do not have. It was published on January 21, 1987, in the* San Miguel Journal, *after the first of four avalanche fatalities in the Telluride area that winter.]*

# Buddhist Road Patrol

*Come, let's go*
*Snowviewing*
*'Til we're buried.*
—Matsuo-Basho (1644-94)

AVALANCHE FORECASTER JERRY ROBERTS AND I are riding in his orange Colorado Department of Transportation pickup. We're on our way to check storm boards for recent snow totals. It's the middle of the night. The road to Red Mountain Pass is white. Our tires leave tracks several inches deep. Snowflakes in the air stop, eerily, strobe-like, in each sweep of the yellow flashing light on the roof. We're driving directly underneath the Brooklyns, a series of slide paths that regularly hit the highway. Roberts chants an impromptu haiku: "Travelling under Brooklyns paths/fear/is my companion."

Some hours earlier, Roberts had phoned. "I've been looking at the confuser. We've got a hundred-mile-an-hour jet stream over us. The dynamics look good. I don't want to overforecast, but we could see a foot and a half, two feet. Come on over. We could be rockin' and rollin'."

I grabbed my gear and headed south on Highway 550, up the Uncompahgre River canyon and over Red to Silverton on the other side. The last time Roberts had called to invite me to ride with him, they'd closed the pass before I could get across. I didn't want to miss this one.

Silverton, elevation 9,308 feet, is one of four forecast centers, run jointly by CDOT and the Colorado Avalanche Information Center, and charged with managing the state's slide-prone highways. Between 1963 and 1992, six people, including three plow drivers, were swept to their deaths on Red Mountain Pass. Since the forecasting program was initiated in 1992-93, no one has died in a snow slide on the highway. When Roberts, or his cohorts, deem conditions dicey enough, they close the road and try to shoot down avalanches before they grow into monsters.

"Three Mary Fourteen, this is Three Mary Fifty-one. Come in Doug." Safely past the Brooklyns, Roberts calls a snowplow driver working the north side of the pass.

"Yeah, Jerry, this is Three Mary Fourteen. I'm over in Ironton Park on my way up. It's snowing pretty hard. Visibility is pretty poor. See you on the pass."

"I've got a lot of respect for the plow drivers," Roberts says, working the defroster to keep the wipers from icing up completely. "Man, that's a lonely, hateful job. Ninety percent boredom and 10 percent terror."

We can see no more than about 70 feet ahead, and the flakes in the headlights have that onrushing Star Wars effect. Jerry estimates the snowfall rate at "S-plus," or somewhere around two inches an hour. It turns out that the rate the snow comes down is an important factor in predicting instability, along with new snow amounts and densities. Wind speed and direction. Temperatures. Weaknesses in the old snow. The pieces of the puzzle come together haltingly, like scraps of a note tossed to you on the wind.

We speed up again underneath Silver Ledge, even though there's a cliff on our right and no guardrail. "Andy [lead forecaster Andy Gleason] and I have a list of 50-60 paths that we worry about. You know what's hanging above you. Which ones could push you off the road and into the canyon." Roberts is 53 and has been skiing the San Juans and driving this road for 30 years. "The living highway," he calls it, with a thin smile.

"This is where we lose NPR. At the Muleshoe turn [another slidepath]. From here to the top all I can get is this religious station. Then on the north side I can usually pick up an oldies station out of Grand Junction." From the driver's seat out of the dark comes another verse. Palliative. Better than a sermon. "Jesus talk radio./Late night/forecast ride."

Five-fifty a.m. Still pitch dark. At the top, at 11,018 feet, we can't make out the road edges for the drifted snow. "Wind slab layers/thick as…"

"…Van Gogh/brush strokes," I contribute to the form. Roberts grins and pulls over, puts his flashlight between his teeth, flips up his parka hood and sets out for the snow stake in the meadow. While he is gone Doug Follman comes by in the plow, all hissing hydraulics and flashing lights. I climb up the door and we chat for a few minutes over the diesel rumble, the heat from his cab billowing out the window. Turns out his uncle lived in the little fruit-growing town where I live now. Passed away just recently. I notice he's wearing his avalanche transceiver over his flannel shirt, something Roberts says the drivers resisted until few years ago.

Roberts comes back with his waterproof notebook and density tube. "Five inches new at point six inches of water. Add that to the point four we had at midnight, and we've got about an inch of water. I was thinking we'd need an inch and a half to reach critical." Then, "What with the wind and the new snow, I think we oughta pop Blue Point."

To close or not to close the road. There's a natural tension between CDOT, the plow drivers, and the forecasters. It's CDOT's responsibility to keep the road open as much as possible; US 550 is a major north-south corridor. The plow drivers want to keep it open. They need the work, but they also don't want to die. The snow geeks like to shoot as often as they can, which requires closing the road temporarily, in order to keep the risk down into the future.

"That's a 12-year-old boy's wet dream," says Roberts, behind the wheel again. "Playing with high explosives and stopping traffic. Standing around telling people what they can't do."

Seven fifty-three a.m. It's just light enough to see the Blue Point, which isn't very imposing as San Juans slidepaths go. It's only a couple of hundred feet high. But it drops unimpeded to the road from multiple start zones, and the pitch well exceeds snow's natural angle of repose. The plow drivers have a saying about the Blue Point: "A cloud rolls overhead, the Blue Point runs." It ran three times in one night during the last storm.

Roberts and Andy Gleason confer with the avalauncher crew, newly arrived with their compressed-air gun and rocket-like, two-pound rounds. They put six shots into Blue Point and Blue Willow. Three small avalanches pour snow to the centerline. "Kind of disappointing we didn't get a tiger by the tail," Roberts says, his pickup sideways across the road. "That's the

Buddhist road patrol for you. It's kind of like I imagine Vietnam was: no sleep, firefights, an enemy who doesn't always cooperate."

Bud, the Cat driver who uses his huge blade to push the debris off the road and over the edge, shouts as we go by: "It'll keep the plank rats happy!" Indeed. Roberts has one more haiku, for the skiers, who will follow the plows to the top: "Aaaah, the turn. /I can smell it/in the air."

# Buried Alive

At Portillo, 8,500 feet up in the Andes, July storms had dropped several meters of snow. Avalanche forecaster Jerry Roberts, on a "visiting scholarship" to Chile for the summer, emailed that he had just had the "best day of skiing" in his life, in 80 inches of new snow on July 11. But by the time I got there in August, that snow was old and unreplenished. U.S. women and Austrian men's World Cup downhillers were having a sweet time scoring the early-morning bathroom tile with their blade-like ski edges. Then, when the sun rose higher and warmed the snow, the Lycra-ed superheroes disappeared into the gym and those of us with fat skis and no gift for speed headed out in search of ripening corn.

Or any kind of soft snow, hissing snow, snow that would show new-moon crescents, like white scars, after our passing. The hunting took some getting used to, some mental readjustment: down there below the equator, the north-facing aspects softened up first, while the last remnants of cold, winter snow hid in pockets of south-facing shade. Exactly backwards, compass-wise, from the regime at home in Colorado.

Temperatures warmed dramatically by midday, to the point where the area's snow safety director, fearful of wet slides, sometimes closed the entire Roca Jack section of the mountain for the afternoon. With not a lot to do one day after lunch, ski patroller Mark Rawsthorne, a Brit who follows winter from Portillo to Colorado's San Juan Mountains, suggested we give his golden retriever puppy, Reggie, some avalanche rescue practice. This'll be fun, I thought. Then somehow I volunteered myself to be the victim.

I'd never been buried completely in snow, never been completely covered over by any elemental thing, unless you count diving into the ocean, or the times the down comforter got out of control. In forty-some years of skiing, with nearly thirty in the backcountry, I'd never been caught in an avalanche. Some close calls, yes. And I'd had the occasional, literal nightmare. (What a stupid way to go! If only I could have left a note goodbye!) But no, never actually buried.

Roberts pointed to a coffin-shaped trench he'd dug in the center of a large snowfield, an off-piste meadow that had been churned by a snowcat to resemble the frozen cottage-cheese texture of avalanche debris. "Climb in," he said nonchalantly, while Rawsthorne kept Reggie well out of sight.

Roberts and I had skied a lot together in the San Juans, where Rawsthorne was one of his protégés. He regularly chalks up a hundred twenty days in the backcountry each winter. I get in fewer days, but still enough to reacquaint myself every year with that range's high-elevation, dry powder snow and its infamous, complicated, slide-prone stratification. Roberts is known at home as the Rev. He is, in fact, ordained in the Universal Life Church. He performs a couple of weddings a year, for friends in the snow world, and now that we're in our fifties, he's beginning to do some funerals, too. But the other reason he's called the Rev is his reverence for the power and unpredictability of snow. It's made him conservative and skeptical. And it's kept him alive.

"So, Jer," I said, peering into the shovel trench. "That doesn't look like a whole lot of breathing space there where my noggin goes." A small blue cavity of maybe a cubic foot extended forward of where my head would be.

"Just get in," Roberts said, ignoring my query. "Face down. I'm going to try to put these heavy chunks on you as gently as I can. Then I'll fill in with loose snow."

Rawsthorne had given me his patrol radio, in case I panicked, which I held in my left hand out in front of my goggles. I squirmed to get comfortable, head down on my right arm jammed awkwardly into the air space."

Roberts wasn't kidding about the heavy chunks. They took the breath right out of me, pressed by ribs hard down onto snow as solid as rock. Muscles tensed reflexively as I tried to create room for my lungs to expand. The air space wasn't going to do me any good if I couldn't expand my chest to inhale.

He finished with the big blocks and began shoveling in the fine stuff, which filtered down around every bone, crept into my collar and up to my chin. It was rapidly becoming darker. I had to fight an instinct to arch my back like a bucking horse to hurl the weight off me, but a little experimenting soon made it clear I couldn't move if my life depended on it. I was paralyzed. Entombed. Voluntarily entombed.

Panic was not an option, so I focused consciously, practically mouthing the words as I thought them: okay; relax; remember the ABCs of avalanche rescue. If you're buried, you'll have a lot more time if you can slow down and breathe normally. I took one long, meditative breath – as long as my limited chest space would allow – and then wondered if I'd just used up half of my air supply.

I couldn't tell if Roberts was done heaping snow on me or if the density of the cover simply precluded feeling, or hearing, further shoveling. Thoughts drifted back to one of the closer calls from my past, to a stormy day on Red Mountain Pass when Mr. Roberts (as it happened) kicked off an avalanche above me. I had dropped through the trees with my camera to leave an inviting open swath of snow for Jerry to ski. I set up near the bottom of the pitch, punched my poles into the snow, took off my gloves and called up, "Ready!"

Roberts hadn't moved five feet onto the slope when it collapsed and took his feet out from under him. "Sliding!" he called out helpfully.

I saw very little after that given my mad scramble, gloveless and missing one pole, but able somehow to grab my pack and keep hold of the camera while sprinting (if such a thing is possible in thigh-deep powder) off to the side and out of harm's way. We were both fine.

I looked at the radio. Felt the call button under my thumb. I remembered an unsuccessful short story I'd written, early in my backcountry skiing days, in which I attempted to recast Hemingway's "The Snows of Kilimanjaro." Instead of a man slowly dying of gangrene on the plains of Africa, my narrator's voice recalled his life and regrets from under the snow, wondering until the end of consciousness if his ski buddies would be able to find and dig him out in time. I'd written it to see if I could imagine a thing I feared, and also as a kind of ritual warding off, as if imagining (and writing it) could somehow prevent the nightmare from happening. Maybe the exercise helped bend my judgment, if not my karma. Maybe I became more cautious afterward, "turned Republican," in Roberts's phrase. In any case, the bad thing hadn't happened. So far.

Earlier, Rawsthorne had allowed as how Reggie was "too smart," and that simple burials were no longer challenging enough for him. "We need to make things more difficult. There's a pretty good breeze coming up from the south. I think I'll bring him in upwind so he really has to search for the scent." Meanwhile, up above on the snow surface, Roberts took the difficulty factor into his own hands. First he scattered my ski poles across hundreds of feet of "debris." Then he peed at two different spots around the perimeter. And finally he went and lay down himself at the opposite end of the slope, as if he were another victim who happened to have been spit out by the slide. If I'd known what he was doing to make things harder for Reggie, I probably would have jerked the radio to life involuntarily. But, of course, I had no way of knowing.

The quiet inside my full-body cast approached – dared I even think it? – dead quiet. I was aware of a kink in one leg and another in my shoulder where my head and neck pinched unnaturally. What kind of pain might there be, I wondered, if one were locked in some grotesque contortion after a laundromat ride in a real avalanche? This discomfort was nothing. This was only a game.

But what if Reggie didn't get here soon? What if he tired of the game altogether? At what point would the men above decide that enough was enough and dig me out? If they could remember where I was. Reggie was only seven months old. Not quite grown and still a little goofy. I'd met him a couple of days before, below the snowline, in the village of Rio Blanco, at a welcome *asado* thrown by expatriate snow guru Tim Lane. It had been a glorious early spring day. We sat in t-shirts under Tim's arbor sipping pisco sours and gazing at the view through a laden orange tree. Reggie had taken little notice of me. Why should he? He was focused on his ball, various sticks, and a puppy's dim calculations regarding his master's commands and the consequences, if any, of just blowing them off.

What if Reggie were blowing them off right now?

How will I know if I'm running low on oxygen? What does it feel like? Do you get stupid? Might there be a prelude to the odd peacefulness one reads about in drowning victims, once they give up trying to breathe? The calm between the mind letting go and the organs shutting down? What might I think about when the time, like a wave receding on a beach, runs out? Did I remember to change the oil in the car before I left Colorado? When the end comes, will my life story, like a supraorbital Stan Brakhage film, flicker across the inside of my forehead: lovers, children, cats, sunsets, mingled ecstasies and self-recriminations, goodbyes unsaid…?

Something that might have been a new weight pressed into my reverie. And barking. Faint. Yes, something was happening. Loose snow filtered into my ear and down my neck. The barking grew louder, right on top of me now, and a scratching, digging, yelping sound, snow pushing at my goggles, snow spraying everywhere. Someone was yelling, "Go, Reggie, go! Good boy! Get him!"

It was my voice yelling.

Roberts went to work again with the shovel, and I stood up finally, coated in snow, like a gingerbread boy dunked in powdered sugar. I felt lighter than air, elated, limbs loose as straw. Reggie raced around with a squeaky rubber chicken in his mouth, his reward for a job well done.

I listened to the recounting of the search. Rawsthorne had indeed brought Reggie over to the debris field with the wind at his tail. He had streaked straight to Roberts lying on top of the snow, realized that this wasn't his goal, and moved on. He ignored Jerry's urine samples, checked out the ski poles, rejected them as well, and raced along in a sweeping curve until he picked up my scent. Coming in from downwind now, he galloped directly to the burial site and started digging. Total elapsed time from Mark's search command: 30 seconds.

My euphoria lasted well into the next day, when I volunteered again. This time I didn't worry about the oil in the car, or death. I spent my time underground on an astronomy problem: trying to figure out, with no topside distractions, how the August sun here traced its path across the sky, low in the north, just the opposite of what it should be doing in the heart of winter.

# The Nightmare

OK, THIS IS NOT A DRILL.

It's happened. This is real. And surreal.

Jerry's down there somewhere in that river of fallen snow. And we've got to find him.

Fast.

The day had begun with such promise. If Jerry Roberts was at all nervous, he didn't show it. He had a chance to guide visiting dignitaries, as he called them, tongue firmly in cheek, on a cold, beautiful, mid-winter Colorado day, with new overnight snow, on his home turf, Red Mountain Pass.

I say guide in the most informal sense. Jerry is not a guide, he is an avalanche forecaster for the highway department and a modest member of the tiny circle of American snow-science geeks. As a measure of respect, he is known to friends as the Reverend, Rev for short. The dignitaries (they would laugh at the word) were two ski pros met during a southern-hemisphere sojourn, in Portillo, Chile, new friends with snow cred nearly equal to the Rev's. Matt Wylie is a ski instructor and guide from Vancouver, B.C. And Greg Harms guides for the heliskiing operation out of Portillo and for another one up in Alaska. Our group of five included Jerry's girlfriend, artist and telemark skier Lisa Issenberg, and me, a long-time acolyte of the Rev's, a sponge for snow knowledge and a greedy collector of the exquisite high lines available on Red.

Where to go? It would be the Rev's call. He decided on a Pass classic, the Prospect-Powerline loop. We followed his lead up the long approach, out of the trees and onto the alpine plain of McMillan Peak. The storm had blown through quickly, leaving six plus inches of snow unevenly distributed by shifting winds. Jerry noted that southwesterly winds had ushered the new snow in, but then had switched to northwest as the system moved out. That brisk northerly was still lifting diaphanous banners from the exposed ridgelines.

Lots of terrain features were cross-loaded, from both directions, and striped with subtle surface ripples. But the skiing would be fine heading down into Prospect on the Silverton side of the divide. A tad inconsistent, yes, with hidden patches of stiffer snow, but floury and billowing in our wakes all the way to lunch at the old collapsed mine building. I was especially impressed with Harms's and Wylie's skiing. Strapping, tall boys who know how to apply smooth force to the center of their boards, they blasted through the tough spots as if they weren't there.

After eating, we skinned up out of that basin toward our second descent, to the west, back to the Pass. The late January sun was just strong enough on this climb, at this aspect, to wet the snow surface, causing Wylie's skins to stick. Jerry and Lisa kept to their leaders' pace, while Harms and I slowed to assist Wylie. I had a scraper in my chest pocket and twice played farrier to Wylie's hoof, hacking away at the snowballs accumulating under his feet.

By the time we reached the divide Jerry and Lisa had already stowed their skins and, chilled by the wind whipping through the gap, were ready to shove off. I wasn't worried. We'd follow their tracks, and they'd wait, surely.

But Jerry didn't wait. This is one of the unanswered – unanswerable, apparently – mysteries of that day. He decided, once he and Lisa got down around treeline, to change destinations. Another group of skiers had tracked up Powerline, our intended route, and were, in fact, heading back up for another lap. So, Jerry traversed to his right across a thinly covered rock bench, to the top of a seldom-skied face on the shoulder of Red Mountain Number Three.

Following behind, I came around the corner and spied the two of them at a distance. Jerry was drawing a square in the snow with his pole and reaching down to feel the layers with his gloved hand. Resistance. Weakness. Clues, maybe, to instability. This is one of his quick tests, something he often does to get a brief, tactile sense of near-surface snow structure.

As I stepped gingerly across the rocks – the new snow barely covered their sharp facets – I expected our group would soon reconvene; Harms and Wylie were a just little ways behind me. But before I reached the lovers, Jerry slid over the edge into the pitch. Lisa watched him go. I couldn't see beyond the convex roll of the shoulder.

Before I saw anything, I heard a woman screaming. It wasn't Lisa. It was a woman's voice somewhere below shrieking in horror: insistent, piercing, like a hawk cry. And then I saw the powder cloud billowing up from the bottom of the basin a very long ways down the mountain.

So this is it. This is not a test. You've thought about this. Dreamed it. Danced around the possibility for years. Now you need to think clearly, think smart. Peering over the edge, I see Jerry's track: eight turns, then the fracture line. No sign of his faded red jacket. No sign at all. The quickest way onto the debris would be to ski right down the bed surface, but there appears to be enough hang fire, enough steep slab that *didn't* release, to make that choice risky. Harms and Wylie haven't started into the rock field yet. They are unaware of what has happened. But, from where they are, they can ski directly around to the side of the path and start searching from there. I yell to them, and the words are alien, the sound of my voice strained.

The screaming bird is a woman we know, a member of the party that had been climbing for Powerline seconds. Harms and Wylie have skied past her and are already on the debris, zigzagging in search mode. We all have our beacons turned to receive. I ask the woman if she's sure she saw Jerry swept along below the spot where we are standing. It's not possible he's buried somewhere above us? No, she says, shaking uncontrollably.

I'm on the debris, moving fast, traversing right and left, beacon on one hand, poles in the other, listening. Then from below Wylie calls out that he has a signal, and everything focuses, and he's got a stronger signal, and everybody's skiing down over the lumpy surface as fast as they can, homing in, hearing it too, and Wylie is already into fine search mode and yelling for probes and shovels, and I'm flinging down my pack and staggering forward, ramming together shovel handle and blade, while Harms is shouting with his probe in the ground like a golden aluminum thread, "I've got something!"

Dig! Dig! Come on! And sure enough, a couple of feet down, there is

Jerry's backpack. Now which end is up? This end, Jesus, yes, come on dig!

His face is blue. And a cut on his forehead drips red blood onto his blue brow. In a flash, the bird woman is here and jumps into the hole. She is a doctor. The blue face looks grave to her, and she thinks out loud that we may need a helicopter evacuation. But she can feel Jerry's blood moving, feel his heart pumping, and she thrusts her hand down underneath his chest, pushing snow aside to open up space for his lungs to expand.

Meanwhile, everyone is pleading with the blue face. Lisa is crying and talking: "Come on, Jerry! Breathe! Jerry! Jerry!" We're here, man. You're gonna make it. Breathe, dammit! And in a matter of a few more excruciating seconds, he does. And the color begins to return to his face, and he blinks his eyes, moves the fingers on his right hand, and a pink flush works across his cheeks and mouth.

Thirty minutes later I'm lugging Jerry's big backpack (he carries more shit than any two skiers I know) out the snow-covered logging road toward the pass and the cars. There are no straps on the pack. We cut it off his body in order to free him from the compacted snow. It's awkward dragging the heavy thing along, and I've fallen behind the rest of the group, which includes Jerry, wearing someone else's down parka (against the possibility of shock), sliding on someone else's ski (one of his had vanished), moving out on his own, insisting that he is fine. Really.

I don't mind the effort. In fact, the work seems to be flushing some of the spent adrenaline from my system, pushing the nightmare back into its corner. Mostly. The Rev is the last person I would have expected to get caught in a slide of his own making. Then again, there is a kind of indisputable math that says: the more you're out there, the more likely you are one day to ski over that trigger point, to have that bit of bad luck, to get whupped by the Zen stick. And Jerry's been out here, 120 days a season, for 40 years. Was it bound to happen? Or were mistakes made?

A week or so later, we would saddle up and ski together again. It was Jerry's first time out since the burial. Mine, too. We lagged behind the rest of the posse and talked. He remembered tumbling, and pushing off the bed surface, coming up for air, going down again. When the snow stopped moving, "I knew I was buried," he said. "I thought, I'm fucked. I gambled and lost. I wasn't upset. I had a good life, filled with good friends. My mind was just in neutral. Then I blacked out." The weight of the snow on his back kept him from inhaling even once. Had there been an air pocket, he couldn't have taken advantage of it.

Seven minutes, I said. That's how long it took to find him and uncover his face. Greg Harms had checked his watch. Some people survive being buried for longer, but they have room to expand their chest, to breathe the air that remains in the matrix. According to the screaming bird, Dr. Debbie Hackett, Jerry didn't have much margin; another minute of asphyxia and he might not have made it back.

I confessed my bafflement at his decision to jump in before the rest of us had had a chance to regroup, to ponder the slope together. At clinics and seminars Jerry sometimes lectures on "the human factor" in avalanche accidents, heuristic traps that have more to do with group dynamics and human nature than with snow physics. Things like: familiarity with the terrain (Jerry calls this one "going to the office"); scarcity, or competition for first tracks ("seeing with your powder eyes"); seeking acceptance within the party ("is there a pretty girl along?"); and the problem of the "expert halo," the crowning of a de facto leader, with the rest of the group behaving like sheep.

Jerry's talks are illustrated with humorous slides. One day on our way to skiing the Pass, we stopped at a local sheep ranch to take a photo of lambs in a line, blindly following their leader.

Jerry's response to my bafflement was muted. "Should I have consulted the wisdom of the group? Was I trying to impress the pretty girl? I hope not."

I thought it more likely he wanted to provide untracked pow for the visiting ski pros (the scarcity scenario), and that that had colored his judgment. Still, why not wait before dropping in?

"Was it the familiarity," he asked rhetorically, "going to the office? Maybe. The snow looked like it was holding together pretty well..."

"It's the San Juans," he concluded, finally, with a shrug, referring to the infamously hard-to-predict snowpack, and subsequent danger, of the home mountains. As if that answered the questions.

In the end, of course, it doesn't matter why. The what of this slide was documented the day after by a Colorado Avalanche Information Center investigator, who determined that, yes, a fragile, 200-foot wide slab of wind-loaded storm snow, eight to eighteen inches deep, skier-triggered, had released on an older wind crust and run nearly full path, about 1,000 feet into the big timber. The victim had been located and dug out near the tongue of the debris.

Some days after that, Debbie Hackett came up with a name for this path, described only as Path 42 in the *Ouray County Avalanche Atlas* (Armstrong, et al). It may never make it onto the map, but to us it will forever be Rev's Resurrection.

# Independence Day

NORMALLY, I WOULD HAVE SLEPT LATE then driven into Ouray in time for the parade, the picnic in the park, and the infamous Main Street water fights. But this Fourth of July the pull of the high country was just too strong.

Late snow locked much of Yankee Boy Basin in a white vice, while just below the snow line wildflowers bloomed and the aspens flashed midsummer, dark-green canopies.

Four inches of snow had fallen overnight, and it looked as if it might storm again as we ground through town and up the old mining road in four-wheel drive. We bumped past the Camp Bird Mine, tucked against its protective cliff, wary of the avalanches that come off U.S. Mountain to the south. The Camp Bird was the last big mine in the area to close, in 1990. The mill had been dismantled a few years before that and shipped to a gold mining operation in Mongolia. A couple of the Victorian houses remain, including the steep-gabled superintendent's home and the one-room schoolhouse with its white siding and gingerbread trim.

Another mile up the road we passed the ghost town of Sneffels, surrounded by towering piles of waste rock, beached freighters of toxic, rusted tailings. Most of the buildings are skeletons now, having been picked apart board-by-board by souvenir-hunting jeepers.

My ski partner Todd Cline is a native of Ouray, blond and boyish, in his mid-twenties. His parents are teachers, not miners, but Todd and his brother have scrambled all over these mountains, courtesy of the miners' audacious double-track roads, some steep as elk trails, that offer a way up nearly every creek and ridgeline.

At 11,400 feet the snow on the road stopped us. It melted back reluctantly to allow light and air to marsh marigolds along the creek. We parked on a gravel bar next to a familiar pickup, the only other vehicle up this high this early. We weren't surprised. Soft-spoken Ouray carpenter Rick Blackford gets out more than most local skiers, especially when there's new snow. He often skis alone, which worries people, but it's his choice. He's been doing it for 30 years now.

Todd and I caught up with Rick on the Emma Rollers, giant cascading benches off the north flank of Mount Emma, treeless terrain as white and smooth as the folds of cloth on Michelangelo's Pieta. We hiked the rest of the way together, skis strapped to our packs, kicking steps up the final steep pitch to the ridge.

From the knife edge at 13,200 feet, we looked down on Telluride's airport – an asphalt Band-Aid on a green mesa – and then back north at the great, horseshoe sweep of Yankee Boy Basin, crowned by Mount Sneffels' jagged pyramid at 14,150 feet.

We couldn't see Ouray around the corner 5,000 feet below, or Telluride, hidden by intervening peaks, but we felt the pull of both towns, linked as they are by history and the hundreds of miles of tunnels honeycombing the mountains separating them. Silver was discovered first, then gold. Both towns hummed with populations pushing 5,000 in the 1890s. (Telluride has about 2,000 people now, Ouray fewer than 1,000.) Sarah Bernhardt played Telluride's Opera House. At the Camp Bird, the owner's daughter bought herself the 45.5-carat Hope Diamond. Greed and high culture combined for a time on the continental divide.

When the silver crash of 1893 turned Aspen overnight from the "Queen City of the Rockies" to a virtual ghost town, Ouray and Telluride survived on gold, copper, and zinc. The mining is finished now, replaced by skiing and ice climbing. And in summer commercial jeep tours crawl up the passes separating the sister towns, giving visitors an eagle's view of tundra and crumbling time.

Both towns draw on their past for Independence Day celebrations. At dawn on the Telluride side, the remnant crew at the Idorado Mine ignites a dynamite blast so powerful the shock wave sets babies to crying and windows rattling all over town. Volunteer firemen roast whole beef halves in

Town Park and, come dark, shoot fireworks between echoing canyon walls.

Following the parade, Ouray closes the highway between brick storefronts to allow teams of men, women, and juniors to pummel each other with water from high-pressure fire hoses. Contestants are swaddled in motocross pads, slickers and full-face helmets, every seam sealed with duct tape. And still survivors of long bouts stagger away bruised from head to toe. It's crazy and riveting, and the encircling crowd, well lubricated by then, usually gets soaked as well.

Below our perch on the ridge, fast moving clouds tore themselves apart on the crags, pooled like fog in the deep holes. We would learn later that the parade went off bravely despite a pounding hail, little girls on the dance squad marching in leotards and parkas. Rick dug out the cherries. "Gotta have cherries on the Fourth of July!" And these were good ones, dark and sweet, from orchards two hours north (and 8,000 feet down) in the valley of the North Fork of the Gunnison.

We felt wild, high and free. And that was before we swooped down the Emma Rollers on our "winged boards." Yankee boys indeed. Where the miners of old would have given their eyeteeth to get down out of the mountains and into the comforts of town, we chose the heights. Mostly, those men despised the snow. It mystified them, buried their roads, entombed unlucky animals and friends. It avalanched in the night during storms or sometimes on the brightest days, weeks after the last big dump. But for the mailmen on skis, and a few Scandinavians who coasted their long wooden "snowshoes" to town on weekends, snow was the enemy.

We had the luxury of loving it, and loving it especially in July and with a surface texture like soft ball bearings. Unexpected, generous, benign, the way down promised sweeping turns independent, almost, of gravity. We gave silent nods to our old miners, and to the visionaries of 1776. Then we stepped into bindings and shoved off the top.

Down near the cars, walking again, skis on shoulders, we confronted a commercial jeep full of tourists. They stared with incredulity. One spoke up. "You boys skiin'? How'd you get up there?" We smiled and kept moving. If we hurried, we might just make the water fights.

# PART V

# Highlands

# Totally Hip

I HAD HIP REPLACEMENT SURGERY one month before my first grandchild was born.

The decision to do it, to go for the new hip, had not come easily. Back and forth I'd gone over the previous winters: I'm too young (I was 59). I can still ski. I can barely walk back to the car after a morning on the slopes, but I can still do it, dammit!

Then on the other side of the coin: I'm bone-on-bone. I've seen the pictures. Yoga isn't helping. I'm eating ibuprofen by the handful, day and night. That can't be good. That for sure isn't good.

I can still sleep. Pretty well. Most nights. Except when I can't because there are no more positions to try, no way to silence the ache.

But what if the new hip turns out to mean an end to skiing? It could happen. A friend in Alta had his arthritic hips replaced and then couldn't do the thing he most loved, which was skate ski.

Isn't skiing, even skiing in pain, better than not skiing?

One Denver surgeon I consulted rolled his eyes when I said it was important to me to be able to keep doing this thing that I loved. It was the reason, in fact, that we'd come to Colorado 35 years before. He didn't think I should risk it. Ski, that is. He didn't get it. I found another surgeon.

But I'd never had any kind of surgery before. What if I didn't wake up? It's happened. Yes, I knew hip replacement is one of the most common elective surgeries in the world. Hundreds of thousands of us used-and-abused Baby Boomers do it every year. The new parts are made of the hardest, smoothest ceramics known to man, and space-age titanium alloys, and third-generation, cross-braided polyethylene. On-line testimonials are legion.

I researched all of the options. Resurfacing versus total joint replacement. Metal versus ceramic. Each surgeon has a preferred "approach" – cutting you open from the front, or the back, or the side. Each approach had advantages and disadvantages.

Failure rates overall were low. But there were any number of ways a new joint could fail. The one recurring bugaboo was dislocation. Artificial hips don't have the range of motion your original equipment affords. You're going to have to be careful, my surgeon said. For the rest of your life. "You don't ski in the backcountry alone do you?" No. "Good. Because no one should die of a hip dislocation." If it were to happen, he promised me, "you won't be able to move." The dislocation wouldn't kill me, exposure would.

The pain was turning me into an old man before my time. My daughter Cloe, who's a doctor, said she could see it in my eyes. She mentioned the d-word, depression. "Dad," she said earnestly, "pain is bad."

Then Cloe told us she was pregnant. The same Cloe whom Ellen and I taught to ski at age three by scooting her back and forth between us, catch-and-release, catch-and-release, down the beginner meadows at Telluride, letting her glide a little farther on her own each time. Little Cloe bubbling with pleasure in our backwards-snowplow arms. Cloe was going to have a baby, and that was the kicker. I wanted to ski with my grandson. And for that to happen, I was going to have to trust in modern orthopedic miracles.

Alexander was born in September 2008, a month into my rehab. We were there. Cloe and her husband Adam wanted us in the birthing room with them. Three generations now. The cycle of life continuing.

I could walk on the new joint by then. Carefully. In the hospital Cloe put Alex in my arms and I rocked him in place, whispering sweet powder nothings to his perfect innocence.

In December, four and a half months out from surgery, I decided to test the new hip on the slopes. After the first run I knew. On the following chairlift ride I relaxed as I hadn't in years. I conjured a ski day with little Alex just a few winters hence.

My lift-mates on the quad chair might have wondered about the stranger with his head thrown back, the closed eyes, the long involuntary smile of relief and celebration.

# Living With Addiction

Easter, and the ski season seems to be rushing to a close. The suddenness of it feels like going cold turkey, and the prospect has me trembling.

I'm an addict, you see.

Robert Woody, a 79-year-old World War II veteran and fellow addict confirmed our problem in the bluntest terms. "It is an addiction," he said, as we slid through remnants of the last powder storm at Alta. "Skiing releases endorphins in the brain, and after a while you have to have them."

Woody is no stoner. He fought in the Italian Apennines with the 10th Mountain Division in 1945. He worked for decades as the business editor of the *Salt Lake Tribune*. He told me that 40 years ago he still harbored dreams of being a foreign correspondent. "But then one day I was up on Sun Spot [at Alta] in the powder and well, that was that. I never left Salt Lake."

I knew the truth of what he was saying, I just didn't want to admit it. I still clung to skiing as this romance, this healthy fraternity of brothers and sisters with an admirable, if fanatical, lineage going back through Killy and Stein, to Andy Lawrence and Gretchen Fraser, Dartmouth's Otto ("Skiing is a way of life") Schniebs, to Otto Lang's frivolous and fantastic *Sun Valley Serenade* (1941) – all the way back to Arnold Fanck's *The White Ecstasy* (1931), starring Hannes Schneider and Leni Riefenstahl in some of the most outrageous powder sequences ever filmed. I even flirted with the idea that what I sought was a mountain-based spirituality, reverence and practice leading to wisdom.

But no. The sad fact is I'm physically addicted to those bliss chemicals my brain produces when hopscotching through a tilted spruce forest.

We're talking total escape here, not so far removed from a junkie nodding oblivious against a wall.

I cannot, no matter how I might try, think about the Middle East while skiing. Not while calculating trajectories on a sheet of corduroy (cloth of kings). And I certainly am incapable of brooding, as I inevitably do during non-skiing hours, on a looming writing deadline. Not while balancing gravity, momentum and the soft marshmallow resistance of a powder pitch.

Similarly, a day in the backcountry requires devotional attention to the moment. Safety demands it. Your buddies deserve it. Addiction sinks gratefully into the palm of wild terrain. Another minute, another hour where grace has nothing to do with being a good person, but only with how true you are to the physics of controlled falling.

I used to think of Easter in the traditional, non-religious way, as a celebration of spring, a harbinger of summer's freedom and warmth. But now, I realize, I dread the holiday, for it signals the near end to the skiing season. Summer offers but a few sun-pocked turns on isolated patches of snow. Barely enough to scratch an addict's itch.

But this is good, I think then, grudgingly. Hard but good, in that I have not become an habitué of river sports or of rock climbing and am not much more than a casual mountain biker. Otherwise, these methadone substitutes for skiing might keep me from producing any useful work at all.

Thank god, I guess, for summer, when the craving subsides to a dull ache. Manageable, for the most part, until fall, when the magazines start arriving with their gear reviews and luscious travel pics, and the need for a fix becomes a gnawing, and then an obsession, and a four-hour drive over four mountain passes to Wolf Creek for opening day seems not only doable but sensible. Enlightened even. The snow is back! And the world once again has to get in line for a piece of my time.

Yes, I'm in denial. What is wrong, I say to myself with giddy, barely confinable joy, with a glimpse now and then of heaven?

# Hot Buttered Corn

Closing day delivered perfect corn.

Corn snow, that is. There were plenty of corny outfits at Powderhorn Resort up on Grand Mesa, from corn pone to candy corn to soft-core porn. Then there were the two ladies of a certain age, telemark skiers, who donned flower-print dresses and glued Easter-egg baskets to the tops of their helmets: sweet corn.

But the day's real star was the corn snow. Repeated melt-freeze cycles, over clear days and cold nights, had frozen all surfaces. Then, by 10:30-11:00, the sunny edges of the trails started to melt, *comme velours*, as the French say, and by 3 p.m. the whole mountain skied like a giant Slurpy. The classic compendium *Avalanche Handbook* (Ron Perla, et al) – not generally known for its lyricism – describes corn's "large, coarse grained aggregates... [which] provide easy maneuverability and delightful downhill skiing conditions."

Given the conditions, my mantra for the day, my instruction to myself, was "get out in front of your skis."

While this may sound dangerous (see: "going over the handlebars" on your mountain bike), it is actually sound advice, and one of the vaguest and most useful clichés in skiing.

What I mean by getting out in front is actually two things. There is a physical, and a psychic component.

Physically, you need to get your core, your center of mass, your belly button, going downhill before your skis begin their direction change. This is what all the great skiers do. You can see it in the videos of Mikaela Shriffrin and Marcel Hirscher: their torsos balanced well inside, out in front of, the path their skis take. It allows them to put their skis way up on edge where side-cut can do its thing. And it helps them resist the merry-go-round forces in a turn with their bones, stacked hips and femurs and tib-fibs, rather than with thigh power alone.

From this "out in front" place, the early-turning skis need only be lightly weighted. You are floating, in transition. (Aspen pied piper John Clendenin calls it "the love spot.") You have options. You can drive your edges into a roundy carve, or swish them sideways in a drift, or fashion a turn shape between these extremes. You're in the driver's seat, not the back seat.

Second, and equally important, is to be out in front with your eyes, your brain – seeing, gauging, projecting a path through these particular folds in the mountain. Then, lickety-split, deciding on an appropriate course: go round, go straight, accelerate, scrub speed. It's that piece of the skiing whole so aptly (and unintentionally) defined by President George H. W. Bush as "the vision thing."

In business we say it's good to be out in front of the market – ahead of the curve. In politics, too, it's good to be out in front of an issue, like being all for gay marriage years ago.

(In baseball, it's more complicated. To be out in front of a changeup is to swing too soon at a pitch you thought was going to be a fastball.)

In skiing, being out in front is pretty much all good. Physically, it's where you want to be to effectively press the skis into the snow, to draw your line precisely. Mentally, visually, you are imagining and then going there – preceding yourself down the mountain. The best turns have a déjà vu quality to them; you live the moment twice, cheating time. Maybe that's why skiing is so addictive.

On slushy corn-snow days getting out in front is easy. All that water in the snow holds your feet back. Just a little. Making it easy for your center to ride forward. A little is all it takes.

I used to suggest to students that they imagine themselves a bowsprit on a sailboat. One of those mythical painted ladies with head up, chest out, and nothing ahead of them but the waves. Pulling the ship along, figuratively at least, behind them.

Unlike the feeling on hard snow when in a blink skis can skitter ahead, putting you back on your heels, on corn you may have the feeling that you are so far forward, so in control, you are pulling your skis along for the ride.

All around the mountain Sunday, closing day, people were skiing out of their heads, out in front of their skis: sinuous, continuous, invincible. The lift operator on the West End chair was just a kid. But he made a wise, if unintentionally flattering, comment. We had spied each other earlier, from a distance, when he was out on break taking a run in the slush bumps. Now, as he loaded me into the old double chair and had a good look at my gray stubble, he said, "Dude, you look younger out on the hill."

# Outthinking the Snowy Torrents

I WROTE A NEWS STORY THIS WEEK about the death of 18-year-old Norwood high-school student Garrett Carothers, and it broke my heart.

"Dear, sweet Garrett," read the caption on a Facebook photo.

By all accounts Carothers and his three snowmobiling buddies were not behaving badly on Saturday when the last in line of their little motorized train was snuffed by an avalanche that released above them. They weren't pushing the envelope. They weren't high-marking some wind-loaded, primed-to-slide alpine bowl. They were struggling uphill, in deep snow, on a summer road in the La Sal Mountains, near Moab, and had decided to turn around. Too late, as it turned out. Innocents abroad.

Other accidents recently in the news did reveal evidence of hubris. In November, there was famous skier, cliff jumper Jamie Pierre, ignoring all the classic signs of instability – including natural and triggered releases everywhere around him – to attempt a narrow, thinly covered chute at Snowbird, before the ski area was open. The moving snow he kicked off didn't kill him, the rocks he bashed over did. Like Carothers, he was beloved, too.

In February, on Stevens Pass in Washington, a giant, unwieldy group of "experts and industry insiders," 13 of them, decided to ski off the backside of the ski area immediately following a two-day, 26-inch storm that came with strong winds. They claimed they were using proper protocol – skiing one at a time, stopping in safe zones, etc. – but somehow five of them got caught in a single slide. Three were buried and killed.

Then, there was Telluride's own Nate Soules tragedy, though I don't use that word. Tragedy is something else, something ennobling. Soules chose to snowboard out-of-bounds into Bear Creek, alone, on the first real powder day in a long time, with two inches of new snow-water equivalent – all of that weight added to an especially rotten San Juans snowpack. He knew what he was doing. But he was blinded by what long-time avalanche forecaster Jerry Roberts calls powder shock: the rational mind succumbing to lust for deep turns.

You're not supposed to speak ill of the dead, but I was mad at Soules then, and I'm still mad. As a father and grandfather. Yes, as many have said, he died doing what he loved. But he also loved his wife and young son. What was he thinking?

I haven't skied the backcountry for a few years now, after devoting the better part of the last 40 years to it. The reasons are complex and include two hip-replacement surgeries and the digging out, in 2005, of the self-same Mr. Roberts, who barely survived an avalanche on Red Mountain Pass. He was one of the most knowledgeable and conservative wild-snow skiers I have known. His triggering a big slide and being crushed blue by the weight of the snow on top of him seemed to prove the adage: if you are out there enough, you will eventually get caught.

I didn't necessarily believe that axiom then, and I'm not sure I understand probabilities well enough to believe it now. There are lots of old skiers in the world, people who have danced the fine line between skill and luck. I once spent a day with a chestnut-skinned 80-year-old climber/skier in Zermatt who was about to guide his 500th Matterhorn. The finger of fate does not choose incompetence over competence, the deserving over the undeserving.

Even part-time observers might remember the random obliteration of revered mountaineer Alex Lowe on Shishapangma in 1999. Lowe was the unquestioned "greatest climber in the world": humble, graceful, and supremely athletic. He and two teammates were out after dinner on a casual reconnoiter from base camp, ski touring across a flat glacier, when a serac broke off the peak 6,000 feet above them. The resulting monster avalanche spared only one of the three. And it was not the greatest ski mountaineer in the world. Dear, sweet Alex.

In 1980, during the Mountainfilm weekend, I listened as Patagonia founder Yvon Chouinard told a story outside Telluride's Opera House. He had just survived an avalanche while retreating down a big peak in China. The slide was an unseen storm-within-a-storm that partially buried Yvon and claimed the life of expedition cameraman Jonathan Wright. He was still shaken weeks afterward and, in fact, vowed during the festival that he was finished with the kinds of big-mountain dangers that respected no level of skill, including decision-making. Sometimes the only decision that matters is the fact that you are there.

This has not actually been an exceptionally deadly avalanche year. The average is 25 deaths across the U.S. in a winter season. We're at 24 now. Of course, March could bring more, but not likely a great many more. Given that so many more recreationists (skiers, snowboarders, snowmobilers, ice climbers) are out testing the snow's strength these days, it's a wonder the numbers aren't higher.

I don't want to be a statistic. I don't fully understand my reasons for backing away. For the longest time, the high, pure-white world seemed as important as breathing. My change of heart has caused some rifts in relationships with old ski partners, changes that give me pain.

Perhaps I'm just getting old. More risk averse. More fragile. More mortal. Roberts says, "Peter, we've lost our edge."

I do know one thing: I want to keep skiing, with my wife, my daughters, and my grandchildren. My dear, sweet grandchildren.

# Lessons Learned

One of the first ski lessons I taught at Mt. Bachelor this winter, in my return to teaching after many years away, was a group of four, first-time beginners. They were Chinese grad students: a brother-sister duo, a cousin of theirs, and a friend. Three of them were attending Oregon State University, in Corvallis, the fourth was at UO, in Eugene. Three Beavers and one Duck. Yizi and Jining and I laughed briefly about that as Jilin and Xuanhan stumbled up, rental skis akimbo, struggling as first-timers often do to walk in stiff plastic ski boots.

Yizi did the introductions. Tall and smiley, he said to pronounce his name "Easy." Jining told me she and her brother were from Inner Mongolia – so they knew about winter. The hardest name to pronounce, by far, was Xuanhan, the sibs' cousin. Her shy attempts to help me say it right were all sliding swishy breathy sounds. Would that Xuanhan's skiing experience had been similarly fluid.

Ellen has said more than once that it is "brave" of me to go back to ski teaching. She's proud of me, for getting out of the house, for bringing home a little bacon. But behind the words I sense incredulousness. I'm 65. I've got two artificial hips. I like my skiing – indeed, after all these years I may be clinically addicted to it – but since the two of us gave up the ski-school ski-bum life in 1980, in Telluride, I have spoiled myself as a strictly recreational skier. No uniform. No morning line-up. No ski school bureaucracy with its certification levels, its priority lists, its tautology and fealty to the Professional Ski Instructors of America and its tome-like manual.

It's a job for young people. Ellen and I met, as twenty-something ski teachers, at Keystone in the early 1970s, when that Colorado area was still in thrall to its founder and ski school director, Max Dercum. Max's enthusiasm extended to the lowliest apprentice, and included inviting all staff to his Ski Tip Ranch home of an evening to project Super 8 film on the wall, film he shot of the latest movement innovations from the Austrian master, Professor Stefan Kruckenhauser. It was all new to us then.

Ellen and I worked for three winters in the California Sierra, at a brainy, tight-knit ski school in Bear Valley. Then we went back to Colorado, to Telluride, for four years' work during that resort's promising infancy. Promising was the operative term; hardly anyone in the skiing public had heard of the place in 1976.

It was hard to make a living at it. And with two children by then, we knew it was time to move on. Ellen got involved in Telluride's film festivals, and I launched a career as a freelance writer, which advanced in part because editors at *Powder* and *Outside* could count on my writing convincingly (not to say authoritatively) about the mechanics of sliding on snow.

That was 35 years ago. When we moved to Bend last year to be close to our first-born and her two kids, I needed a job and thought for the first time in ages about joining a ski school. I'm not the oldest on staff. Ray is 70, I think. And there's another guy I haven't met who is 72. I am at the bottom of the priority list. Mt. Bachelor is one of eight resorts in the Powdr Corp. stable. The powers that be didn't care – didn't know and by rights needn't care – about my ancient history. I was brought on board as a "non-cert(ified) new hire." I battled through the on-line application, submitted to the drug test, attended orientation (where we learned that a lost child is never a "lost child" but always, euphemistically, a "huckleberry"), signed up to have my minimum-wage pay deposited directly into my checking account, was issued a locker and my orange-and-black uniform. Brave was maybe not the word.

My Chinese millennials were all four pursuing advanced degrees in computing or coding – eminently practical things for their futures back home. By contrast, skiing is impractical, completely sensual, of the moment, all slippery feet and gravity. We started out with one ski off and one ski on, scooting gently back and forth across the snow, skateboard style. Yizi and

Jining got it right away. They had the kinesthetic sense, the ability to lift their gaze, balance and glide. Jilin was more tentative, inclined to stare at his feet. And Xuanhan was really suffering. She took tiny, mincing steps, achieving no glide at all.

She told me her feet hurt, so we stopped and investigated. Her feet were not the problem; it was her calves. She was a big girl with large calves, and the boots were cutting painfully into her lower legs. It's well known – it's been known for decades – that a woman's calf muscles are likely to sit lower on the leg than a man's do. Many women-specific ski boots are designed to accommodate this physiology. Xuanhan's unisex rental boots did not.

I tried loosening the buckles on the cuffs to little effect then unbuckled them completely. She tried again, gamely, but finally, near tears, asked to sit out the rest of the lesson. Her friends spoke to her in Mandarin (or maybe it was Mongolian?), but she insisted, sitting at one of the children's tables in the ski school yurt and working through layers of tight jeans and long johns to get the boots off. For such a big person her feet were tiny. Yizi promised to retrieve her street shoes from the rental shop and bring them to her after the lesson.

The rest of us went back to the business of controlling, of crafting a descent over snow. They were quick studies. After a couple of successful, slow-motion, practice turns, we rode the beginner chair lift. Yizi and Jining especially took their new tools, their gliding wedge turns, and ran with them. They learned that turning was the key to speed control. They steered their ski prows downriver left and right at will. On the flatter sections Jining in particular was able to let go, give herself over, comfortably, joyfully, to sliding, the wind in her hair. "So happy!" she beamed at the bottom. "I am a skier!" I was almost as pleased as she was.

Back at the yurt Yizi handed Xuanhan her street shoes while I repeated an offer from the rental shop folks to comp her next time around. No, no, she said, perhaps out of cultural reticence. Or maybe she was saying there would be no next time.

In any case, her final words seemed a kind of Taoist koan. After thanking me for my efforts, she said, apparently without irony, "Where we come from, my name, Xuanhan, means 'snow.'"

# Code White

My new skis are German-made Völkls, the Völkl Code Speedwall S. They came in a box from New Hampshire a couple of weeks ago. I leaned them against a wall downstairs and admired their sleek shape. And then I took them out for a first test ride.

The S stands for slalom. They are built like a slalom racing ski, with a laminated wood core and stiff titanium top and bottom sheets. They are small-waisted, and curvy. (Back when I used to be part of the annual equipment test at *SKI* magazine, someone correctly described the new "shaped" skis as having figures "like Betty Boop.") Thanks to this deep sidecut, the Codes come with a built-in hairpin turn – if you can stay on top of them.

I bought them sight unseen. And untried. Risky business. But the guy I know at Völkl USA promised they were "outrageously fun." So I took a chance.

Speedwall refers to the skis' sidewalls, which can be waxed to make them more slippery. The factory supplies a little tube of fast fairy dust with an applicator lid. Just rub on and polish.

Why wax the sidewalls? Part of the Code. You wax the sidewalls because these babies beg to be tilted up on their sides—way up—so far up on edge the resulting grooves in the snow are etched by both the base and the sidewall. You wax your ski bases, so why not the sidewalls.

My regular five-year-old, all-mountain skis carve pretty darn well. They were once described, in a *SKI* magazine gear review, as "double-wide giant slalom skis." They are curvy, too, compared to old-fashioned "straight" skis.

But they are much beamier than the Codes. Their built-in turn is more like a bend in the road than a hairpin. A gifted skier can carve them down almost any hill, but I have to apply the brakes when it gets steep. I reach a point where I can't handle the speed, or the g-forces, in a giant slalom-radius, pure-carved turn. So on the old skis I'm on-carve and off, scrubbing speed. On-carve and off. Carving and skidding, where the skidding can feel like a concession.

With the Codes, and their tighter natural turn shape, I learned right away I could carve more terrain more of the time. This is huge. I struggle to relay just how huge. Carving is not like run-of-the-mill steering, not like the skiing we used to do. (Back in the '70s and '80s we thought we were carving when we left a relatively narrow, steered trace on the snow.) There is no play, no sloppiness, no brushing sideways at all in a true carved turn. The resulting lines in the snow are sometimes referred to as railroad tracks. The feeling the skier gets is one of pure precision joined with perfect stability, because the ski is in fact slicing a trench in the snow. It's building a tiny curved wall against which you, the driver, the giddy beneficiary, lean. Insouciant. Invincible. Leaning against a wall. That's the feeling.

Think of a bobsled run with its banked vertical curves along which the sleds ride. It's as if an alternate gravity, one pulling 90 degrees off vertical, were pinning them to that wall. (Or picture mountain bike wheels cleaving to banked singletrack berms.) Carving skiing is like that. Except you don't have to ride down a refrigerated track (or go where the singletrack says you must go). You gouge your own tiny walls with each turn, anywhere you want, anywhere you are bold enough to stand firm against that knifing edge.

Right away on that first day the Codes drew such round-y perfect lines in the snow, I could ski entire runs, top to bottom, without once throwing my skis sideways. Not until reaching the lift line again. I felt like an engraver writing on soft silver. Ted Ligety, the American master of giant slalom, can do this. So can Mikaela Shriffrin, the slalom prodigy from Vail whose balanced stance and precocious sense of touch have made her, at 18, the world's best slalom racer. Carving has been the Holy Grail of efficient, ecstatic skiing, especially for ski racers, forever. Sixty-four-year-old guys who started late and have never raced aren't supposed to be able to do this. To feel this in-control freedom, this pressed-against-the-wall line drawing. And yet now…

The Code makes it possible. Maybe it's code for cheating? No. I don't believe there is such a thing as cheating in skiing. In the early 1970s, when I was trying out for the ski school at Keystone, my Uncle Hal took me into his garage and showed me his Dynastar MV2s. He called them his "cheaters," said they already knew how to turn and somehow transferred that gift, deserved or not, to him. They were beautiful, white metal, with a small red logo near the tip. I bought a used pair like his in Denver and aced my apprentice clinic.

Those skis were primitive approximations, many design generations ago, of the surgical tools available today. I couldn't have made a true carved turn on those MV2s to save my life.

The Codes are white, too, a beautiful pearlescent white, with a small red Völkl chevron near one tip. Sometimes, riding them, I feel as if I've been given the code for bending space-time.

# Highlands

I DIDN'T PLAN IT. HONEST. The same six CDs had been in the car changer for weeks. But there it was, a coincidence too perfect to invent.

Driving to Aspen Highlands – in fact, just rounding the corner on Colorado State Highway 82 where the ski trails first come into view – Bob Dylan's "Highlands" twanged out of the speakers. "My heart's in the Highlands, gentle and fair..." The final talking blues on his elegiac album from 1997, *Time Out of Mind.*

I had decided, selfishly, to spend this Saturday in April driving, and skiing, on one of the extra weekends the Aspen Skiing Company had added to the calendar. Great late-season snow made it possible, and SkiCo decided to generate some good will, if not big profits, among skiers who weren't ready for the season to end.

The timing of this musical coincidence went beyond serendipity. And not just because of the word "Highlands." The whole album is one big, beautiful, incisive, indulgent, mid-life crisis. And I'd been feeling kind of rudderless and low.

I'd been guilting since the night before. How to justify driving three hours and 150 miles, each way, with gas prices the way they were, just to ride chairlifts and have fun? I should have stayed home to help Ellen prepare the garden for summer. I could have pruned the spirea, at least. Or perhaps I could have made myself useful up at Cecily and Mike's place as our daughter and son-in-law struggled to finish a long punch list and move in to their new house. Or try to figure out a way to generate some income. Or whatever.

Truth be told, Ellen was down a bit, too. We were both of us suffering a sort of ill-defined malaise as we entered our sixties, a temporary – we hoped – inability to see the future with the kind of energizing clarity we used to take for granted. Dylan describes his own (or his character's) ennui this way: "I'm in Boston town in some restaurant. I have no idea what I want. Or maybe I do but I'm just really not sure. Waitress comes over, nobody in the place but me and her."

This scene always makes me smile. The way Dylan finds humor and pathos in the absolutely mundane: "She got a pretty face and long white shiny legs. I said 'Tell me what I want.' She say 'You probably want hard boiled eggs.' I said 'That's right, bring me some.' She says 'We ain't got any, you picked the wrong time to come.'"

The song is about more than flirting, or boredom, it's about loneliness. Existential and otherwise. And the inevitability of death. "Big white clouds like chariots swing low. Well my heart's in The Highlands, only place left to go."

I wasn't feeling the nearness of that particular end. Far from it. Aspen Highlands, as opposed to Robert Burns' Scottish Highlands, was right there in front of me. And it was an "actual spring day," according to the ski patrolman I rode one chair with. He explained that the year before, spring had arrived overnight, in March. It was, he said, a "nuclear meltdown." It had become a disconcerting pattern in the age of global warming. But this year had been different, cooler, as we used to assume the seasons would go. On cue a hard freeze had set the whole mountain up, set the table for a corn feast.

Corn snow – frozen granular warming gradually to slush – appeared first on the east-facing slopes, then, eventually, around on the west. With ski edges sunk in wet, forgiving snow, the steeps of Temerity and Olympic Bowl didn't feel steep. Turns flowed from one to the next. Everything was possible and nothing was scary.

A diverse skier clan materialized to join in the celebration. Day-trippers like me from Telluride and Vail, Denver and the Front Range. Hard-core locals, too. There was a pond-skimming contest out in front of the Merry-Go-Round restaurant. And a reggae band. And beer, and girls baring their shoulders in the sun.

A supremely self-indulgent thing, I said to myself, driving back west into the sunset. No higher purpose, no worthy cause. I had no assignment to write about it, no friends in tow with whom to share the day. But I hadn't been lonely. There was joy, real joy in the grace of large forces: gravity, weather, the skill of years. "Well, my heart's in the Highlands at the break of day, over the hills and far away. There's a way to get there and I'll figure it out somehow. But I'm already there in my mind, and that's good enough for now."

Now it's several years later. We've moved to Bend, Oregon, to be near two of our three grandchildren, but also in an effort to shake free of the rut we were in. It's a big change. Ridgway, though it has grown since we moved there in 1981, still counts fewer than 1,000 residents. Bend's population has skyrocketed from about 17,000 the first time I skied here, in the mid-1980s, to well over 80,000 now. It's a big town. No longer dependent on logging and the railroad, it has embraced, like few places I can think of, a recreation paradigm: skiing, mountain biking, the marijuana business, craft brewing, climbing, music, beer, river sports, beer.

The freelance writing gigs, in Colorado and now here in central Oregon, have become about as rare as trumpeter swans. But, in many ways, the skiing has come full circle. That is, the pleasure in skiing, at the new home mountain, Mt. Bachelor, has come full circle. If not in body, then in my mind.

I haven't exactly returned to childhood. But I do get to ski with eight-year-old Alexander and six-year-old Lily, and their delight is contagious. They like nothing better than to lead their Bup down Dilly Dally Alley, a natural halfpipe that meanders playfully through sheltering hemlocks.

Bachelor is what's known as a shield volcano, after the conical shields used by soldiers in ancient Greece. It stands alone 20 miles west of Bend, Fuji like. (The taller Three Sisters volcanoes huddle, uninterested, a little ways to the north.) Bachelor's top half is alpine – pure white – skirted 360 degrees around by dark hemlock forest. A bird's-eye view from above the summit crater shows erosion furrows running out and down like the spokes of a wheel. Heavy snow and wind sculpt these furrows into white waves. The grandkids already know to bank off the lips and swoop like falcons through the belly of the grooves. One of my surfing heroes, Gerry Lopez, moved to Bend from Hawaii decades ago to surf Bachelor's frozen waves on his snowboard.

I'm too old to take up the uni-plank now. But, thanks to the years, and the carving/floating abilities of the new skis, I don't have to. My skiing obsession has evolved. I look back on the coastal California boy for whom the Sierra snow was the most exotic, the most tantalizing thing. All he wanted to do was float downhill on the easy stuff like his father, upright and (seemingly) effortless. That boy went next to a passion for imitation: to lock feet together à la Stein, and Leo, his beautiful spring-break instructor at Sun Valley. Style was the key to the kingdom. Or so he thought. From there the young man dove feet first into the pedagogy, the familial orthodoxy of his ski school years. (Feet apart! Independent leg action!) Then came the prolonged love affair with the backcountry, its special lexicon, its crucial knowledge and camaraderie, its necessarily restrained ecstasies, its wild soul.

I thought I'd never give up the backcountry, but I have. I may yet return to its siren song. But for now, the turn has once again become the goal. Ah, the turn. Something I can control. But now it's not a how-do-I-look thing, an am-I-doing-it-right thing. Instead it's a reaching for the perfect feeling thing. The perfect, deeply etched, sling-shot arc across a blank canvas. Can I, like Bode Miller (not like Bode but in the spirit of Bode), scribe a line I've never scribed before? That arc leading to the next, and the next? The perfectly continuous, not to say never ending, line down one of Bachelor's wave-like funnels?

Years ago on Mt. Bachelor I spied a group of skiers wearing wool flannel shirts, standing around mid-mountain, a little hunched over, talking, before poling off and smoothing down the hill with what looked like an accomplished lack of ambition. Or acceptance. Contentment. Something.

Turned out they were members of an old-timers ski club. Some of them had patches sewn on their flannel that read: 70+. One guy sported an 80+ patch on his sleeve. What a perfect mountain for them, I thought. (I was not yet 40.) So open and undulating – so much flow – with an average pitch well shy of desperate. Now I see that it's the perfect mountain for me in my "fourth quarter."

Dad came for a visit on his own last winter, at 91. His wife didn't want him to make the drive. Neither did my California sibs. He had only one good eye, a pacemaker sewn into his chest, at least one stent, two artificial hips and one new knee. He wasn't skiing any more. But he still loved to drive. He took his time, tuned the satellite radio to classical, set the cruise control for 55 mph, and settled in for what he called his "sojourn." ("Ten days, 2,099 miles, 47 gallons of gas at an average 44 mpg," he wrote when he got home, pleased as punch. "Paradise on Wheels," he titled the email.)

While he was here, I drove him up to Mt. Bachelor so he could see for himself the object of my late desire. It was a beautiful day: blue sky, no clouds, Bachelor's volcanic shapes like rogue waves frozen in time. We walked up to the lodge deck and watched skiers tilting left and right, coming closer, sliding in to a stop. It was his last road trip.

The addiction continues. A new Bend friend, who is 75 and never has a bad day on the hill, refers to the condition we share as "being hard-wired to ski." I like that. It's gentler, less pejorative than addiction. He can't help himself either. We both need to be out there in the highlands, moving through the air and over the snow as serenely and (dare I say?) artistically as possible. Playing. Sculpting space on the tilt. Never growing up completely.

I have a *New Yorker* cartoon (by Arnold Roth, date unknown) pinned to the wall in front of my computer. A skier is confronting the grim reaper. He's an older guy, jowly, in an anorak and stretch pants, his long skis balanced upright in one hand. In the other hand he thrusts his ski pole out, horizontal to the ground, its basket and sharp point inches from the reaper's midsection. The black-robed spirit stares down at this affront, incredulous. He is nonetheless stopped cold, temporarily at least, held at bay.

# Summit Day

The wind was not so loud I couldn't hear the words of the volunteer patrolman at the top of Mt. Bachelor's Summit chairlift. My hood was cinched tight, and for the last thousand feet of the lift ride I'd held my gloved hand up to shield a bit of exposed cheek. It was a sunny morning, single-digits cold, with the wind ripping out of the southeast, rivers of snow like contrails streaming from the peak, gusts rolling over the mountain's ribs like waves breaking over jetties.

The patroller was standing in the middle of a vibrating thicket of signs at the entrance to the backside runs. All of the signs said, basically: Whoa! Don't ski this area without a partner. I asked him if this was prohibition or recommendation. A week prior, when the Northwest Chair first opened for the season, patrol was enforcing a buddy system, on account of the deep, unconsolidated snow and the worry that tree wells could swallow an occasional powderhound. Patrol is concerned, my gatekeeper told me, about "the difficulty of hauling a wreck out of here." And, he added, "not many people go back here. You could get hurt and no one might see you for quite a while."

Message received. But the policy was voluntary; tree wells were not an issue in the alpine, and the deep snow had all blown away. Or rather, I was hoping some of it had blown – was blowing – into favored bowers on the west side, 90 degrees around the circumference of Mt. Bachelor's bald cone, one long right-hand traverse from this point at the south end of the compass.

He let me go, and right away a hundred feet past him I saw the logic behind the caution. The south face with its myriad ribs and gullies was a ravaged icescape. Banks of giant, unskiable "coral heads," gleaming with wind-polished rime ice, choked off any conceivable descent route. Maybe Killy could have skied it in his prime. Not me. Not in this lifetime. There was a traverse line, though. Set by skiers and boarders when the snow had been softer, it contoured now a step above the surrounding scour, like a rock-hard welt. I wasn't the first skier out here. But I was alone, as far as I could see, on my powder mission.

It was my first summit run of the season. I'd missed opening day and missed, too, the last brace of days when the Summit chair had not opened at all thanks to steady 80-plus mph winds. (They store the chairs in the cavernous bottom terminal when it gets like this, to let the wind sing through the cables unimpeded.) I'd missed those first soft days. But I was here now. I was stoked. This was big weather. Wild weather. Exploratory skiing, with no promise of any reward. I had to go find out.

I hadn't counted on the wind sailing me out the traverse with quite so much force. Right at my back, it shot me along faster than I wanted to go. Braking was tricky on the frozen-brick rubble. I didn't want to scrape skis sideways any more than I had to, and only in spots that looked to have collected a few soft grains, like stray electrons, that might offer a bit of resistance. Twice I got myself into dead-end alleys of coral heads and lava rock and had to turn around step-by-step into the wind to rattle down to a better line, a through line.

From one ridgeback to another I scudded, feet spread, anchor dragging, looking to keep the speed down. Off to my left, way down at the base of the volcano, Sparks Lake looked like a frozen paw print on the forest floor. Not that I could afford an extra second gazing at it. The wind felt like a feral, boiling thing, something alive, if not actually conscious.

I was beginning to think all of the December snow was gone, blown across the Cascade Lakes to settle on the Three Sisters, or farther still, to Mounts Jefferson, Hood, Rainier – all the big volcanoes in the chain north to Seattle. But then I crossed the first small shield of wind buff, a nascent patch of grains coalesced in a hollow, like sand. In place of the constant clatter, my skis went quiet for a bit.

On I went around the horn to my right. Over fields of "chicken heads," millions of rime-ice nodules poking their little necks out of the firmament. These were not the worst chicken heads I'd seen. These at least toppled over, like dominoes, under my edges. Out onto the west-facing Serengeti Plain.

Which is not a single plain but a series of fluted gullies and ridgelines. "Furrows," the volcanologists call them, each one skewed to a slightly different point on the clock face. They're mostly not continuous. They overlap. They split around moraines. They stop. They start. They roll into bowls and wave shapes. None of them makes a straight shot to treeline but each one is striped with bands of tortured, dune-rippled snow.

I picked one furrow at random and dropped in along its left-hand flank, the wind ushering me forward and down. Snow grains rushed past on all sides, hugging the ground and whipping into diaphanous, undulating snow scarves that partially obscured the surface beneath. Sunlight came from straight behind me, too. The angle of the light so paralleled the terrain that my shadow danced many hundreds of feet down slope.

When I could see it. Mostly I couldn't. Every turn I made kicked up a universe of crystalline air, each murmuration caught by the wind and flung downhill faster than I could ski. Each cloud-wake exploded with infiltrated, golden light. Exploded around me before vanishing down the hill. Golden face shots from behind.

Down I curved, adrenalin fizzing in my veins. I felt barely human, hollow. No past. No future beyond the start of the next turn. Slicing left and right through this angled, yielding world of airborne crystals, sideways light, wind made visible – everything moving at once.

Less than an hour later the wind had built a lenticular cloud, a cardinal's brimmed galero, over the summit. The swirl of ice particles let almost no light through. Snow underfoot blurred to gray. And it was over. Memories lodged in that part of the brain that sees mirages. That part that craves an insoluble bliss.

# Author's notes:

*Each of these stories has been edited, in some cases substantially modified, from their original published versions. Each one remains true, to the best of my recollection.*

---

*I am indebted to a slew of editors who encouraged, assigned, accepted, and improved these stories:*

Neil Stebbins and Pat Cochran at *Powder*

Steve Cohen, Ed Pitoniak, and Andy Bigford at *SKI*

Al Greenberg and Bill Grout at *Skiing*

Mark Bryant at *Outside*

Harriet Choice at *Universal Press Syndicate*

Joan Yee at the airline magazines

John Fry, Dick Needham, and Seth Masia at *Skiing History*

Jim Davidson at the *San Miguel Journal*

Marta Tarbell at *The Watch Newspapers*

And, always, Lito Tejada-Flores, a poet on skis and on the page.

---

**A Kind of Grace**

*first appeared in Wasatch Journal, Winter 2008*

**ChapStick Kiss**

*a version of this piece was published in SKI Magazine, October 1992*

**All Go Anywhere**

*appeared in SKI Magazine, December 1995*

**Sanctuary**

*was published in SKI Magazine, October 1994*

**Private Lessons**

*was published first in Outside Magazine, November 1983*

**Curtains of Time**

*appeared in SKI Magazine, February 1994*

**The Education of a Ski Instructor**

*appeared in the Watch Newspapers, October 28, 2012*

**Gliders of the Storm**

*ran in SKI Magazine, February 1993*

**On the Brink**
*was published on Wordpress* (peterhshelton@wordpress.com), March 2010*
**Bear Lessons**
*a version of this piece appeared in Outside Magazine, November 1983*
**Ski Bum Alum**
*was first published in the Telluride Times-Journal, 1987*
**Gear and Clothing in Las Vegas**
*appeared in Powder Magazine, September 1984*
**The Need for Speed**
*a version appeared in SKI Magazine, September 1983*
**E.T. and the Mind of Expectation**
*appeared in Powder Magazine, sometime in 1987*
**Letter to My Girls**
*was published in the Telluride Mountain Journal, March 24, 1988*
**Christmas Tree**
*appeared in the Telluride Times-Journal, December 19, 1991*
**My Girls on Boards**
*appeared in SKI Magazine, December 1994*
**Le Raid Blanc**
*a version appeared in Powder Magazine, Spring 1988*
**Sugar Shacks**
*appeared in SKI Magazine, March/April 1997*
**Let Bode Be**
*was published in the Telluride Watch, February 24, 2006*
**Life of Velocity**
*appeared in Outside Magazine, February 1991*
**Largemouth Bass**
*was published on Wordpress*, July 31, 2015*
**Tears in the Snow**
*ran in the Watch Newspapers, March 3, 2011*
**L'Espace Killy**
*was published by Universal Press Syndicate, Winter 1991*
**The Games are Already Won**
*appeared in SKI Magazine, April 1992*
**Late Storm**
*ran in the Watch Newspapers, April 11, 2013*

**Powder Epiphanies**
*appeared in SKI Magazine, January 1997*
**Fat Skis, Dad & Me**
*appeared in SKI Magazine, September 1995*
**Go Down Easy**
*appeared in SKI Magazine, December 1988*
**A Heartbeat Away**
*ran in the Telluride Times-Journal, January 25, 1990*
**Today's 10th**
*appeared in SKI Magazine, February 1999*
**David Light**
*ran in the Watch Newspapers, May 17, 2002*
**Otto Pilot**
*appeared in SKI Magazine, November 1995*
**High Route to Telluride**
*first appeared in Peaking Out, Autumn 1978*
**The Accidental Bivouac**
*was published by the Telluride Watch, January 2012*
**A Wedding of Opposites**
*appeared in Cross Country Skier, December 1984*
**On Suspect Slopes**
*a version appeared in Outside Magazine, March 1985*
**Promise Me This**
*appeared in the San Miguel Journal, January 21, 1987*
**Buddhist Road Patrol**
*appeared in the Silverton Mountain Journal, January 18, 2002*
**Buried Alive**
*was published in Mountain Gazette 99, December 2003*
**The Nightmare**
*was adapted from a piece in the Telluride Watch, February 18, 2005*
**Independence Day**
*ran in SKI Magazine, May/June 2002*
**Totally Hip**
*appeared in SKI Magazine, 2009*
**Living with Addiction**
*was published by the Telluride Watch, April 5, 2002*
**Hot Buttered Corn**

*appeared in the Watch Newspapers, April 4, 2013*

**Outthinking the Snowy Torrents**

*appeared in the Watch Newspapers, March 8, 2012*

**Lessons Learned**

*appeared on Wordpress* , February 6, 2015*

**Code White**

*was published on Wordpress*, December 15, 2013*

**Highlands**

*incorporated parts of a story from the Ouray County Watch, April 22, 2008*

**Summit Day**

*was published on Wordpress*, January 3, 2016*

** peterhshelton@wordpress.com*

---

## *Photo Credits*

*and special thanks to some very creative skiing friends, starting with ski photographer par excellence, Robert Chamberlain, for the cover photo.*

page ii — Frontespiece: tracks beneath the Matterhorn, circa 1928
*photo E. Gyger, courtesy Museo Nazionale della Montagna, Torino*

page xii — Peter and his father, at Little Sweden, March 1953
*photo Miriam Shelton*

page 46 — Downhill racer, Aspen, Colorado
*photo Alan Becker*

page 100 — Peter in deep, in Kashmir
*photo Chaco Mohler*

page 156 — Red Mountain Lifetime Pass
*created by Jerry Roberts and Lisa Issenberg*

page 204 — Summer skiing in the high country, San Miguel Peak
*photo Robert Chamberlain*

page 236 — Peter in his preferred medium
*photo Tom Lippert*

rear cover — Peter above Battle Abbey, British Columbia
*author's colection*

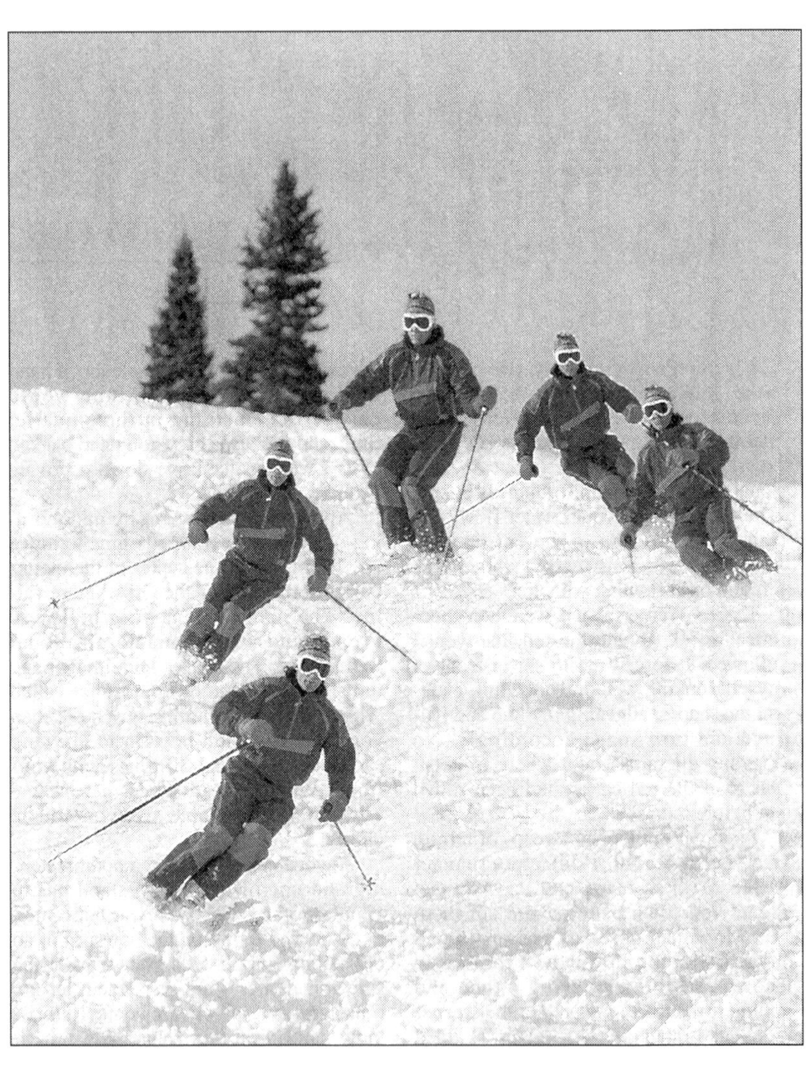